Air Traffic Control Handbook

Front cover: London Heathrow Control Tower. *Steve Flint/Air Team Images*
with background of the radar picture around Manchester Airport.

Rear cover: Stansted tower controllers. *NATS*
with background of the radar picture around Manchester Airport.

Air Traffic Control Handbook

The complete guide for all aviation and air band enthusiasts

David Smith

Crécy Publishing Limited

Air Traffic Control Handbook

First published as *Air Band Radio Handbook* in 1986 by Patrick Stephens Limited
Second edition 1987
Reprinted (with revisions) July 1988
Third edition February 1990
Reprinted (with revisions) July 1990
Reprinted August 1991
Fourth edition October 1992
Reprinted (with revisions) August 1993
Fifth edition November 1994
Sixth edition February 1997
Seventh edition 2002
Eighth edition, published by Sutton Publishing Limited, 2005
Ninth edition, retitled *Air Traffic Control Handbook,* published by Haynes Publishing, 2010
Tenth edition, published in 2015 by Crécy Publishing Limited
Eleventh edition, published in 2021 by Crécy Publishing Limited

Unless otherwise credited, the photographs are by the author

A CIP record for this book is available from the British Library

ISBN 9781910809990

Printed in Bulgaria by Multiprint

Crécy Publishing Limited
1a Ringway Trading Estate, Shadowmoss Road, Manchester M22 5LH
www.crecy.co.uk

Contents

Acknowledgements

I should like to thank NATS Media Centre for their kind co-operation and permission for the use of photographs and charts, also to Alex Newberry of Nevada Radio (www.nevadaradio.co.uk) for supplying scanner photographs. I am grateful also to John Locker for his guidance and comments on virtual radars. John is a satellite communications consultant, broadcaster and freelance journalist and his fascinating website is at www.satcom.website.orange.co.uk. He is also a major contributor to PlanePlotter. My friend, Dave Traynor, an avid airband listener for very many years, was a great help with advice and information. There is now only one commercial magazine that publishes airband and ATC information in a regular feature. This is *RadioUser Magazine*, whose content includes my Airband News column, about various aspects of airband listening and ATC developments. Thanks go to Georg Wiessala, Editor of *RadioUser*, for his advice and support, also to Mark Allen, Chief Engineer of PanAm World Radio, a Texas-based Long Distance Operational Control station for commercial aircraft. Thanks to my friends and former colleagues, Marc Hill and Ryan Swann. Marc arranged for Graham Hocquard to take a photo inside Jersey's control tower and Ryan sent me a selection of images from his personal archive. Finally my wife, Paula, for her enduring support.

Boeing 777 at Manchester.

Introduction

In effect, this is the 11th edition of a volume that first appeared in 1986. By 2010, the publisher and author both felt that the previous title of *Air Band Radio Handbook* was not sufficiently indicative of its content and wider-ranging appeal. Hence the change in that year's ninth edition to *Air Traffic Control Handbook*, with subtitle *And Guide to Air Band Monitoring*, to reassure enthusiasts that their interests were still in focus. I have now divided the book into two sections; the first describes how ATC is organised and performed, the second is an outline of the phraseology to be heard on airband. A few examples of the latter can also be found in the first section when they are particularly relevant to the topic described.

I have always aimed the content at several distinct groups of readers, primarily the airband listener for whom it is an aircraft spotting tool, but also the aviation enthusiast who is fascinated by air traffic control and wants to know how it all works. Then there is both the student and qualified private pilot who, I hope, will learn a lot from this book. Finally, the person who is considering a career in ATC but has only a rudimentary knowledge of its workings. In fact a colleague assures me that it was reading my book that inspired him to choose ATC as a career! He now works at a major UK airport.

A great many enthusiasts have bought airband radios and found that the jargon they hear is almost incomprehensible. It is easy to pick out callsigns but many VHF listeners I have talked to would like to build up a better picture of what is going on and to unravel the 'mysteries' of Air Traffic Control. This book aims to do just that. Persons embarking upon a course of flying lessons for a Private Pilot's Licence will find it very useful to acquire an airband radio and listen to how the professionals do their R/T.

My experience shows that, for the majority of trainee pilots, learning how to use the radio is almost as big a hurdle as mastering their aircraft. The terse messages, so confusing at first hearing, follow a definite pattern known as 'standard phraseology'. This verbal shorthand is designed to impart the maximum amount of unambiguous information in the shortest possible time. Since English is the international language of Air Traffic Control it must be understood easily by those with a different native tongue. With careful listening, and the aid of the examples in this book, the R/T exchanges on the airband will soon become both logical and familiar.

The Civil Aviation Authority's Future Airspace Strategy (FAS), developed in collaboration with airlines, airports, ATC bodies, general and business aviation, is a blueprint for how the airspace structure in the UK will develop over the next 20 years. The basic layout of the UK's airspace was developed more than forty years ago. Since then there have been huge changes, including an enormous increase in demand for aviation.

Before the pandemic drastically reduced air traffic, the point had been reached where localised optimisation of airspace had been all but exhausted. When normality finally returns and air traffic resumes its relentless growth, fundamental redesign of the UK airspace network will be required to smooth flows and reduce bottlenecks. Projects with public consultations are already in place for radical changes to London and Manchester/Liverpool airspace. Undoubtedly, there will be objections on the grounds of noise and air pollution.

The aim is to integrate airspace changes with new ATC technologies and to take advantage of improved aircraft navigation systems. These enhance pilots' ability to fly on preset routes with far less controller intervention. More direct routeing of aircraft from departure to destination will be accommodated. This will result in closer spaced routes, enabling aircraft to fly their optimal or most fuel efficient flight profile more often during the en-route phase of flight.

What of the future of airband listening? The spread of datalink has reduced some listening opportunities, mainly so-called 'housekeeping' tasks to reduce controller workload. Some of these services are already operational in the UK; Oceanic Route Clearance Authorisation service (ORCA), Datalink Volmet (D-Volmet) and Datalink Automatic Terminal Information Service (D-ATIS). D-ATIS is currently restricted to a few airports, including Heathrow, Gatwick, Edinburgh and Glasgow. These four airports also feature Pre Departure Clearance where the route clearance is sent directly to the flight deck for print out.

Eurocontrol and other ATC service providers, the International Civil Aviation Organisation (ICAO), the US Federal Aviation Administration and industry have been planning the implementation of Voice over Internet Protocol (VoIP) in ATM (Air Traffic Management) for several years. Reported results show good voice quality and in effect this is similar to a Skype telephone call. Much work is taking place behind the scenes to develop a global standard and the eventual aim is for VoIP to be adopted by ICAO. It is already in use for military applications and can be encrypted. Whether it will ever entirely replace conventional airband VHF/UHF radio is open to question.

I hope that I have distilled a readable narrative from the mass of official data listed in Chapter 20 as primary sources. Most of this is available for download or reading online if you really want to immerse yourself in the subject. I have attempted to demystify a very complex subject that is growing ever more specialised.

For example, Air Traffic Control itself is part of what is known as Air Traffic Services, which is defined as comprising Flight Information Service, Alerting Service, Air Traffic Advisory Service and Air Traffic Control Service (itself divided into Area Control Service, Approach Control Service or Aerodrome Service). In turn this is incorporated into Air Traffic Management, defined as the aggregation of the airborne and ground-based functions (Air Traffic Services, Airspace Management and Air Traffic Flow Management) required to ensure the safe and efficient movement of aircraft during all phases of operations.

Since this book's last edition, there have been some radical improvements in the management of air traffic. To cite a major example, space-based ADS-B has enabled an almost realtime virtual radar picture of traffic over the North Atlantic. The success of the remote digital tower to conduct operations at London City Airport is likely to lead to its adoption at other UK locations. Some Artificial Intelligence aids to traffic handling are already operational and more are currently being evaluated.

As for the effects of Brexit, the UK is, of course, no longer constrained by EU law and may choose to amend the retained EU aviation law as it sees fit. In effect, despite having left the European Union Aviation Safety Agency (EASA) system, the UK has adopted more or less wholesale the body of EU law that governs aviation safety. This was formalised by the Air Safety Agreement that was signed between the UK and EU in December 2020. In May 2021, it was reinforced by an agreement between EASA and the UK CAA on their future working relationship, known as Technical Implementation Procedures. Since Eurocontrol is not an EU body, the UK remains a Eurocontrol member and will continue to receive its Air Traffic Flow Management (ATFM) service and other important cross-border traffic management systems.

The complex nature of ATC is reflected in the ever-increasing number of titles, abbreviations and acronyms. I regret having to use so many but it is impossible to write a book of this nature without them. All, however, are listed below and explained in the text.

Abbreviations and Q-Codes

*Abbreviations marked with an asterisk are normally spoken on R/T alphabetically or as a complete word

AAC	Air Arrivals Control Army Air Corps
AAR	Air-to-Air Refuelling
ACARS*	Aircraft Communication Addressing and Reporting System
ACC	Area Control Centre
ADF	Automatic Direction Finder
ADS-B*	Automatic Dependent Surveillance – Broadcast
ADS-C*	Automatic Dependent Surveillance – Contract
ADT	Approved Departure Time
AEF	Air Experience Flight
AEW	Airborne Early Warning
AFIS*	Aerodrome Flight Information Service
A/G	Air/Ground
AGL*	Above Ground Level
AIAA	Area of Intense Aerial Activity
AIP	Aeronautical Information Publication
AIS	Aeronautical Information Service
AIRPROX*	Aircraft Proximity
AMSL	Above Mean Sea Level
ANSP	Air Navigation Service Provider
ANO	Air Navigation Order
APU	Auxiliary Power Unit
ARCC	Aeronautical Rescue Co-ordination Centre
ASACS	Air Surveillance and Control Systems
ARINC*	Aeronautical Radio Inc
ATA	Aerial Tactics Area
ATCRU	Air Traffic Control Radar Unit
ATD	Actual Time of Departure
ATIS*	Automatic Terminal Information Service
ATM	Air Traffic Monitor
ATS	Air Traffic Services
ATU	Aerial Tuning Unit
ATZ	Aerodrome Traffic Zone
BAA	British Airports Authority
BFO	Beat Frequency Oscillator
CAA	Civil Aviation Authority
CAS	Controlled Airspace
CAVOK*	Ceiling and Visibility OK
CCAMS	Centralised Code Assignment & Management System
CCD	Continuous Climb Departure
CDA	Continuous Descent Approach
CHAPI*	Compact Helicopter Approach Path Indicator
CPDLC	Controller-Pilot Datalink Communications
CVR	Cockpit Voice Recorder
DAAIS	Danger Area Activity Information Service
D&D	Distress and Diversion
D/F	Direction Finding
DFR	Departure Flow Regulation
DGPS	Differential Global Positioning System
DME	Distance Measuring Equipment
DVOR	Doppler VHF Omni-Directional Range
DVP	Digital Voice Protection
EASA*	European Aviation Safety Agency
EAT	Expected Approach Time
EFPS	Electronic Flight Progress Strip

EGNOS*	European Geostationary Navigation Overlay Service
EOBT	Estimated Off Blocks Time
ETA	Estimated Time of arrival
ETD	Estimated Time of Departure
FAB	Functional Airspace Block
FAS	Future Airspace Strategy
FDPS	Flight data Processing System
FDR	Flight Deck Recorder
FIR	Flight Information Region
FISO	Flight Information Service Officer
FL	Flight Level
FM	Frequency Modulation
FMC	Flight Management Computer
FMS	Flight Management System
FMU	Flow Management Unit
FPS	Flight Progress Strip
FTR	Fighter
FTU	Flying Training Unit
FUA	Flexible Use of Airspace
GA	General Aviation
GAT	General Air Traffic
GBAS	Ground Based Augmentation System
GHFS	Global High Frequency System
GLONASS*	Global Orbiting Navigation Satellite System
GMC	Ground Movement Control
GMP	Ground Movement Planning
GNSS	Global Navigation Satellite System
GPS	Global Positioning System
GPU	Ground Power Unit
GPWS	Ground Proximity Warning System
HAPI*	Helicopter Approach Path Indicator
HF	High Frequency
HEMS*	Helicopter Emergency Medical Service
HIRO*	High Intensity Runway Operations ('Hero')
HMR	Helicopter Main Route
HPZ	Helicopter Protected Zone
IAA	Irish Aviation Authority
IAS	Indicated Air Speed
IATA	International Air Transport Association
ICAO	International Civil Aviation Organisation
ICF	Initial Contact Frequency
IFR	Instrument Flight Rules
ILS	Instrument Landing System
IMC	Instrument Meteorological Conditions
INS	Inertial Navigation System
IRVR	Instrumented Runway Visual Range
ISTAR*	Intelligence, Surveillance, Target Acquisition and Reconnaissance
kHz	Kilohertz
Kt	Knots
LARS*	Lower Airspace Radar Service
LATCC*	London Area and Terminal Control Centre
LDOCF	Long Distance Operational Control Facilities
LITAS*	Low Intensity Two-colour Approach Slope Indicator
LJAO	London Joint Area Organisation
LSB	Lower Side Band
LVPs	Low-Visibility Procedures
M	Metres
MACS	Military Aeronautical Communication System
MARSA*	Military Accepts Responsibility for Separation of Aircraft
MATO*	Military Air Traffic Operations

MATS*	Manual of Air Traffic Services
MATZ*	Military Aerodrome Traffic Zone
MDA	Managed Danger Area
MDH	Minimum Descent Height
MDI	Minimum Departure Interval
MEDA*	Military Emergency Diversion Aerodrome
METAR*	Routine Aviation Aerodrome Weather Report
METRO*	US Military Met Office
MHz	Megahertz
MLS	Microwave Landing System
MMRSA	Military Mandatory Radar Service Area
MNPS	Minimum Navigation Performance Specification
MoD*	Ministry of Defence
MOR	Mandatory Occurrence Report
MRA	Military Reserved Airspace
MRSA	Mandatory Radar Service Area
MTA	Military Training Area
MTOM	Maximum Take Off Mass
NATS*	Adopted as company title but originally stood for National Air Traffic Services
NDB	Non-Directional Beacon
NERL	NATS En Route Plc
NERS	North Atlantic European Routeing Scheme
NFM	Narrow (band) Frequency Modulation
NM	Nautical Miles
NMOC*	Network Manager Operations Centre
NOTAM*	Notice to Airmen
NPR	Noise-Preferential Route
OACC	Oceanic Area Control Centre
OAT	Operational Air Traffic or Outside Air Temperature
OCA	Oceanic Control Area
OCH	Obstacle Clearance Height
OTS	Organised Track System
PAPI*	Precision Approach Path Indicator
PAR	Precision Approach Radar
PBN	Performance Based Navigation
PIREP*	Pilot Report of weather conditions encountered en route
PPR	Prior Permission Required
QDM	Magnetic track to the airfield with no allowance for wind
QFE	Barometric pressure at aerodrome level
QFG	Overhead
QNH	Barometric pressure at sea level
QRA	Quick Reaction Alert
QSY	Change frequency to ...
QTE	True bearing from the aerodrome
RA	Resolution Advisory
RCC	Rescue Co-ordination Centre
RMZ	Radio Mandatory Zone
RNP	Required Navigation Performance
RP	Reporting Point
RPS	Regional Pressure Setting
R/T	Radio Telephony
RTOW	Regulated Take-Off Weight
RTTY*	(Pronounced 'Ritty') Radio Teletype
RVR	Runway Visual Range
RVSM	Reduced Vertical Separation Minimum
SAATS	Shanwick Automated Air Traffic System
SAR	Search and Rescue
SBAS	Satellite-Based Augmentation System
SES	Single European Sky
SID*	Standard Instrument Departure
SLP	Speed Limit Point

SLOP*	Strategic Lateral Offset Procedure
SMGCS	Surface Movement Guidance and Control System
SMR	Surface Movement Radar
SOP	Standard Operating Procedure
SOTA*	Shannon Oceanic Transition Area
SPECI*	Special Met Observation
SRA	Surveillance Radar Approach
SSB	Single Side Band
SSR*	Secondary Surveillance Radar
STAR*	Standard Terminal Arrival Route
STOL*	Short Take-Off and Landing
TA	Traffic Advisory
TACAN*	Tactical Air Navigation
TAD*	Tactical Air Designator
TAF*	Terminal Aerodrome Forecast
TAS	True Air Speed
TASCOM*	Terrestrial Air Sea Communication (said as TAZCOM)
TC	Terminal Control
TCA	Terminal Control Area
TCAS*	Traffic Alert and Collision Avoidance System
TMA	Terminal Control Area
TMZ	Transponder Mandatory Zone
TOS	Traffic Orientation Scheme
TRA	Temporary Restricted Area
TRACON*	Terminal Radar Control (USA)
UAC	Upper Area (Control) Centre
UAR	Upper Air Route
UAS	Unmanned Aircraft System
UAS	University Air Squadron
UAV	Unmanned Aerial Vehicle
UHF	Ultra High Frequency
UIR	Upper (Flight) Information Region
USAF	United States Air Force
USB	Upper Side Band
UTC	Universal Time Constant (or Co-ordinated)
VASI*	Visual Approach Slope Indicator
VCR	Visual Control Room
VDF	VHF Direction Finder
VDGS	Visual Docking Guidance System
VFR	Visual Flight Rules
VGS	Volunteer Gliding Squadron
VHF	Very High Frequency
VMC	Visual Meteorological Conditions
VOR	VHF Omni-directional Range
VRP	Visual Reference Point
WFM	Wide (band) Frequency Modulation

Opposite: Farnborough tower.

Section 1

Chapter 1

Air Traffic Control Basic Principles

An Air Traffic Service is a generic term meaning variously: Air Traffic Control Service, Air Traffic Advisory Service, Flight Information Service, and Alerting Service. The objectives of the air traffic services are to: 1. Prevent collisions between aircraft. 2. Prevent collisions between aircraft on the manoeuvring area of an aerodrome and obstructions on that area. 3. Expedite and maintain an orderly flow of air traffic. 4. Provide advice and information useful for the safe and efficient conduct of flights 5. Notify appropriate organisations regarding aircraft in need of search and rescue aid and assist such organisations as required.

It must be emphasised that the provision of an air traffic service must be based upon expedition consistent with safety. In complex environments any deviation from basic procedures in order to expedite traffic should be carefully considered against the extent of co-ordination required and the attendant risk of error. The controller should only deviate from the basic procedures when they are quite sure that the resultant co-ordination can be carried out without excessive workload and without detriment to the safety of aircraft under their control.

Aberdeen's 'ziggurat' tower. *NATS*

The type of air traffic service (ATS) to be provided will depend on the class of airspace within which the aircraft is flying (see Chapter 2) and the type of ATS unit, ie Area, Aerodrome, or Approach. Operations at some smaller aerodromes are conducted by Aerodrome Flight Information Service Officers (AFISOs) who do not actually control aircraft. They provide information to pilots useful for the safe and efficient conduct of aerodrome traffic. This includes assisting pilots in the prevention of collisions, and to give taxi instructions on the apron and manoeuvring area. From the information received, pilots will be able to decide the appropriate course of action to be taken to ensure the safety of flight.

Air Traffic Control Clearances

Clearances are issued solely for expediting and separating air traffic and are based on known traffic conditions that affect safety in aircraft operation. Such traffic conditions include not only aircraft in the air and on the manoeuvring area of an airfield over which control is being exercised, but also any vehicular traffic or other obstructions not permanently installed on the manoeuvring area in use.

The issuance of air traffic control clearances by ATC units constitutes authority for an aircraft to proceed only in so far as known air traffic is concerned. ATC clearances do not constitute authority to violate any applicable regulations for promoting the safety of flight operations, or for any other purpose. Neither do clearances relieve a pilot-in-command of any responsibility whatsoever in connection with a possible violation of applicable rules and regulations.

Categories of Priority

Requests for clearances are normally dealt with in the order in which they are received and issued according to the traffic situation. However, certain aircraft are given priority over others in the following descending order:

Category A Aircraft in emergency and ambulance/medical aircraft when the safety of life is involved. Aircraft that have declared a 'Police Emergency'

Category B Operating for search and rescue or other humanitarian reasons. Post-accident flight checks. Other flights, including Open Skies Flights authorised by CAA. Police flights under normal operational priority

Category C Royal Flights. Flights carrying visiting Heads of State. In both cases, having been notified by NOTAM or Temporary Supplement

Category D Certain flights carrying Heads of Government or very senior government ministers

Category E Flight check aircraft engaged in, or in transit to, time or weather-critical calibration flights. Other flights authorised by the CAA. Note that Police Emergency Flight callsigns will be suffixed by the letter 'A' to highlight the requested priority status to controllers, eg 'Police 22A'.

Normal Flights Those that have filed a flight plan in the normal way and are conforming with normal route procedures. Initial instrument flight tests conducted by the CAA Flight Examining Unit (callsign 'Exam')

Category Z Non-standard and other flights, particularly training

Non-deviating Status: aircraft, both civil and military, which have been allocated this status have an operational requirement to maintain a specific track and level(s) or a particular route and level(s). It is imperative that an NDS aircraft is not moved from its pre-planned flight path unless absolutely necessary because this could render it operationally ineffective.

Visual Flight Rules (VFR) and Instrument Flight Rules (IFR)

Of paramount importance in ATC, flight conditions are divided thus:

Instrument Flight Rules (IFR) which apply under Instrument Meteorological Conditions (IMC).

Visual Flight Rules (VFR) which apply under Visual Meteorological Conditions (VMC);

The minima for VFR flight are quite complicated but can be summarised as follows. At or below 3,000ft AMSL at an indicated air speed (IAS) of 140 knots or less, an aircraft must remain in sight of ground or water and clear of cloud in a flight visibility of at least 1,500m. Above 3,000ft up to FL100 the minima are 5km visibility and at least 1,500m horizontally, or 1,000ft vertically clear of cloud. At FL100 and above, the visibility minimum is increased to 8km.

Since it is his or her responsibility to keep clear of other traffic, the pilot must maintain a good lookout. Furthermore, under certain conditions, climbs or descents maintaining VMC may be authorised for aircraft flying under IFR so as to expedite traffic, it is then the pilot's responsibility to avoid other traffic. In R/T transmissions the terms VFR or Victor Fox are used freely by pilots. In the same way, VMC may be referred to as Victor Mike. The phrase 'VMC on top' means that the aircraft is flying in VMC conditions above a cloud layer.

IFR comes into force when the visibility requirements described above cannot be met, and at all times during the hours of darkness. Instrument flying is mandatory unless the pilot has a valid Night Rating and can thus operate VFR during the hours of darkness. The aircraft must also carry a minimum scale of navigational and other equipment. Commercial aircraft almost always fly IFR irrespective of weather conditions. Within controlled airspace, responsibility for separation from other aircraft rests with ATC.

A final variation on the IFR/VFR theme is Special VFR, an authorisation by ATC for a pilot to fly within a control zone, even though unable to comply with IFR, and in certain airspace where provision is made for such flights. Depending on the visibility, amount of cloud and its height, and the limitations of the pilot's licence, a Special VFR clearance may be requested and issued. Standard separation is provided between all Special VFR flights, and between such flights and other aircraft operating IFR.

In practice much use is made of geographical features to keep Special VFR traffic apart, routeing along opposite banks of an estuary for instance. When flying on this type of clearance pilots must comply with ATC instructions and remain at all times in flight conditions that enable them to determine their flight path and to keep clear of obstructions. It is implicit in all Special VFR clearances that the aircraft stays clear of cloud and in sight of the surface. ATC almost always imposes a height limitation that will require the pilot to fly either at or below a specific level.

Separations

The rules for separation of IFR traffic, particularly when radar is not available, are complicated and probably of little interest to the layman. Suffice it to say that the basic radar separations are 5 miles laterally (but 3 and up to 10 in certain cases) and/or 1,000ft vertically up to FL290. Above this level, 2,000ft vertical separation is applied unless aircraft have been approved for RVSM (Reduced Vertical Separation Minima) operations. RVSM is mandatory over the UK and much of Europe, so aircraft unable to comply with the conditions have to remain below FL290. Above FL410, 2,000ft is the required vertical separation.

For aircraft departing from an airport the minimum separation is one minute, provided the aircraft fly on tracks diverging by 45 degrees or more immediately after take-off. Where aircraft are going the same way, and provided the first has filed a true air speed (TAS) 40kt or faster than the second, the separation is two minutes. With a TAS of 20kt or more faster than the second aircraft it becomes five minutes and in all other cases it is ten minutes. Radar will reduce some of these times and they are also affected by the demands of vortex wake separation and local procedures.

Speed control

Used to facilitate a safe and orderly flow of traffic. It is achieved by instructions to adjust speed in a specified manner. Speed adjustments should be limited to those necessary to establish and/or maintain a desired separation minimum or spacing. Instructions involving frequent changes of speed, including alternate speed increases and decreases, should be avoided. Aircraft should be advised when a speed control restriction is no longer required. The flight crew should inform ATC if unable to comply with a speed instruction.

The future position of an aircraft (and, consequently, separation) is determined by the ground speed. Since it is impractical to use it directly, the indicated airspeed (IAS) or Mach number are used instead to achieve the desired ground speed. At levels at or above FL250, speed adjustments should be expressed in multiples of 0.01 Mach. At levels below FL250, speed adjustments should be expressed in multiples of 10kt based on IAS. It is the controller's task to calculate the necessary IAS or Mach number that would result in the appropriate ground speed.

The following factors need to be taken into account: Aircraft type (range of appropriate speeds), wind speed and direction (in case the two aircraft are not on the same flight path), phase of flight (climb, cruise, descent), aircraft level (especially if the two aircraft are at different levels). Speed control is not to be applied to aircraft in a holding pattern. Only minor speed adjustments not exceeding 20kt IAS should be used for aircraft on intermediate and final approach. Speed control should not be applied to aircraft after passing 4 nautical miles (nm) from the threshold on final approach.

Speed Rules of Thumb

Generally, 0.01 Mach equals 6kt

Speed difference of 6kt gives 1nm in ten minutes

Speed difference of 30kt gives 1nm per two minutes

Speed difference of 60kt gives 1nm per minute

Transition Altitude

The Transition Altitude is the point at which aircraft change from reference to an altitude derived from a local pressure setting, expressed in feet above mean sea level, to a standard pressure setting of 1013.2 Hectopascals. This allows flights to be conducted using an internationally agreed set of flight levels based on the standard setting. It removes the necessity of continually adjusting the altimeter to allow for local pressure variations along the route, any error being common to all aircraft in the system. This ensures that they can easily be separated vertically by the required amount. The Transition Altitude is not currently consistent across the UK and varies between 3,000ft and 6,000ft depending on location and type of airspace.

Chapter 2

Types of Airspace

Flight Information Regions (FIRs)

The United Kingdom is divided into two FIRs, the London and the Scottish, the boundary between them being the 55 degrees North line of latitude. Above 24,500ft, these areas are known as Upper Flight Information Regions, abbreviated to UIR. The London Area Control Centre (LACC) at Swanwick in Hampshire manages en route traffic in the London FIR/UIR. This includes upper airspace over England and Wales up to the Scottish border. It also houses the London Terminal Control Centre (LTCC), which handles traffic below 24,500ft flying into or out of London's airports. This area, one of the busiest in Europe, extends south and east towards the coast, west towards Bristol and north to near Birmingham.

The Scottish FIR/UIR comes under the Scottish Area Control Centre at Atlantic House near Prestwick Airport. Its operations room controls aircraft over Scotland, Northern Ireland, Northern England and North Wales up to FL660. Co-located is the Manchester Area Centre, which is responsible for much of the north of England, the Midlands and North Wales from 2,500ft up to

Birmingham control towers, the old and the new, with an ILS glide path antenna in the foreground. *RW*

28,500ft. At both London and Scottish ACCs, military controllers provide services to civil and military aircraft operating outside controlled airspace. They work closely with civilian controllers to ensure safe co-ordination of traffic. Also at Scottish Centre is the Oceanic Area Control Centre (OACC), which controls the airspace over the eastern half of the North Atlantic from the Azores (45 degrees North) to a boundary with Iceland (61 degrees North).

Southern Ireland comes under the jurisdiction of the ACCs at Shannon and Dublin, the stretches of the Atlantic to north and south being controlled by Reykjavik and Shanwick Oceanic Control Centres, respectively.

Two states can agree, through a bilateral letter of agreement, to delegate the responsibility for providing air traffic services within a certain airspace from one state to the other. There can be numerous reasons for this. For example, a part of Scottish airspace is delegated to the Danish air navigation service provider because Denmark has better radar coverage within the specific area. Over the Irish Sea, a considerable amount of UK airspace is delegated to Dublin Area Control Centre for more efficient handling of traffic into and out of Dublin Airport, principally its Point Merge approach procedure. Conversely, sections of French and Dutch airspace are delegated to London Control to better handle the traffic flows.

The UK follows the ICAO system, which aims to classify airspace internationally so that it is perfectly clear to users from anywhere in the world which flight rules apply and what air traffic services they can expect within a particular airspace. The seven different categories of airspace are represented by the letters A to G, although Class B has not been adopted in the UK and Class F has been discontinued.

Airspace Classification

Class A

Controlled Airspace. Consists mainly of airways, which are normally 10 miles wide (5 miles each side of centreline) and generally have a base between 3,000ft and FL55. With some exceptions, they extend vertically to FL245, the base of upper airspace in Britain. Aircraft flying in them are required to operate under IFR and are separated positively by ATC, using radar or procedural methods. 'Westbound' flights, which could in practice also be on north-west or south-west headings, fly at even-numbered flight levels and 'eastbound' flights at odd numbers. Some airways are activated for peak periods only, usually weekends and national holidays. Certain airways are 'one way' only,

Other Class A airspace includes the London Control Zone and Control Area, the Worthing, Daventry and Clacton Control Areas, and the Shanwick Oceanic Control Area.

A, B, G, and R signify regional air routes that are not RNAV routes. L, M, N and P indicate European Regional area navigation (RNAV) routes. H, J, V and W are routes that do not form part of the regional networks of ATS routes and are not area navigation routes. Q, T, Y or Z are non-regional RNAV routes. These designators are prefixed by U when in the upper airspace (ie above FL245). Conditional Routes (CDRs) are ATS Routes that are usable only under specified conditions.

Free Route Airspace (FRA) has now been deployed above 25,000ft over Scotland, Northern Ireland and a small portion of northern England. Further deployments are expected in the near future. FRA is specified airspace within which users can freely plan a route between a defined entry point and a defined exit point, with the possibility of routeing via intermediate (published or unpublished) waypoints, without reference to the air traffic services (ATS) route network, subject to availability. Within such airspace, flights remain subject to ATC.

Class B

Controlled Airspace. No UK airspace is currently designated as Class B.

Class C

Controlled Airspace. The London and Scottish FIR above FL195, including all Control Areas, Airways and Upper Air Routes, plus the London and Scottish UIR between FL245 and FL660 (which includes the Hebrides Upper Control Area. Below FL195, certain Control Areas, including Cotswold and Daventry are Class C.

Class D

Controlled Airspace. Control Zones and Control Areas around airports.

Class E

Controlled Airspace. Parts of Scottish TMA airspace below 6,000ft (above 6,000ft is Class D), Belfast TCA and Prestwick TCA.

Class F

Advisory airspace. No UK airspace is currently designated as Class F.

Class G

Uncontrolled. All UK airspace, including that above FL660, not included in Classes A to F. This is unregulated airspace in the open FIR within which pilots are allowed to fly as they wish without hindrance or radio calls.

Flight Rules and Services Applied

The classification of the airspace within a Flight Information Region determines the flight rules that apply and the minimum services that are to be provided. These are summarised below:

Class A: IFR only, ATC clearance before entry. All aircraft are separated from each other and must comply with ATC instructions.

Class B: Not applicable.

Class C: IFR and VFR. ATC clearance before entry. Comply with ATC instructions. IFR flights separated from other IFR and VFR flights. VFR flights given traffic information on other VFR flights and traffic avoidance if requested.

Class D: IFR and VFR. For IFR traffic ATC clearance before entry. Comply with ATC instructions. IFR flights separated from other IFR flights and traffic information provided on VFR flights, with traffic avoidance advice on request. Traffic information to VFR flights on IFR flights and other VFR flights.

Class E: IFR and VFR. IFR flights separated from other IFR flights. Comply with ATC instructions. Traffic information on known VFR flights. VFR flights do not have to contact ATC but are encouraged to do so in order to receive traffic information and comply with any instruction given.

Class F: Not applicable.

Class G: IFR and VFR. Flight Information Services as required. Separation cannot be provided owing to the possible presence of unknown traffic. Pilots have no obligation to contact anyone while operating in Class G airspace.

Special zones and areas

Aerodrome Traffic Zone (ATZ)

The dimensions of ATZs relate to the midpoint of the longest runway and its length. For example, if the longest runway is greater than 1,850m, the boundary of the ATZ will be a circle of radius 2nm from the midpoint of that runway. Aerodromes with shorter runways have smaller ATZs but the vertical limit remains 2,000ft above aerodrome level. Both within or outside controlled airspace pilots must either avoid the ATZ or obtain permission to fly through it.

Control Zone (CTZ)

Aerodrome Control Zones afford protection to aircraft within the immediate vicinity of aerodromes.

Terminal Manoeuvring Area (TMA)

Designated areas of controlled airspace surrounding a major airport where there is a high volume of traffic. The London TMA is one of the busiest and most complex in the world.

Control Area (CTA)

Control Areas are generally established around airports, but also in any area where the density of air traffic is high. Control Areas afford protection over a larger area than an airway to a specified upper limit. Terminal Control Areas are normally established at the junction of airways in the vicinity of one or more major airports.

Helicopter Main Routeing Indicators and Protected Zones

The concentration of offshore oil and gas installations in the North Sea and Irish Sea, with their busy helicopter support operations, has resulted in the introduction of protected airspace. Helicopter Main Routeing Indicators (HMRI and formerly known as Helicopter Main Routes) and Overland Corridors have been established when helicopters operate on a regular basis from and to the mainland or between platforms. A Helicopter Protected Zone (HPZ) is sometimes established around two or more installations and a Helicopter Flight Information Service may also be provided. Apart from the East Shetland Basin in which procedural separation is provided, the airspace is uncontrolled but its dimensions are published, and military and civil pilots must obtain clearance to penetrate an HPZ and keep a good lookout when in proximity to an HMRI.

Military Mandatory Radar Service Area (MMRSA)

A large part of the Upper Airspace CTA within which military aircraft flying between FL245 and FL660 are required to operate under a radar control/procedural control service.

Radio Mandatory Zone (RMZ)

VFR flights operating in parts of Classes E or G airspace and IFR flights operating in parts of Class G airspace designated as an RMZ must maintain continuous air-ground voice communication watch and establish two-way communication, as necessary, on the appropriate communication channel before entering.

Transponder Mandatory Zone (TMZ)

All flights operating in airspace designated as a Transponder Mandatory Zone (TMZ) must carry and operate SSR transponders capable of operating on Modes A and C or on Mode S.

Areas of Intense Aerial Activity (AIAA)

Not controlled as such, but since military aircraft regularly conduct unusual manoeuvres, pilots of non-participating aircraft unable to avoid the area are strongly advised to make use of a radar service. AIAAs include the Vale of York, Lincolnshire and The Wash.

UNITED KINGDOM ALTIMETER SETTING AND FLIGHT INFORMATION REGIONS

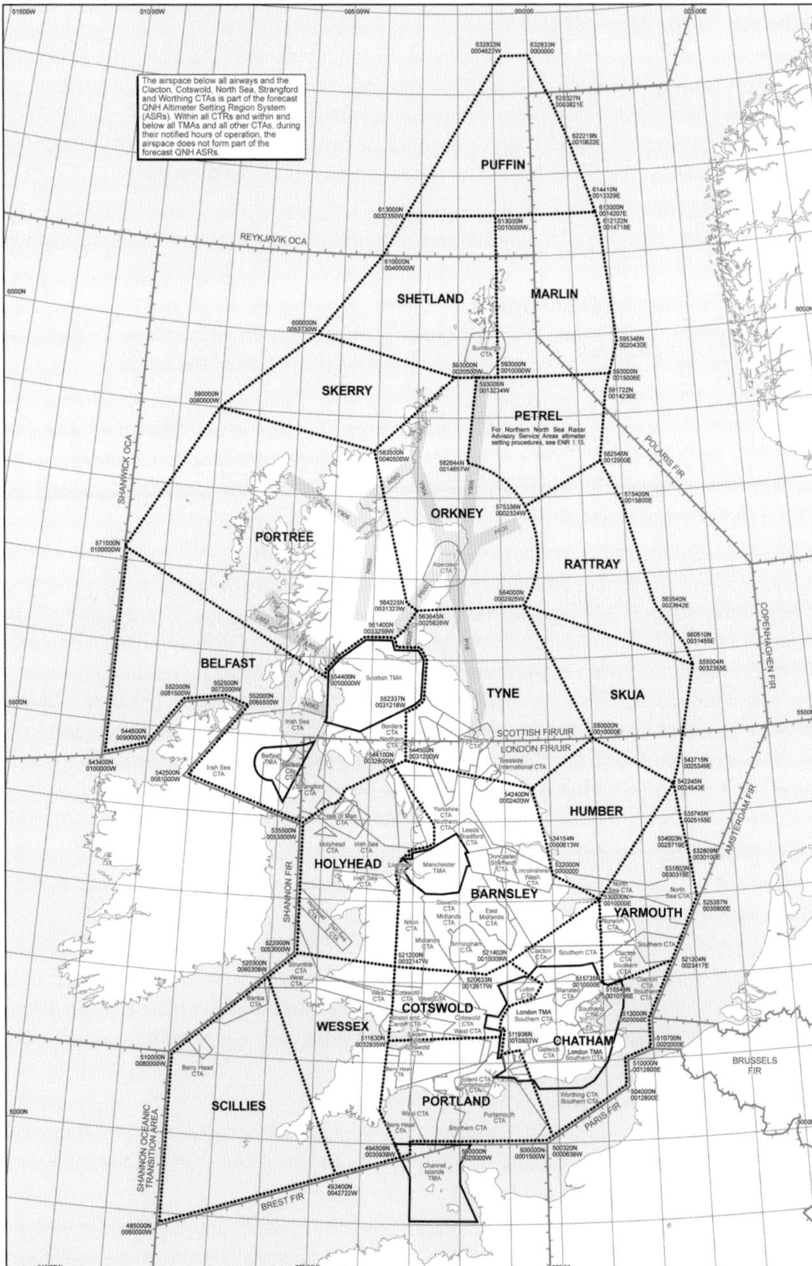

CHANGE (2/21): BORDERS CTA ADDED. NORTHERN CTA ADDED. YORKSHIRE CTA ADDED.

AERO INFO DATE 13 NOV 20 FOR THE LATEST CHANGE IN INFORMATION THIS CHART SHOULD BE CHECKED AGAINST THE ENR SECTION OF THE U.K. AIP ENR 6-18

Danger Areas

The most common Danger Areas are weapons ranges, but the term also embraces parachuting and other activities potentially hazardous to aircraft, including unmanned aircraft systems. Radar crossing services are available for some of them, depending on activity status. In the initial stages of a disaster or emergency incident, a Temporary Danger Area is always introduced to prevent flight by aircraft not engaged in the associated support or rescue action. The eight prospective UK vertical and horizontal spaceports, as well as balloon and sea launchers, will all require specially segregated airspace to safely manage their launches. The required volume of airspace for each launch is expected to be large to protect other airspace users.

Prohibited and Restricted Areas

Most Prohibited Areas are centred on nuclear power stations, over-flight being prohibited below 2,000ft above ground level within a radius of 2 miles. Restricted Areas include certain prison sites.

Temporary Reserved Areas

Airspace temporarily allocated for the exclusive use of a specific user, military or civil, during a determined period of time. A Red Arrows display, for example.

Flexible Use of Airspace (FUA)

A concept based on the fundamental principle that airspace should not be designated as either pure civil or military airspace, but rather be considered as one continuum in which all user requirements have to be accommodated to the extent possible.

Military Airspace

See Chapter 15 for information on TACAN Routes, Military Aerodrome Traffic Zones, Military Training Areas, Aerial Tactics Areas, Low Flying Areas, Air-to-Air Refuelling Areas, and AWACS Orbit Areas.

Opposite: United Kingdom altimeter setting regions. *NATS*

Chapter 3

Navigational Aids and ATC-Related Equipment

Radio navigational aids or 'navaids' assist pilots in threading their way through the airways, letting down at destination and then, if an Instrument Landing System is installed, following its beam down to the runway, a so-called precision approach. Non-precision approaches do not incorporate ground-based electronic descent guidance and include Localiser only, Localiser/DME, VOR, VOR/DME, NDB, NDB/DME, RNAV (LNAV) and SRAs. Non-precision approaches rely on the pilot being in a position to cross the published Final Approach Fix at the specified altitude/height in order to safely complete the approach. The main types of navaid in the United Kingdom are described briefly below.

NDB Non-Directional Beacon

The most common, and one of the simplest of aids, is the Non-Directional Beacon (NDB). The introduction of Area Navigation (RNAV) has rendered NDBs redundant in operation on the ATS route structure. As a result, en route NDBs have been withdrawn and replaced with waypoints. By contrast, there are still a relatively large number of instrument flight procedures based upon

ILS localiser antenna at Birmingham. *RW*

NDBs sited on or near to aerodromes. Here, it continues in operation as an approach and landing aid, sometimes referred to as a Locator Beacon, when its range will be about 15 miles. It consists merely of a radio transmitter in the medium frequency band that sends out a continuous steady note in all directions. A callsign of three letters in Morse code (two for airport locator beacons) is superimposed at regular intervals as a check that the desired beacon has been selected.

Doppler Very High Frequency Omni-directional Radio Range (DVOR)

DVORs broadcast their signals in all directions, but the signals vary around the compass in such a way that each direction has its own signal that cannot be confused with that of any other direction. If an aircraft receiver can pick up and decode the signal from a DVOR, it can tell the bearing (or radial as it is termed) from the station. Doppler VOR is a development of the original VOR beacon system, which improves the accuracy of the signal and reduces errors caused by obstructions and high ground. A number of long-standing UK DVORs have already been decommissioned, although if there was a co-located DME it has been retained in service. These will act as backup for aircraft RNAV failures, which of course are dependent upon satnav.

This is part of a European plan for future navigation, based on the ability of area navigation systems to work out the most accurate track keeping by means of multiple DMEs. Responsibility for the upkeep of the beacons rests with NATS En Route Plc, known as NERL. It assumes that the use of satellite navigation for all phases of flight will become progressively more dominant until a point is reached when NDB and VOR will not be required at all.

Distance Measuring Equipment (DME)

While VOR gives accurate, specific directional information, it cannot make explicit distance measurements. The solution is DME, which is associated closely with VOR, the combination providing an accurate position fix. A special transmitter in the aircraft sends out pulses in all directions and these are received at the DME station on the ground. As each pulse is received. an answering pulse is transmitted automatically and this is picked up in the aircraft. It is in fact the reverse of secondary radar (see below). As the speed of radio waves is constant at 186,000 miles per second, a computer in the aircraft that measures the time interval between the transmission of the pulse and the receipt of the response can convert this time interval into a distance and display it to the pilot in nautical miles and tenths. More advanced equipment will also display 'time to go' to the beacon.

DMEs are normally co-located with VORs and the frequencies of the two installations are 'paired'. For example, the VOR frequency of 112.7MHz is always matched by a DME on Channel 74, a VOR on 114.9 by a DME on Channel 96 and so on. This means that aircraft equipment can be arranged so that the selection of a particular VOR frequency means that the related DME channel is selected at the same time.

Instrument Landing System (ILS)

ILS is a pilot-interpreted aid that gives a continuous indication of whether the aircraft is left or right of the final approach track and also its position in relation to an ideal glide path to the runway. The latter is a standard 3 degrees, giving an approximate rate of descent of 300ft per minute. Certain airfields may have greater angles owing to high ground on the approach or other local considerations. London City Airport, with its steep 5.5 degrees approach to reduce noise footprint, is one example. An associated DME sited on the airport pilot provides a continuous read-out of range from touchdown.

A transmitter with a large aerial system known as the Localiser is sited at the far end of the runway, transmitting its signals on either side of the centreline of the runway and approach. These signals, called blue on the right of the approach path and yellow on the left, overlap in a beam about 5 degrees wide exactly along the approach centreline. A second unit, the glide path transmitter, is sited at the nearer end and slightly to one side of the runway. ILS Localiser/DME systems dispense with the glide path beam but the DME ranges enable the pilot to monitor his or her rate of descent.

Initial approach on to the ILS is normally achieved by Approach Radar, the aim being to place the aircraft on a closing heading of about 30 degrees to the final approach at a range of between 7 and 9 miles. The aircraft should be at an appropriate altitude so that the glide path can be intercepted from below rather than attempting to 'chase' it from above. The final turn-on can be done by radar direction, but these days it is usually done automatically by coupling the ILS with the Flight Director. Where no radar is available, a procedural ILS is flown, similar to an NDB approach with the exception that the procedure turn will intercept the ILS and enable the pilot to establish himself on the Localiser.

ILSs are divided into categories based on the lowest operating minima below which an approach should only be continued with the required visual reference as follows:

Category I: Decision Height not lower than 200ft and with either a visibility not less than 800m or Runway Visual Range not less than 550m.

Category II: Decision Height lower than 200ft but not less than 100ft, with Runway Visual Range not less than 300m.

Category IIIA: Decision Height lower than 100ft, or no Decision Height and a Runway Visual Range not less than 175m.

Category IIIB: Decision Height lower than 50ft, or no Decision Height and a Runway Visual Range less than 175m, but not less than 50m.

Category IIIC: No Decision Height and no Runway Visual Range limitations.

Localiser/DME ILSs are non-precision and therefore uncategorised.

Microwave Landing System (MLS)

Once expected to replace ILS, but ground and aircraft-based augmentation systems using GPS produced similar accuracy without the cost of new equipment. London Heathrow was the only UK airport to install MLS (on all four runway directions), eventually decommissioning it in May 2017.

Inertial Navigation System (INS)

INS operates independently of ground stations, being based on a computer aboard the aircraft that derives its input from gyroscopic accelerometers. A pre-determined journey can be programmed in, the output of which will enable the Flight Director to fly the required tracks. This allows aircraft to fly direct routeings without reference to radio beacons if first requested from, and approved by, ATC. INS is now usually combined with satnav systems.

Global Navigation Satellite System (GNSS)

GNSS is a general term describing any satellite constellation that provides positioning, navigation, and timing services on a global or regional basis. While GPS (Global Positioning System) is the most prevalent GNSS, other nations are fielding, or have fielded, their own systems to provide complementary, independent capability. Apart from GPS, the United Nations currently recognises three other systems. These are the EU's Galileo;

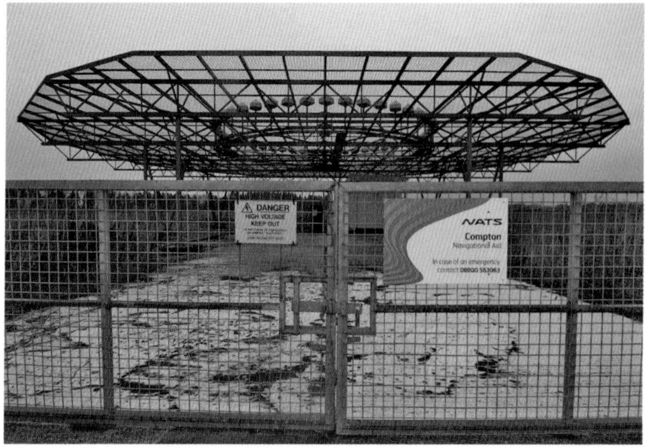

Compton DVOR site.

GLONASS, the Russian GLobal Orbiting NAvigation Satellite System; and China's BeiDou, formerly known as Compass. India and Japan have their own systems, but coverage is limited to their respective regions.

Europe's Galileo is interoperable with the US GPS, improving the accuracy and reliability of navigation and timing signals received across the planet. The constellation of thirty satellites considerably increases the number providing GPS. More importantly, it eliminates reliance on GPS, which is operated and maintained by the US Air Force and theoretically could be withdrawn, or at least rendered less accurate, at times of international crisis.

However, Washington and Brussels have signed an agreement to adopt compatible operating standards. These technical parameters will allow either side to jam effectively the other's signal in a small area, such as a battlefield, without shutting down the whole system. More importantly, from the civilian perspective, the agreement allows the systems to be meshed seamlessly, greatly benefiting manufacturers, service providers and consumers. Better accuracy, especially in built-up areas where the current GPS signal can be patchy, should lead to an even bigger demand for positioning systems. Remember that aviation is just one of many users of satellite navigation.

GLONASS (Globalnaya Navigazionnaya Sputnikovaya Sistema, or Global Navigation Satellite System) is owned and operated by the Russian Federation.

The Chinese BeiDou ('Northern Dipper' after the Ursa Major constellation) became operational in 2020. Both are interoperable with GPS and Galileo.

The European Geostationary Navigation Overlay Service (EGNOS)

EGNOS is Europe's regional Satellite-Based Augmentation System (SBAS). SBAS augments the core satellite constellation by providing ranging, integrity and correction information via geostationary satellites. This system comprises a network of ground monitoring stations distributed throughout Europe and North Africa. These measurements are transferred to a central computing centre where differential corrections and integrity messages are calculated. These calculations are then broadcast over the covered area using geostationary satellites that serve as an augmentation, or overlay, to the original GNSS signal. However, since June 2021 EGNOS has no longer been available for UK airfields apart from Channel Islands locations, which have a separate and continuing agreement with the European Satellite Service Provider.

Performance-Based Navigation (PBN)

PBN forms a significant part of the Future Airspace Strategy Two (FAS 2) and consequential modernisation of the UK Airspace system. That modernisation envisages transition from airspace, routes and instrument flight procedures (including holds), based on conventional navigation systems eg VOR, DME, NDB, to airspace described in terms of Performance-Based Navigation. This provides the opportunity for a significant airspace redesign, especially of the terminal airspace structure, which will enable the ATC system to be modernised and deliver a series of safety, environmental, capacity and efficiency benefits.

The airspace concept relies on a greater systemisation of the airspace route structure and therefore the ability of aircraft to fly the required route and profile accurately and consistently. Aircraft are currently equipped to differing standards and specifications, as well as varying levels of certification and crew authorisations to use the equipment. The aim is to achieve a consistent standard of precision navigation based on Area Navigation (RNAV) and Required Navigation Performance (RNP).

RNP is a family of navigation specifications under Performance Based Navigation (PBN) that allows an aircraft to fly a specific path between two three-dimensionally defined points in space. Although RNAV and RNP systems are fundamentally similar, the key difference between them is the requirement for on-board performance monitoring and alerting. A navigation specification that includes a requirement for on-board navigation performance monitoring and alerting is referred to as an RNP specification. One not having such a requirement is referred to as an RNAV specification.

The level of performance requirements for an RNP system include the capability to follow a desired ground track with reliability, repeatability and predictability, including curved paths. Where vertical profiles are included, vertical angles or specific altitude constraints are applied to define a desired vertical path. Aircraft are required to arrive in terminal airspace to an accuracy of plus or minus thirty seconds. Positional accuracy at any stage of a flight will be within a box of 0.3 nautical miles.

Precision Area Navigation (P-RNAV)

With the anticipated growth in air traffic, it is envisaged that P-RNAV will be employed to a greater extent for the design of terminal procedures, including Standard Instrument Departures (SIDs), Standard Terminal Arrival Routes (STARs) and Transitions to final approach. Both London Heathrow and Gatwick already use many procedures based on P-RNAV, as do Stansted, Luton, Newcastle and other major UK airports. The aim is to make much greater use of the potential of RNAV. One of the main benefits is environmental, because conventional departure and arrival procedure design requires aircraft to overfly ground-based navigational aids. If it is possible to remove this restriction safely, it will enable aircraft to be more easily routed round noise sensitive or built-up areas. The accuracy and functionality afforded by modern RNAV systems means that aircraft can fly noise preferential routes with a greater degree of accuracy than was previously possible. Continuous Descent Approaches can also be designed into the procedure, meaning reduced noise, fuel burn and therefore carbon emissions. An ability to separate arrival and departure routes strategically will reduce controller workload.

Required Navigation Performance (RNP) Approaches

Formerly known as RNAV approaches and now renamed RNP Approaches

These procedures have a predetermined path that is stored in the aircraft's navigation database and used by its Flight Management System (FMS) to provide lateral and vertical guidance on the approach. Reduced minima apply if Localiser Performance with Vertical Guidance (LPV) is available.

In simple terms, this is an instrument approach based on a navigation system that is not required to meet precision approach standards, but which provides both course and glide path deviation information.

The fundamental difference between LPV and ILS is the source of the guidance signals. Whilst an ILS is a ground-based approach, necessitating the associated transmitters and antennae for each individual runway, the source for RNAV LPV guidance is the space-based GNSS, which can be used to simultaneously provide the guidance to an unlimited number of aircraft conducting concurrent approaches at multiple locations. However, as stated above in the EGNOS section, LPV approaches have been suspended in the UK, apart from the Channel Islands Airports.

ILS localiser antenna at Birmingham. *RW*

Automatic Dependent Surveillance-Broadcast (ADS-B)

For an aircraft to be capable of employing ADS-B, it must have a transponder that broadcasts not just Mode C but ADS-B information. Essentially, a GPS receiver (or the output from the aircraft's primary GPS) is piped into the transponder, along with other information from flight instruments. Then, once per second, the transponder transmits a code that contains the aircraft ID, its altitude, and its position as derived from GPS, along with information such as its rate of climb or descent and whether it is presently turning and in what direction. This transmission is intended to be received by two different types of receivers. First, it is intended to be received by other aircraft within approximately 200 miles. Those aircraft, if they are also equipped for ADS-B, will have a special computerised display in their cockpits that is able to show the position of every ADS-B transponder-equipped aircraft and its relative position and heading from the display aircraft. ADS-B updates once per second, and its transmissions are also meant to be received by ground stations, being nearly ten times more accurate than radar.

To illustrate this, whether primary or secondary, the controller's radar picture updates only as fast as the radar antenna rotates, which can mean anything up to twelve seconds per sweep. During that time a jet aircraft can travel a mile or more, and usually the radar location information isn't very precise either, which means that, in congested airspace, a substantial margin of error must be maintained. This in turn means fewer aircraft can move through a given amount of airspace, leading to delays.

ADS-C Over the North Atlantic

The basic concept of ADS-C (Automatic Dependent Surveillance-Contract) is that the ground system will 'set up a contract' with the aircraft. This means that the aircraft will automatically provide information obtained from its own on-board sensors, and pass this information to the ground system under specific circumstances dictated by the ground system). Contracts are initiated by the ground and *cannot* be modified by the pilot. Note that the contract is a 'dynamic agreement' between the ground system and the aircraft. It is not, as one might think, a piece of paper that has some legal value. All aircraft intending to conduct flights in certain portions of the North Atlantic (NAT) Regional airspace have to be fitted with and operate CPDLC (see below) and ADS-C equipment. Apart from ensuring that separation is maintained, the use of ADS-C will also greatly facilitate search and rescue operations and location of an aircraft following an accident in oceanic airspace.

Controller Pilot Datalink Communications (CPDLC)

This enables controllers and pilots to communicate on a one-to-one basis via a simple, text-based messaging system. This is a two-way system, meaning that communication can be initiated by either side. ATC messages are displayed to pilots in the cockpit via the Flight Management System. Pilots can then respond to ATC clearances by datalink. They also have the capability to make requests by datalink, for example requested Levels, Routes etc. Either side will also be able to send a 'free text' message to the other.

Transponders and Secondary Surveillance Radar (SSR)

The transponder is not a navigational aid in the true sense, but its use is vital to the service that ATC is able to provide. A small airborne transmitter waits until a radar pulse strikes its antenna and then instantly broadcasts, at a different frequency, a radar reply of its own – a strong synthetic echo. Since ordinary 'skin return' (the reflection of the ground radar pulse from the aircraft structure) is sometimes quite weak, especially at great distances or with small aircraft, the transponder helps the radar operator to track targets that might return an echo too weak to display. Interference from weather and other causes is virtually eliminated.

The transponder is simple in concept but in practice is a complex, sophisticated device. It is triggered into either of two modes of reply by the nature of the ground radar pulse. Without delving too deeply into the technicalities, Mode A is employed for identification and Mode C for altitude information. Mode B is in military use only and Mode S (S standing for Select) is a datalink for the exchange of operational information. At UK Control Centres and airports, radar replies are channelled into a computer that decodes the pulses, converts them into a letter and number display, and places a label alongside the appropriate target on the radar display. The information includes the callsign and altitude of the aircraft. Secondary Surveillance Radar (SSR) has many advantages. One of the most important is that aircraft identification is easy to achieve. R/T loading is reduced considerably because altitude information is presented continuously to the controller.

Traffic Alert and Collision Avoidance System (TCAS)

When TCAS is fitted to aircraft, the equipment reacts to the transponders of other aircraft in the vicinity to determine whether or not there is the potential for a collision. TCAS is mandatory within UK airspace for all jet and turboprop aircraft of maximum take-off weight of 5,000kg or more, or passenger capacity of more than thirty.

Warnings are given in two steps: typically forty-five seconds before the assumed collision, a Traffic Advisory (TA) warning indicates where the pilot must look for the traffic; then between twenty and thirty seconds before the assumed collision a Resolution Advisory (RA) gives the pilot advice to climb, descend or remain level. The two warnings, TA followed by RA, can only be received if the conflicting aircraft is transponding on Mode C or Mode S. Where both aircraft in an encounter are fitted with TCAS Mode S, the transponders will communicate with each other to agree which aircraft is to pass below, and which above, the other. Warnings appear on the flight deck display indicating the relative positions of the conflicting aircraft in plan view and elevation, together with an aural warning spoken by a synthetic voice.

FLARM

Taking its name from a fusion of 'flight' and 'alarm, it is an electronic system used to selectively alert pilots to potential collisions between aircraft. Using ADS-B, it is optimised for the specific needs of light aircraft, helicopters and gliders, not for long-range communication or interaction with ATC. The aircraft's position and altitude are broadcast and at the same time its receiver listens for other FLARM devices within range and processes the information received. Advanced motion prediction algorithms predict potential conflicts for other aircraft and alert the pilot using visual and aural warnings. Obviously, its effectiveness depends upon the number of FLARM-fitted aircraft but current numbers in the UK are said to be more than 7,000, almost half being gliders.

Unlike conventional transponders, FLARM has low power consumption and is relatively inexpensive to purchase and install. Furthermore, conventional TCAS is not effective in preventing light aircraft collisions, as these can be close to each other without danger of collision. TCAS would issue continuous and unnecessary warnings about all aircraft in the vicinity, whereas FLARM only issues selective warnings about collision risks.

Ground Proximity Warning System (GPWS)

GPWS is also not a navigational aid but it provides an audible warning to the pilot if an aircraft experiences any of the following conditions:

(a) Excessive sink rate

(b) Excessive terrain closure rate

(c) Altitude loss after take-off or overshoot

(d) Proximity to terrain when not in the landing configuration

(e) Deviation below the glide slope

In the first four conditions, the warning consists of an audible tone and a spoken warning over a cockpit loudspeaker, 'Whoop, whoop. Pull up'. For the last condition the warning 'Glide slope, glide slope' is used. The warning is repeated as long as the conditions exist.

Aircraft Flight manuals instruct pilots to climb immediately to a level where the warning is no longer being received. If a pilot gets a 'pull up' warning, his recovery action is to establish the power setting and attitude that will produce the maximum climb gradient consistent with the aircraft configuration. If a 'glide slope' warning is received, recovery action is to apply power to regain the ILS glide slope.

Unfortunately, the GPWS is an extremely sensitive piece of equipment and spurious warnings can be caused by several factors. One of these is a sudden variation in terrain, even though it is well below the aircraft. Enhanced GPWS (EGPWS) has made the system even more effective by issuing earlier warnings and reducing the number of failure alerts.

Flight Checks

Navaids, particularly ILS, require regular flight checks to ensure that their performance remains consistent. These checks, which are mainly flown by a Beech Super King Air of Cobham Flight Inspection, are not as intensive as those made when the equipment was first installed at a specific location, but they are still quite time-consuming. As a more immediate safeguard, most navaids are self-checking and will shut down automatically if they are not operating within the correct parameters.

Tools of ATC

Flight Plans

Flight Plans are the standard method of providing ATC units with details of intended flights. They are mandatory for most IFR flights, any flight across international borders and flights into designated areas such as Air Defence Identification Zones (ADIZ) or anywhere the authorities deem to be difficult for search and rescue operations. For VFR flights in relatively populated countries such as the UK, Flight Plans are not required but pilots are encouraged to file them, if they are flying over water or mountainous areas. A Plan must be filed at least thirty minutes before departure but sophisticated ATC systems such as the United Kingdom's may require considerably more than this if the flight is to operate within a complex route network.

Scheduled flights to a regular timetable are covered by the so called Repetitive Flight Plan, better known as a 'stored plan'. This refers to the fact that when a computer is being used to support the air traffic services, the information can be placed in what is termed the 'bulk store' and the computer programmed to produce the relevant data at a predetermined time. Where there is no ATC unit at destination, Flight Plans have to be 'closed' by the pilot as soon as practicable after landing to avoid unnecessary search and rescue operations.

Typical Flight Plan

Transmitted in abbreviated form on the AFTN, the flight plan message reads: FPL RYR953 IN B738/M SDHIR/C EGGP0700 NO436F370 UB3 HON UA1 VEULE UL612 PAS UA41 GRO UA26 CMP DCT LIRA0223 LIRN EET/LFFF0031 LSAS0116 LFFF0117 LIMM0124 LIRR0151 REG/EIDAZ

Decoded, this means Ryanair Boeing 737-800, wake turbulence category Medium, callsign RYR953, IFR flight Liverpool to Rome Ciampino, standard navigation equipment, ETD 0700, true air speed 436kt at Flight Level 370, routeing via Honiley VOR, VEULE on the French coast near Dieppe, Passeiry VOR near Geneva, Pisa VOR, Grosseto VOR, Ciampino NDB, estimated elapsed time to Rome two hours twenty-three minutes, alternate airfield Naples. The estimated elapsed times to each FIR boundary en route are also included, as well as the aircraft registration EI-DAZ. The supplementary information (fuel endurance, total number on board, survival equipment, etc) is not sent but held on file at the departure airport.

Flight Progress Strips (FPS)

Amidst all the hi-tech hardware of modern ATC, the humble paper flight progress strip, which is slotted into a plastic holder, still has an important part to play. It carries all the basic details of each aircraft's flight plan; its callsign, type, required flight level, true air speed, route and destination, along with spaces in which the controller can annotate and update the information. They are still handwritten at some locations but machine-printed in busier ATC environments. The controller will annotate and update them with such information as take-off or landing times, route clearances (ticked when passed and acknowledged correctly), slot times, pressure settings and current ATIS code. Different colour pens may be used where several controllers write on the same strip, ie Clearance Delivery, GMC and Tower.

Electronic Flight Progress System (EFPS)

Major UK airports have now replaced paper flight strips with the Electronic Flight Progress System (EFPS). It allows Tower Controllers to manage electronic flight data online, using touch-sensitive display screens. This significantly reduces the need for voice communications between controllers and replaces the traditional method described above. It increases efficiencies by ensuring an instantaneous sharing of relevant flight information between workstations within the tower, and between the tower and terminal control. EFPS is fully interfaced with the Integrated Initial Flight Plan System (IFPS) and other flow management systems located at the Network Manager Operations Centre in Brussels. It also interfaces with the BAA's Stand (or gate) Management System, NATS' National Airspace System (NAS), and performs datalink Departure Clearance (DCL) with aircraft flight decks.

Electronic flight progress strip board, Birmingham Radar. *RW*

This means that suitably equipped aircraft may request and receive their ATC route clearance via datalink. As a basic requirement, the crew must have received training in the use of their equipment for requesting and handling datalink clearances. The message is routed via the international communications providers SITA or ARINC. Datalink Departure Clearance may be requested from EOBT (Estimated Off Blocks Time) minus twenty-five minutes until EOBT plus ten minutes. The request will be processed by the same controller who is also carrying out the voice clearances and will normally be returned to the aircraft within a short period of time.

Once a clearance has been requested, one member of crew should remain available to acknowledge the returned clearance. If receipt of the clearance has not been acknowledged within five minutes, the system will consider an error has occurred. Under these circumstances, or when any messaging error occurs, a message requiring the crew to 'revert to voice' will be sent and the datalink clearance cancelled. No further pilot or system- generated departure datalink requests should be made once a successful clearance has been received. The system cannot be used for re-clearance or checking for any updates, nor can ATC respond via datalink to any additional information added in the remarks field. One the aircraft is ready to depart, voice contact should be established stating 'With datalink clearance', the aircraft type and series and the QNH.

Radar Data Processing (RDP)

On advanced radar systems, automatic radar data processing removes unwanted signals such as ground and weather echoes and limits the information on the radar display to aircraft responses. This computer technology is used to decode the combined radar information from several antenna to produce the best possible picture. It also enables the transponder information to be displayed as a label alongside the radar position symbol, a computer-generated 'blip'. RDP can be correlated with Flight Data Processing to display callsign, actual flight level and destination. The aircraft's ground speed and other information can also be displayed as required. All modern radar displays use colour to identify different types of airspace, land and water areas, active and pending traffic, as well as a variety of other operational features specified by the customer.

iFACTS (Interim Future Area Control Tools Support)

Some advanced tools are still under development, but those already operational include Trajectory Prediction (TP) and Medium Term Conflict Detection (MTCD), a system that identifies and display predicted conflict information to controllers to support decision making. Software algorithms compare the predicted future trajectories of multiple aircraft in order to identify potential conflicts.

Short Term Conflict Alert

Again not a navaid as such, STCA (Short Term Conflict Alert, known colloquially as 'Stacker'), uses sophisticated software to examine radar track data in order to look for possible conflicts between pairs of aircraft. In London Terminal Control, for example, aircraft tracks are projected ahead and a low severity alert generated when the aircraft are predicted to come close vertically and laterally in the same time interval. The target labels on the controller's radar display change from green to white to indicate that a conflict is predicted and a white pairing line joins them. As the conflict situation becomes imminent, the labels change to red to indicate that the situation has deteriorated.

See Chapter 7 for more tools related to London Terminal Control.

Chapter 4

Area Control

There are two Area Control Centres operated by NATS, situated at Swanwick in Hampshire and Prestwick in Ayrshire, Scotland. The operations room at Swanwick combines:

- London Area Control Centre (LACC), which manages en route traffic in the London Flight Information Region. This includes en route airspace over England and Wales up to the Scottish border.
- London Terminal Control Centre (LTCC), which handles traffic below 24,500ft flying to or from London's airports.
- Military ATC. Military controllers provide services to civil and military aircraft operating outside controlled airspace. They work closely with civilian controllers to ensure safe co-ordination of traffic.

Prestwick ACC combines:

- Manchester Area Control Centre (MACC), which controls aircraft over much of the north of England, the Midlands and North Wales from 2,500ft up to 28,500ft.

Scottish Control Ops Room at Prestwick. *NATS*

- Scottish Area Control Centre (ScACC), which controls aircraft over Scotland, Northern Ireland, Northern England and the North Sea from 2,500ft up to 66,000ft.
- Oceanic Area Control Centre (OACC), which controls the airspace over the eastern half of the North Atlantic from the Azores (45 degrees north) to a boundary with Iceland (61 degrees north).

Transmitter/receiver stations are sited at various strategic positions around Britain and linked to the ACCs by land line. The aim is to achieve a balanced coverage over the whole area with no 'dead' spots. Similarly, the radar stations are 'remoted' on high ground where possible, to improve range. London ATCC (LATCC) is served by radar heads at Heathrow, Ash near Canterbury, Ventnor on the Isle of Wight, Clee Hill in Shropshire, Burrington, Devon, and St Annes, near Blackpool. Additional service is provided on a Eurocontrol agency basis from Mount Gabriel in Eire, a station that extends SSR cover out to 15 degrees West in the south-west approaches.

More information on SSR will be found in Chapter 3 but, briefly, the main function of primary radar is to provide aircraft position. Secondary Radar, or SSR, depends for its operation on a transponder carried in the aircraft that, on receipt of pulses from a ground interrogator, will transmit coded reply pulses back to the ground. When these are decoded by the display equipment, they give the altitude or flight level of the aircraft together with a four-figure identifying number known as a 'squawk'. The primary and secondary information received by the radar stations is processed in a common 'plot extractor', converting the base radar data into digital form and automatically sending the information to the ACCs over land lines.

At the ACC, display processing equipment employing computer technology is used to decode the combined radar information from several antennae and displays, either a manually selected radar station or a composite area mosaic picture. The SSR squawk is paired with the aircraft callsign in the computer and this callsign label is displayed on the screen instead of the code. This is known as callsign conversion and enables the controller to match the radar picture with the electronic strips on his flight progress board.

When the mosaic picture is selected at LATCC, the computer divides the London FIR into 16-mile squares, each of which has radar cover from a 'preferred' radar and a 'supplementary' radar. This avoids the blind spots possible if only one radar were in operation. Should the preferred radar fail, the supplementary will take over automatically, information from a third radar head being upgraded in turn to supplement it.

All incoming primary and secondary digital data is continuously recorded. The same applies to all ATC radio messages, whether they be Area, Tower or Approach. The purpose of these recordings is to help an investigating authority to build up a picture of the events surrounding an accident or incident.

To facilitate traffic handling, airspace under Area Control is broken up into sectors, each with its own radio frequencies, a primary and several 'as directed' channels to enable the sector to be split during busy periods. To eliminate confusion, the sector is vertically 'gated'. In other words, traffic above and below the area of responsibility is filtered out.

Aircraft are passed from one sector to the next with co-ordination between the controllers concerned, or electronically where approved. See 'Standing Co-ordination' at the end of this chapter. From mid-evening as traffic decreases, sectors are 'closed down', the frequencies being 'band-boxed', to use the jargon. When the morning shift comes on duty the sectors are activated again to meet the renewed traffic flow.

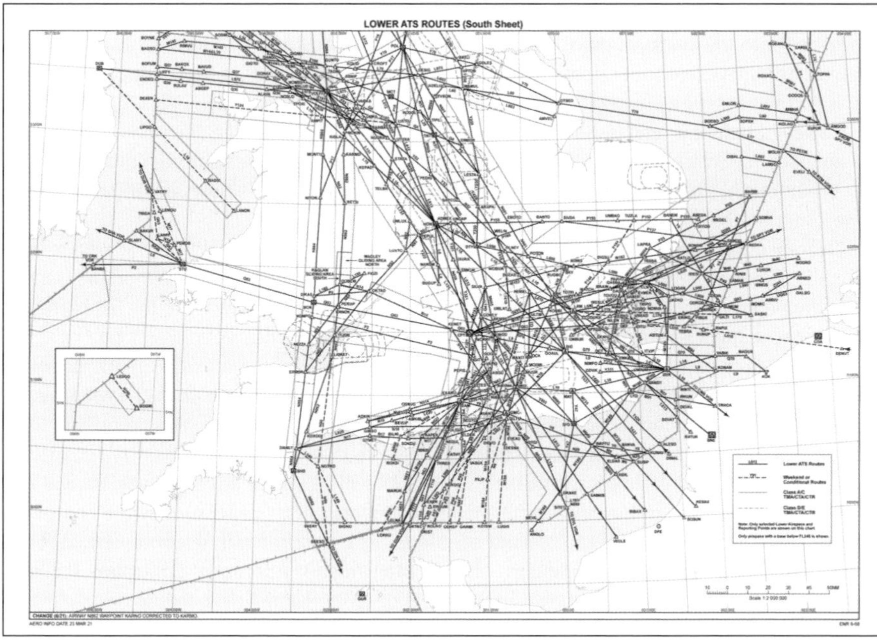

Airspace routes, part of South sheet. *NATS*

Before computers came on the scene in British ATC in the 1970s, flight progress strips at the ACCs were handwritten in vast quantities. Today the system is automated, apart from a shut-off period for computer maintenance in the small hours of the morning, and it would be advantageous to describe briefly what happens when a particular flight leaves, for example, Leeds for London Heathrow.

If the flight is a scheduled one, it will be on a 'stored plan' in the LATCC computer's bulk store file. At the appropriate time as programmed into the computer, usually about forty minutes before Estimated Time of Departure (ETD), the details will be input to the electronic strip display at the Scottish ACC and at any controller position at LATCC where advance information of the flight is required.

When Scottish receives an estimated time of departure from Leeds, based on the aircraft starting up, via a direct telephone link, an activation message will be input to the computer. This will generate an update message for the sectors at Scottish and those sectors at London that will handle the flight. In all cases the computer will have calculated and input times for en route reporting points based upon the airborne time recorded at Scottish. The forecast winds at various levels will have been programmed in and thus automatically taken into account.

The flight of an aircraft from Heathrow to Manchester serves as a good example of how traffic is fed through the airways system. When the departing aircraft comes onto the LATCC Departure Radar Controller's frequency and has complied with the minimum noise routeing element of its Standard Instrument Departure, it is started on its climb to cruising level, using radar separation where necessary between it and other arriving, departing or transiting traffic.

To ease the task of the Departure Controller in regard to co-ordination with other sectors concerned with the airspace, there is an internal procedure that permits him to climb the aircraft to an arbitrary level without reference to other sectors. This is known as Standing Co-ordination and is further described below.

However, before it reaches this flight level or, alternatively, when the aircraft is approaching the airspace for which the next Sector Controller is responsible, prior co-ordination is carried out. When this has been done, the aircraft is instructed to contact the next Sector (still with the same London Control callsign.)

Clearance is given for the aircraft's climb to its cruising level, once again using radar to resolve any conflict with other traffic. By this time it is also possible to check the computer on the elapsed time between reporting points and, if these deviate by three minutes or more, the estimates for the rest of the flight are revised and a new ETA is passed to Manchester.

As the flight nears the Manchester TMA boundary, co-ordination takes place between Daventry Sector and the TMA Controller. Descent instructions dependent upon the Manchester traffic situation are then issued and the aircraft is transferred to the new frequency. The Manchester TMA Controller has a radar display similar to that used by the Daventry Sector and, as the aircraft enters his airspace, its callsign and level will be visible on his display. He will also have displayed in front of him the electronic flight progress strips generated by the computer, which have been updated by any revised estimates. The descent will be continued until the aircraft comes under the jurisdiction of the Manchester Approach Controller (callsign 'Manchester Director') and positioned on the ILS as described in the next chapter.

Ideally, traffic is given an uninterrupted climb to cruising level and, from a convenient point, a continuous descent to final approach. However, the presence of other traffic has to be taken into account. Traffic climbing to, say, FL180 may be given an initial limit of FL120 against conflicting traffic at FL130. By the time it is approaching FL120, the other aircraft may be well out of the way and the controller will be able to instruct the pilot to continue his climb to the required level. Before the days of SSR height read-outs, the Area Controller in this example would ask the pilot to report passing FL110 and then would assess the situation with regard to further climb.

Reduced Vertical Separation Minima (RVSM)

Now in widespread operation. Until technology overcame the problem, altimeter systems were less accurate in the higher levels, and above Flight Level 290 the standard vertical separation of 1,000ft has traditionally been doubled to 2,000ft to allow a greater margin of error. An intensive programme monitoring height-keeping performance proved that RVSM could safely be applied. It has produced a very significant increase in airspace capacity. RVSM operations are mandatory in all UK airspace above FL290, except for certain military aircraft that have a non-RVSM dispensation. Non-compliant civilian aircraft will have to remain below FL290.

Standing Co-ordination

Standing Co-ordination is a written agreement between two sectors about how they will present certain flights to each other. Telephone co-ordination only needs to be done if a flight cannot be presented in the agreed manner for whatever reason, or if the conditions of the standing co-ordination do not apply to a particular flight. Standing Co-ordination often has conditions attached. For example, once an aircraft has been transferred to a particular sector, that sector may immediately climb, descend or turn that aircraft even if it has not yet reached their airspace. It is not uncommon for an aircraft to be transferred up to about 30 miles before it has left a particular

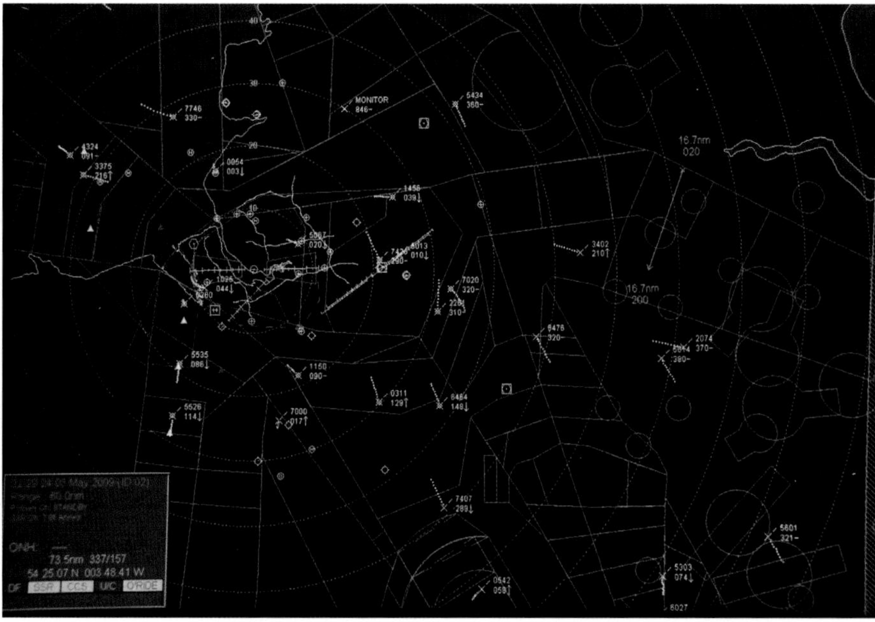

Liverpool's approach radar display 'wound out' to cover much of north-east Wales and north-west England. The graduated lines are Liverpool, Manchester and Hawarden final approaches.

sector, because the present sector does not need to do anything else with it and because controllers can see at least that far beyond the bounds of their sector. These provisions can be quite detailed; an agreement may allow turns to the right but not to the left; descents but not climbs.

If an aircraft does not qualify for the conditions of standing co-ordination it must be individually co-ordinated. The next sector is warned that the flight is on its way, and an agreement made with them about how it will be 'presented': ie, the aircraft's altitude, the approximate time it will enter the next sector and its heading (if applicable). Such a warning usually takes the form of a phone call. Normally, these calls are made between the 'Planner' or 'Co-ordinator'. The one who actually talks to the aircraft is known as the 'Tactical' controller. If all goes well, the aircraft will be accepted as is. If not, it may have to be climbed or descended to a new cruising level before reaching the next sector or maybe put on a heading.

Standing Co-ordination enables a massive through-put of traffic without all the hassle of individual co-ordination between sectors. Just one example in the Woodley/Compton area: London TMA outbounds to west will climb to FL130; London TMA inbounds from west will descend to FL140.

Controller Pilot Datalink Communications (CPDLC)

Currently, CPDLC is provided by the London and Scottish Area Control Centres in UK airspace at Flight Level 285 and above and may be available down to FL195 in certain sectors. It is a form of text messaging that enables communication with ATC without the need for voice contact by radio. The CPDLC system is designed for simplicity. To set the system up, crews must first log on to the ATC unit to which they wish to connect. Each unit has its own four-letter code, which is entered into the login page. For example, London is EGTT.

Once logged on, ATC can use CPDLC to send instructions relating to changes in flight level, heading, speed and radio frequencies. Pilots can also send requests to ATC should they wish to change altitude or change course to deviate around thunderstorms. When a message is received from ATC, for example a clearance to climb to a higher altitude, it pops up on a screen on the flight deck. A reply to the message requires a press of one of three buttons – 'accept', 'cancel' or 'reject'.

It is emphasised that if a flight crew has any doubt regarding the content, validity or execution of a CPDLC message they must revert to voice communication immediately to clarify the situation. Within UK airspace CPDLC is a supplementary means of communication. Voice over R/T remains the primary method. Flight crews are also reminded that following a change of frequency, there is a requirement to check in by voice prior to the use of CPDLC. To send a message to ATC, one of the pre-set pages in the CPDLC menu is used.

Declared Capacity

A measure of the ability of the ATC system or any of its sub-systems or operating positions to provide service to aircraft during normal activities. It is expressed as the number of aircraft entering a specified portion of airspace in a given period of time, taking due account of weather, ATC unit configuration, staff and equipment available, and any other factors that may affect the workload of the controller responsible for the airspace. The term is also used for the hourly capacity of airport runways.

Lowther radome on a southern Scotland hilltop. *NATS*

Chapter 5

Approach Control

An arriving aircraft is transferred from Area to an airport's Approach Control at a specified release point. This is not obvious from R/T transmissions because it is passed by land line or electronically between controllers shortly before the aircraft comes on to the approach radio channel. It may be a position, time or level. The transfer of control is made deliberately flexible to react to differences in the flow of traffic. For example, if the release is 'Leaving Flight Level 50' the Approach Controller may not alter the heading of the aircraft until he has received a 'passing FL50' report. The reason for this is that Area Control may have been separating the inbound aircraft from other traffic above FL50.

Most UK airports have published Standard Terminal Arrival Routes (STARs), an example being the BRI One Bravo for Bristol traffic arriving from the west. Aircraft are expected to cross Speed Limit Points (SLPs) at or below 250kt indicated air speed. Ideally, the arriving aircraft should be released in plenty of time to enable it to carry out a straight-in approach and at the same time to lose height. However, should a busy traffic situation exist, it might be necessary to put it into a holding pattern.

Cardiff Radar room. *NATS*

VOR/DME Holding Procedures

A standard oval 'racetrack' holding pattern for IFR aircraft is based on a holding fix. This fix can be a radio beacon such as an NDB or VOR. Alternatively, it can be at a published named point, created using two crossing VOR radials, or it can be at a specific distance from a VOR using a coupled DME. When DME alone is used, the inbound turn of the racetrack may be permanently defined by distance limits rather than in minutes. The fix is the start of the first turn of the racetrack pattern. Aircraft will fly towards the fix, and once there will enter a predefined oval pattern. A standard holding pattern uses right-hand turns and takes approximately four minutes to complete – one minute for each 180 degree turn, and two one-minute straight ahead sections. For any holds above 14,000ft the straight sections must be one and half minutes.

An example is DAYNE, south of Manchester Airport, an 'offset' holding pattern for traffic inbound to Manchester. Its axis is aligned on Trent VOR Radial 312, its position between Trent DME 13 and 17 miles. The aircraft flies towards the VOR/DME on this designated inbound radial and on reaching the holding fix position carries out a procedure turn onto the reciprocal outbound track. This outbound track is flown until the limiting DME is attained and the aircraft then turns to intercept the inbound VOR radial back to the holding fix position.

In the event of a ground equipment failure at the VOR/DME installation, a standby procedure is published, based on an alternative VOR/DME or other radio beacon. In the case of DAYNE, the holding pattern is defined additionally by a radial and distance from the Manchester VOR/DME.

At airfields without radar, traffic is separated by procedural methods, the first aircraft making an instrument approach from, say, 3,000ft, with aircraft continuing to hold above at 1,000ft vertical intervals. As soon as the first aircraft reports visual with the ground or approach lights, and there is a reasonable likelihood of a successful landing, the second aircraft is cleared for the approach, and so on. If the aircraft carries out a missed approach prior to becoming visual, it must climb to the safe terrain clearance altitude, in this instance 3,000ft. Hence it is not hard to see why this altitude is left vacant at the beacon until the first aircraft breaks cloud.

The Decision Height is the level at which the pilot on a precision approach must carry out a missed approach if he/she fails to achieve the required visual reference to continue the approach to a landing. A precision approach is defined as being provided by an ILS, Precision Approach Radar (PAR), or GNSS supported by ground-based augmentation. All other procedures, including SRAs and Localiser/DME approaches, are non-precision and the term Minimum Descent Height is used instead.

Obstacle Clearance Height is the minimum safe height to which an aircraft may descend either on an instrument approach or in the event of a missed approach. This is published on the approach charts for each airfield, aircraft being divided into five speed-related categories, resulting in a reduction of the Obstacle Clearance Heights for the smaller and more manoeuvrable types.

VHF D/F display. *RW*

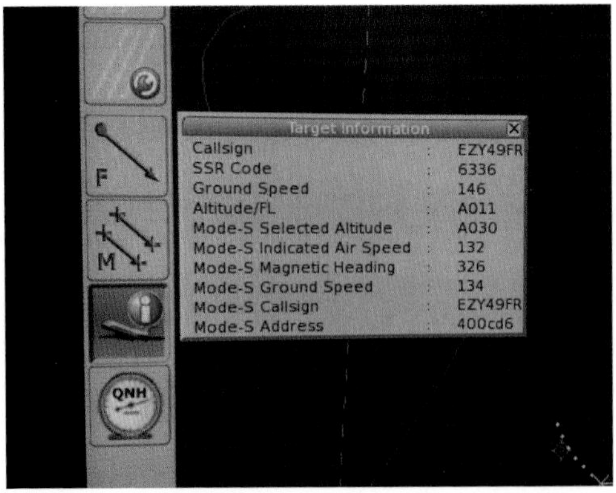

Mode S information on a radar display. *RW*

The obstacle clearance criteria are, of course, tied in with company minima for visibility and cloud base, below which a public transport flight is not allowed even to attempt an approach. There are also statutory provisions for non-public transport flights whereby recommended minima are published for the approach aids at each airfield for the guidance of pilots.

The term Expected Approach Time can be heard at non-radar equipped airports. This is the time at which ATC expects that an arriving aircraft, following a delay, will leave the holding fix to complete its approach for a landing. The actual time of leaving the hold will depend upon the approach clearance. It also indicates to a pilot that if he has a radio failure he must not leave the holding fix to commence an instrument approach until this specific time, in order to allow preceding aircraft to descend and land. 'No delay expected' means that a pilot can begin his approach as soon as he reaches the beacon. If his estimate for the beacon is twelve minutes after the hour, the next aircraft's EAT will be nineteen, the third's twenty-six and so on.

A standard seven minutes is assumed to complete the let-down procedure and three minutes will be added to this if an aircraft arrives from certain points of the compass and has to realign itself in the correct direction for the descent. The controller will calculate the figures and update them as necessary. Note that EATs are not issued in busy TMAs when the delay is likely to be less than twenty minutes. If it is likely to be more, inbound aircraft are given a general statement about anticipated delay and EATs are issued as necessary.

In less well-equipped aircraft, pilots' interpretations of instrument let-downs vary enormously, the seven-minute standard ranging from five to ten or more, depending upon wind strength, aircraft performance and other factors. One other phrase used in connection with EATs is the rarely heard 'delay not determined'. This is used to meet certain eventualities, such as a blocked runway, when it is not known how long an aircraft may have to hold.

Where Approach Radar that is not SSR-enabled is in use, as well as giving a release, the ACC also transfers radar identity in what is called a handover (a 'handoff' to the Americans). The Approach Controller is thus certain that the aircraft he is directing is the correct one on his radar display. The object is to pass headings (vectors) to the pilot to enable him to lock onto the ILS beam by the shortest practicable route commensurate with losing height. If there is no ILS, a Surveillance Radar Approach (SRA) will be given or, when the weather is suitable, radar positioning to a visual final.

A further check on the position of an aircraft is the VHF Direction Finder (VDF). It provides directional information about the origin of a VHF radio transmission. A pilot can be given a magnetic heading to steer – a QDM – in order to come within radar cover. It assumes nil wind conditions, an unlikely occurrence, so the pilot will have to allow for drift.

In effect a radar-directed circuit is flown, the terms downwind, base leg and final (see page 48) all being used where necessary, although the area of sky covered is far bigger than in the normal visual traffic pattern. A closing heading of about 30 to 40 degrees is recommended so that when the aircraft intercepts the ILS, only a gentle turn is necessary to lock on. The aim is to intercept the standard

3 degree glide path at approximately 7 to 8 miles out on the extended centreline of the runway. As a 3 degree glide path is roughly equal to 300ft of descent per mile, the aircraft should be between 2,000ft and 2,500ft at this point.

Subsequent landing aircraft are vectored not less than 5 miles behind, or further depending upon the wake turbulence category of the preceding traffic (See Chapter 14). Bigger gaps may also be built in to give space for departing traffic at single-runway airports. At Heathrow, under certain conditions, reduction of the separation to 2.5 nautical miles is authorised to ensure maximum utilisation of the arrival runway. The wake turbulence separation rules still apply, of course. Sometimes an aircraft may be instructed to make a complete turn (known as an orbit or a 360-degree turn) for delaying purposes or to achieve a required spacing behind preceding traffic.

It requires great skill to arrange traffic in line astern with the correct spacing, particularly at Heathrow where four holding stacks serve the airport. Speed control is also used extensively to even out the flow, a minimum of 170kt being permissible for jets and 160kt for large propeller-driven aircraft. Within the TMAs during the intermediate stages of the approach, a speed limit of 250kt is imposed on all traffic to make the radar controller's task a little easier. The same speed limit applies to outbound traffic, but the controller can lift it by using the phrase 'No ATC speed restriction', often abbreviated to 'No ATC speed'. I once heard a Shorts 360 pilot respond with 'Would that it made any difference!' At the other end of the scale, an inbound aircraft asks Amsterdam Radar if there is any speed restriction, to which the controller replies 'No sir, you can go as fast as you dare!'

Speed control should not be applied to aircraft after passing a point 4 nautical miles from the threshold on final approach. Commercial aircraft operations require that an approach is flown as a 'Stabilised Approach' in which an aircraft should be in its landing configuration and at its final approach speed by at least 1,000ft above the threshold elevation. If agreed by the aircraft operator this may be reduced to 500ft; however, this is not considered normal operations. The higher the speed applied on final approach, the greater the chance of an approach becoming unstable and a go around being initiated.

'Minimum clean speed' signifies the minimum speed at which an aircraft can be flown in a clean configuration, ie without deployment of lift-augmentation devices, speed brakes or landing gear. The use of the phrase 'minimum clean speed' can achieve a reduction in aircraft speed in a very short space of time and is useful in appropriate circumstances. However, the actual speed flown will vary depending on type, and compliance may be affected by other factors such as local turbulence. This instruction to fly at minimum clean speed should be given early to enable aircrew to plan and achieve descent profiles.

The Approach Controller passes an 8-mile check on intercom to his colleague in the tower who will already have details of the arriving aircraft. If there are no pending departures at the runway holding point, a landing clearance may be given at this point but it is more usual to give it at the 4-mile range. Alternatively, once the pilot reports established on the ILS, Approach may tell him to contact the tower, who will give landing clearance when available. Where the Tower Controller has an ATM (Air Traffic Monitor) display, approach will routinely transfer aircraft to his frequency with no prior warning.

Pilots expect to receive a landing clearance at around 4 miles on final approach, but this is not always possible owing to departing traffic or a previous landing aircraft being slow to vacate the runway. Two miles is the absolute minimum for large transport aircraft because a go-around is a fairly major operation. The phrase 'expect late landing clearance' is sometimes heard because spacing has got a little tight in the final stages of the approach and the first aircraft is not yet off the runway. On other occasions, departing traffic may be slower to get airborne than expected.

Aberdeen radar room. *NATS*

Surveillance Radar Approaches

For a runway not equipped with ILS, the radar controller is normally able to offer a Surveillance Radar Approach. If the weather is poor this can be down to half a mile from touchdown, assuming that the radar is approved for this purpose. With certain types of radar, approaches to two miles only may be allowed. This ensures a reasonable chance of seeing the approach lights and making a successful landing in all but the worst weather.

Where only one Approach Controller is on duty and the ILS fails, he may be unable to offer a half-mile SRA because of the necessity for continuous transmissions during the last 4 miles of the approach. This of course means that any other traffic cannot communicate with him until the talkdown is complete. If a second controller is available, the first can do a half-mile SRA on a discrete frequency while his colleague continues to sequence traffic onto long final for handover as soon as the preceding aircraft has completed its approach.

SRAs to 2 miles, however, do not require continuous transmissions and the controller can talk to other traffic as necessary, although he must time his calls so that range checks and the associated advisory heights are passed at the correct intervals. The advisory heights are based upon a glide path of 3 degrees, therefore, at 6½ miles the aircraft should be at a height of 2,000ft. Descent on a 3 degrees glide path is equivalent to about 300ft per mile. Some airfields have non-standard glide path angles because of local obstructions and other considerations, the advisory heights being adjusted accordingly. It is assumed that the aircraft is flying on QFE, but if the pilot advises that he is using QNH, the runway threshold elevation is added to the advisory heights and rounded up to the next 25ft, the term 'altitude' being used in place of 'height'.

In good weather, by day or night, even though nominally flying IFR, a pilot may request permission to make a visual approach. This may be granted subject to certain provisos, the most important of which is that the pilot must have visual reference to the surface, ie the ground or water, and a reasonable assurance exists that he will be able to complete the landing visually. Standard separation continues to be applied between this aircraft and other arriving and departing traffic, unless the pilot states that he can see an aircraft ahead in the approach sequence and follow it down to the runway. During daylight hours only, IFR flights may be cleared to approach maintaining VMC and their own separation, if weather reports indicate that this is possible.

Inbound VFR traffic will be cleared into a control zone via a Visual Reference Point (VRP), which ensures that it remains well away from the flight paths of arriving and departing IFR traffic. An altitude restriction will also be imposed for the same reason, as well as a clearance limit in the vicinity of the airfield. This will be an easily identifiable ground feature over which the aircraft can hold until it can be fitted into the traffic pattern.

Letters of Agreement

ATC Units may establish Letters of Agreement with adjacent aerodromes or airspace users to permit the integrated operation of airspace activities including glider, hang-glider, parachuting and other activities. The document specifies airspace sharing and delegation arrangements, hours of operation and any necessary inter-unit co-ordination arrangements.

Point Merge

Devised by Eurocontrol to take advantage of the precision of current flight navigation, Point Merge is a radical revision of traditional radar Approach Control methods. Already in operation at twenty-five airports worldwide, including Dublin, it was adopted at London City and Biggin Hill Airports in 2016 but has yet to spread to other UK locations. It is a system by which the aircraft queuing to land fly an extended flight path around an arc instead of holding in ovals. They fly along the arc until the next slot in the landing sequence is free. These arcs are generally much higher than the stacks in current use, so reducing noise and fuel burn.

Aircraft fly onto a designated arc and proceed along its curvature until told to turn towards the merge point and fly direct to it. This turn is calculated such that once on the direct leg, the target spacing at the merge point is assured. Aircraft on the sequencing legs are vertically separated from each other. Descent in the direct leg is mainly continuous and speed control is applied as necessary to maintain the required spacing. The merge point may be followed by another direct leg to intercept the final approach course or be itself the start of the final approach. There are no set rules for this and procedures are set up at each location to best fit the circumstances.

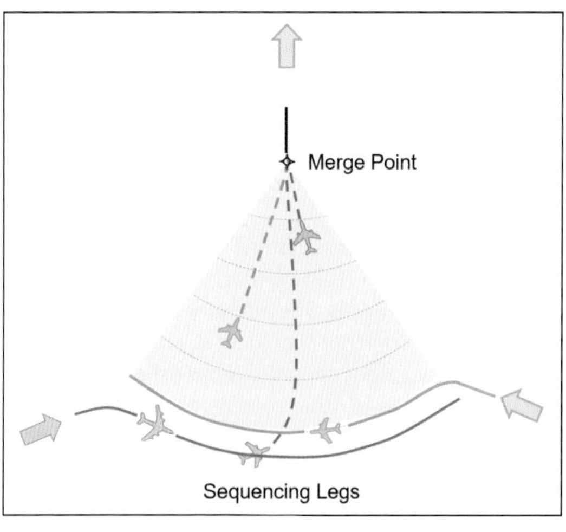

Point Merge diagram.

Chapter 6

Aerodrome Control

The term 'aerodrome' dates from the First World War and is derived from the Ancient Greek meaning 'aerial racecourse'. Surprisingly, it is still official ICAO terminology. The Aerodrome Controller's basic function is defined as the issuing of information and instructions to aircraft to achieve a safe, orderly and expeditious flow of traffic with the objective of preventing collisions between:

(a) Aircraft flying in, and in the vicinity of the Aerodrome Traffic Zone

(b) Aircraft taking off and landing

(c) Aircraft and vehicles, obstructions and other aircraft on the manoeuvring area (ie the runways and taxiways)

(d) Aircraft and other aircraft moving on the apron

It is emphasised that Aerodrome Control is not solely responsible for the prevention of collisions. Pilots and vehicle drivers must also fulfil their own responsibilities in accordance with the Rules of the Air.

Jersey Airport Visual Control Room. *Graham Hocquard of Ports of Jersey, via Marc Hill*

The apron may also come under the jurisdiction of 'Apron Control', a non-ATC function, and/or the marshaller, who makes sure that aircraft are parked in the required places. This is particularly important at airports where all or part of the apron is out of sight of the tower. At larger airports, self-manoeuvring markings are painted on the concrete to guide pilots to the stand that has been allocated on R/T, thus obviating the need for 'the man with the bats'. Major airports have Visual Docking Guidance Systems (VDGS) using lights and symbols. It would be impossible to control all the service vehicles moving about the apron so these are confined, as far as possible, to outline-painted lanes.

Airfield fire and maintenance vehicles that need to go on the runways and taxiways are controlled on a UHF domestic frequency. These are not published but can be found in the range 455–461MHz (NFM). Most operate on a split frequency where the base station transmits on, for example, 455.6375MHz, and the mobile on 460.9375. Sometimes the VHF tower or GMC channel

Aerodrome traffic circuit diagram.

Designated Positions in the Traffic Circuit

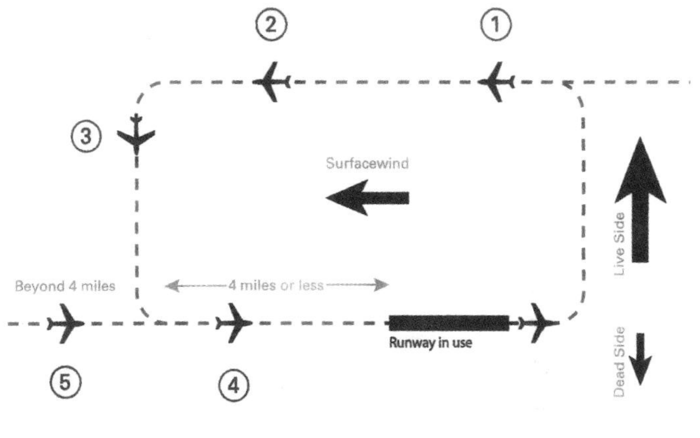

Figure 1 Designated Positions in the Traffic Circuit

Position 1: Aircraft reports on 'downwind' leg when abeam upwind end of the runway.

Position 2: Aircraft reports 'late downwind' if it is on the downwind leg, has been unable to report 'Downwind' and has passed the downwind end of the runway.

Position 3: Aircraft reports 'base' leg (if required).

Position 4: Aircraft reports 'final'. Clearance to land issued here.

Position 5: Aircraft reports 'long final' (between 8 and 4 miles) when aircraft is on a straight-in approach.

Note: For light aircraft operations, circuit dimensions may be reduced, but the relative RTF reporting points are maintained.

is rebroadcast on the UHF frequency so that vehicle drivers can be aware of aircraft movement. At some airfields the tower VHF frequency is used for controlling vehicles. Standard phraseology is in use (aircraft 'taxi', vehicles 'proceed' or 'tow') and vehicles have self-explanatory callsigns such as Sweeper One, Works 36, Security 22, Fire Six, etc.

To smooth the running of the larger airports, it may be necessary to split the duties of Aerodrome Control into Air Control, which has absolute authority over all movements on active runways and their access points, and Ground Movement Control (GMC). The latter's responsibility covers aircraft moving on the apron and aircraft and vehicles on the manoeuvring area, except on runways and their access points. Major airports have a Surface Movement Radar (SMR) to follow aircraft and vehicle movements in bad visibility. R/T loading at some locations, including Heathrow, Gatwick and Manchester, necessitates a further sub-division of GMC known as Ground Movement Planning (GMP), also referred to as Clearance Delivery, callsign 'Delivery', on which start-up and route clearances are passed.

Until quite recently the Tower Controller had few aids apart from his or her 'Mark One eyeball' and a pair of binoculars. Now, many Visual Control Rooms (VCRs) are equipped with an Air Traffic Monitor (ATM). This is a daylight-viewing, colour radar showing the local area out to a radius of about 15 miles. At airports with only one runway and a high movement rate it is invaluable in judging whether there is sufficient space to clear a departing aircraft to take off or to give priority to an aircraft on final approach. It also serves to confirm the turn onto track of a preceding aircraft so that a second aircraft can be permitted to depart. If an ATM is not available, the Radar Controller is required to give an 8-mile check for traffic on final approach to his colleague in the tower, using intercom. The aim is to confirm landing clearance at about 4 miles but normally at not less than 4 miles.

Manchester aerodrome chart. *NATS*

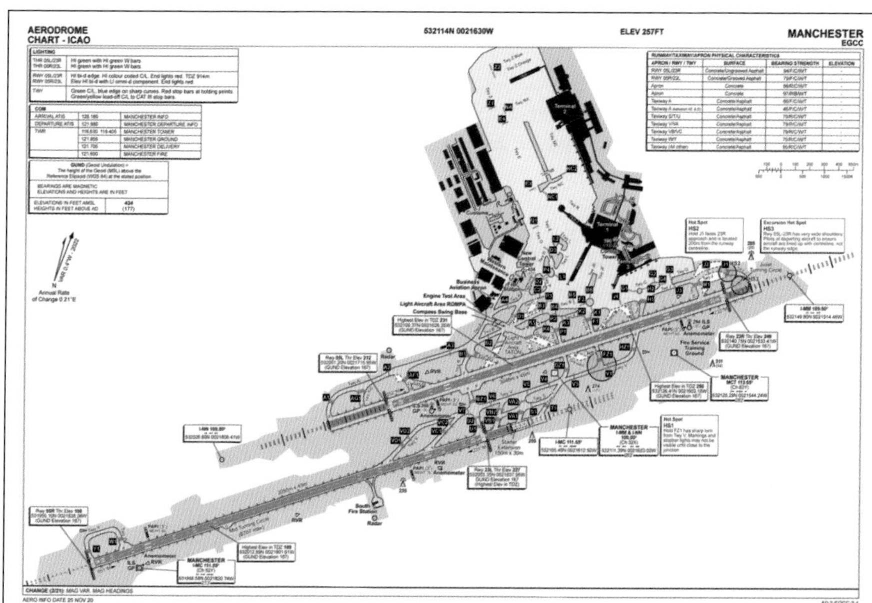

Runway occupancy is governed by the following rules:

(a) An aircraft shall not be permitted to begin take-off until the preceding departing aircraft is seen to be airborne or has reported 'airborne' by R/T and all preceding landing aircraft have vacated the runway-in-use.

(b) A landing aircraft will not be permitted to cross the beginning of the runway on its final approach until a preceding departing aircraft is airborne.

A pilot receiving the ATC instruction 'cleared for immediate take-off' is required to act as follows: If waiting clear of the runway, taxi immediately on to it and begin his take-off run without stopping his aircraft; if already lined up on the runway, take-off without delay; if unable to comply with the instruction, inform ATC immediately.

Frequent use is made of the 'land after' procedure, which seems to puzzle some inexperienced pilots who perhaps think it is a place in Wales! Its purpose is to increase runway utilisation by permitting a landing aircraft to touch down before a preceding aircraft that has landed is clear of the runway. The onus for ensuring adequate separation is transferred from controller to pilot. The provisos are:

(a) The runway is long enough to allow safe separation between the two aircraft and there is no evidence to indicate that braking may be adversely affected.

(b) It is during daylight hours.

(c) The preceding landing aircraft is not required to backtrack in order to vacate the runway.

(d) The controller is satisfied that the landing aircraft will be able to see the preceding aircraft that has landed clearly and continuously until it has vacated the runway.

(e) The pilot of the following aircraft is warned. Responsibility for ensuring adequate separation rests with the pilot of the following aircraft.

At some airfields the tower and approach function may be combined on one frequency. This is perfectly satisfactory with light to medium traffic flows, but on busy weekends the R/T congestion can be serious, pilots having difficulty in getting a word in.

Airfields outside controlled airspace possess an Aerodrome Traffic Zone, through which flight is prohibited without an ATC clearance or traffic information from a Flight Information Officer. The circuit direction is a standard left hand, although this may vary for different runways to avoid overflying built-up areas, hospitals and the like. The reason for the left-hand pattern is said to date back to the First World War when aircraft such as the Sopwith Camel turned much more easily to the left than the right, owing to the torque effect of the rotary engine. When larger aircraft with side-by-side seating were introduced, the pilot sat on the left and this has become traditional. In helicopters, however, this is reversed! Circuit height is normally 1,000ft above ground level (QFE), but at some airfields it is 800ft.

The circuit is divided into four legs: crosswind, downwind, base and final approach. The first aircraft to report downwind will be told to 'report final'. ('Number One' may be added to this.) The second will be told 'Report final number two to the Cherokee on base leg', and so on. New pilots should note that it is 'final' singular, not 'finals'! If the circuit is very busy the tower may instruct a pilot to 'report before turning base, four aircraft ahead'. When he does this he will be given an update on his position in traffic, there perhaps being only two ahead by this time.

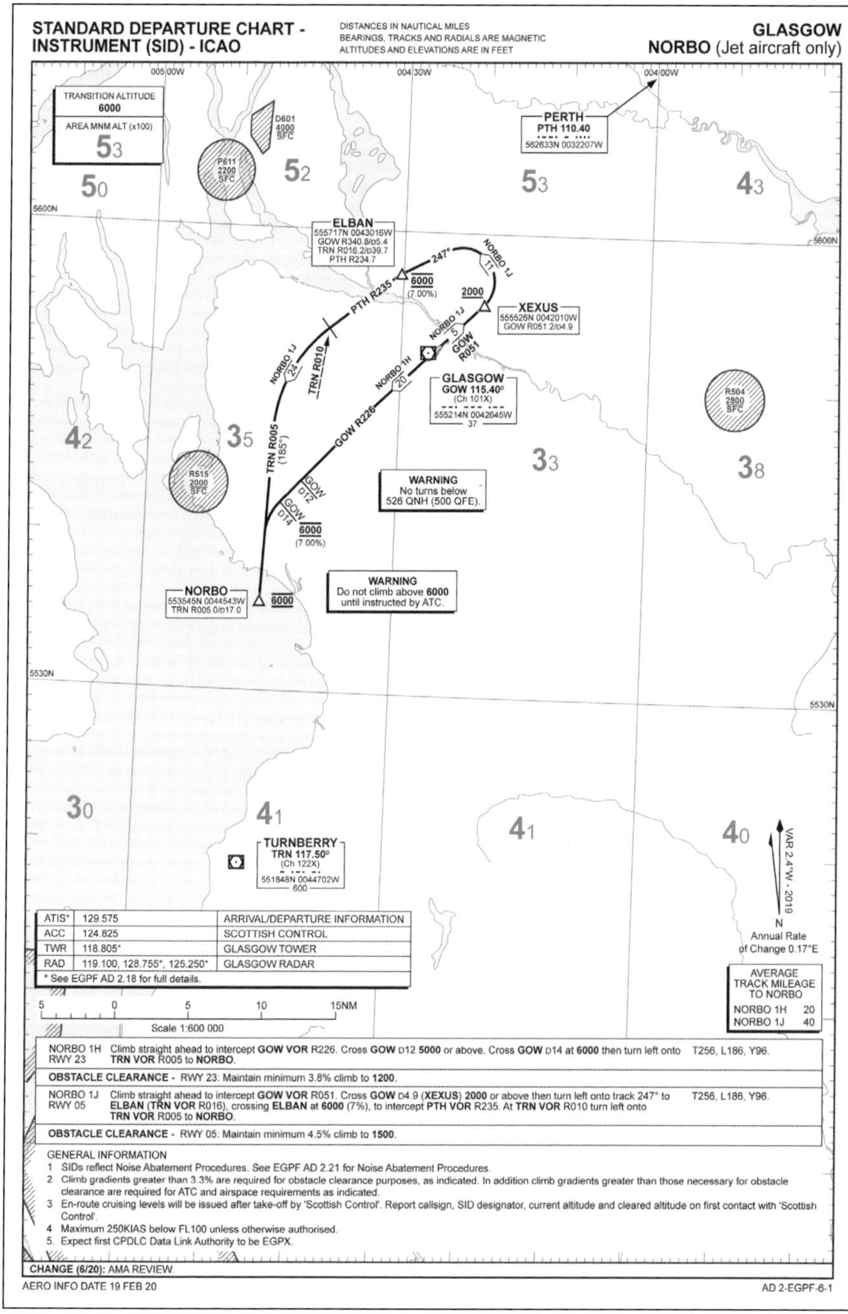

Glasgow NORBO Standard Instrument Departure. *NATS*

The standard circuit-joining procedure is to arrive overhead the field at 2,000ft, descend on the dead side, ie the one opposite the live downwind leg, and let down to 1,000ft. Whilst watching for departing traffic, the pilot then joins the crosswind leg over the upwind end of the active runway. (Humourists should note that there is a cemetery under the dead side at Cambridge Airport.) This should ensure that a joining aircraft does not conflict with one just airborne, as there have been numerous cases in the past of collisions because of careless rejoins a mile or so off the end of the runway. Of course, a high-performance aircraft can easily be at 1,000ft by the time it reaches the end of a longish runway, so it is up to the tower to make sure that a joining aircraft does not cross its path. At many controlled airports the standard join is not used, aircraft being authorised to join directly onto final, base or downwind.

Aircraft flying under IFR are usually fed straight into the final approach, which can sometimes be tricky. One way to achieve this safely if there is circuit traffic is to instruct the training traffic to continue downwind until he has the arriving aircraft in sight and then follow it. A warning about wake turbulence and the recommended spacing to avoid it is passed if necessary. The other solution is an orbit – 360-degree turn – always away from the final approach, to be continued until the traffic is sighted. The first method has the disadvantage that a strong tailwind may carry the aircraft into the next county, with perhaps an inexperienced pilot losing sight of the aerodrome. An orbit may be impracticable because of following traffic in the circuit. There is a limit to the number of aeroplanes you can orbit safely in a circuit!

If traffic is particularly congested and large aircraft are expected, trainers can always be told to land and taxi back to the holding point to await further take-off clearance. Another complication is wake turbulence, a phenomenon once referred to as slipstream or propwash, but now known to be a rapidly revolving cylinder of air from each wingtip. This can be so violent that it can overcome the control forces of a following aircraft and roll it over. Aircraft in the United Kingdom are placed in four categories depending upon maximum total weight at take-off. They are Heavy, Medium (divided into Upper and Lower), Small and Light. Full details are to be found in Chapter 12

Helicopter operations are less of a problem than might be imagined; the main one being crossing the active runway. However, they can clear it quickly and can thus be slotted between arriving and departing aircraft, remaining below 500ft until clear of the traffic zone. The same applies to their arrival. At some locations, helicopters are required to use a runway for take-offs and landings. Some small helicopters have skids rather than wheels so the phrase 'air taxi' will be used when directed to the parking position. Overflying helicopters are treated like any other crossing traffic, either cleared overhead above 2,000ft if the circuit is busy, or asked to report a few miles away and given traffic information so that they can fly through the pattern without conflict.

The Aerodrome Controller is, of course, pre-warned of arriving traffic by Approach or at some places he handles both functions on the same frequency. Similarly, for departing IFR traffic he will have the flight progress strips on his pending board, made up when the flight plan was filed with ATC.

Departing pilots who do not file a flight plan are required to inform the air traffic unit or other responsible agency at the aerodrome of departure, giving their destination, number of persons on board, fuel endurance and time en route. This is referred to as 'booking out'. The actual time of departure is then recorded and no further action is taken. Although such action is not required for circuit training and local flying, at busier locations there may be an agreement for pre-warning ATC. The Tower Controller may refuse to accept more than a certain number of aircraft in the circuits, dependent upon weather conditions, scheduled traffic, existing congestion and other factors. At smaller airfields, pilots merely call for taxi clearance from the parking area stating their requirements.

Aircraft on IFR flight plans must first request permission to start engines so that ATC can warn of any likely delays. Traffic on congested routes over Europe are subject to complex rules known as Departure Flow Regulation. They require the aircraft to take off at a specified time, ATC being allowed a small margin before and after this to cover any taxiing delays or short waits for landing traffic. These Calculated Take-off Times (See-Tots) were formerly known as slot times. Further details will be found below and also on page 92. Busier airports are allowed longer tolerances.

Domestic traffic within the UK is also regulated at peak periods. For example, the Channel Islands airports become very busy during the summer and flow control is often employed to reduce congestion. On occasion, routes over the Irish Sea and Scotland are also subject to flow management. A time band normally of ten minutes, within which an aircraft must cross a specified point, is used as an alternative to a CTOT. On fairly rare occasions, the parent Area Control Centre may impose a Minimum Departure Interval (MDI) between take-offs for a specified period of time. This is normally because of traffic congestion in the vicinity and is totally unrelated to slot times.

Network Manager Operations Centre (NMOC)

Based in Brussels and formerly known as the Central Flow Management Unit. The NMOC computer knows the theoretical capacity of every piece of airspace and every runway in Europe. If it states that a certain sector can take forty-five aircraft per hour at certain levels, but fifty are flight-planned plan into it, five of those have to be shunted into the next hour to accommodate them. Hence a departure slot is issued to delay them. There are other factors as well. For example, if a certain airport has a major weather problem that reduces arrival rate, or has staffing or equipment problems, they notify NMOC of the reduced acceptance rate. Flights inbound to the airport then get delayed so that the rate is adhered to. Note that Runway Slots at major airports are a totally different game, and one of the ways that airports make their money is by auctioning them to the highest bidding airline.

At the London Area Control Centre (ACC) there is a Flow Management Position under a Network Manager, supported by Airspace Capacity Managers. They are responsible for the day-to-day monitoring, planning and co-ordination of all flow measures affecting traffic entering, leaving, overflying or remaining within the UK. Effectively, this is a tactical interface between airport ATC units and NMOC. If a flight's CTOT is some way ahead, passengers will be boarded and the aircraft made ready to start. The crew will then request ATC to send a 'Ready Message' in the hope that the CTOT will be brought forward. Sometimes this works!

Returning to the airport scenario, if there are no problems, taxi instructions will be given to the appropriate runway. In the meantime, ATC will have obtained an airways clearance from the parent ACC by land line and this is passed to the aircraft at a convenient moment, assuming that this has not been done earlier. Now that NATS has introduced Electronic Flight Data Display Systems at some of its airports, suitably equipped aircraft may request and receive their ATC route clearance via datalink.

Standard Instrument Departures (SIDs)

SIDs have been developed for the main runways of major airports, the routes terminating at an airway or at a radio navigational fix. Noise Preferential Routeing is also built in. Assuming SIDs are published for a particular airport, all departing aircraft under IFR are required to follow the appropriate SID, unless and until authorised to do otherwise by the relevant ATC unit. Each SID has a designator that incorporates the name of the radio beacon or fix on which it is based. An example is the BARTN One Tango from Runway 27 at Liverpool, for traffic heading to the east and north-east. Subsequent changes to SIDs result in a new number up to nine, then back to one again. The suffix letter indicates the runway, a BARTN One Victor being the reciprocal Runway 09.

Local procedures vary from one airport to another and it may be necessary to contact the ACC again as the subject nears the runway for permission to let it take off. This is known as a 'release'. On occasion, Approach Radar will have to separate it from inbound conflicting traffic. It will then be given a suitable radar heading to fly after departure and/or a level restriction. An example is: 'After departure, climb straight ahead to maintain altitude 3,000ft.' As soon as it is airborne the aircraft will be transferred to the Approach frequency and it will only be handed over to the Area Control Centre when the confliction has been resolved ('Clean' in ATC slang).

Where no local restrictions are applied, the tower will transfer the aircraft to the ACC immediately after take-off. The departure time may also be passed to the ACC electronically or by telephone to be fed into the computer. At the busiest UK airports, including Heathrow, Gatwick and Manchester, the flow of arrivals and departures is designed so that the two do not conflict. The ideal is a 'conveyor belt' system but, although in practice this is virtually impossible to achieve, it comes quite near to being so. Of necessity the other lesser airfields in a TMA, for example Liverpool in the case of Manchester, are somewhat subservient. Their traffic flows are very much subject to those of their busier neighbours, although on the credit side, sometimes more flexible.

Birmingham Tower Voiceswitch panel for channel selection, intercom and telephone direct lines. *RW*

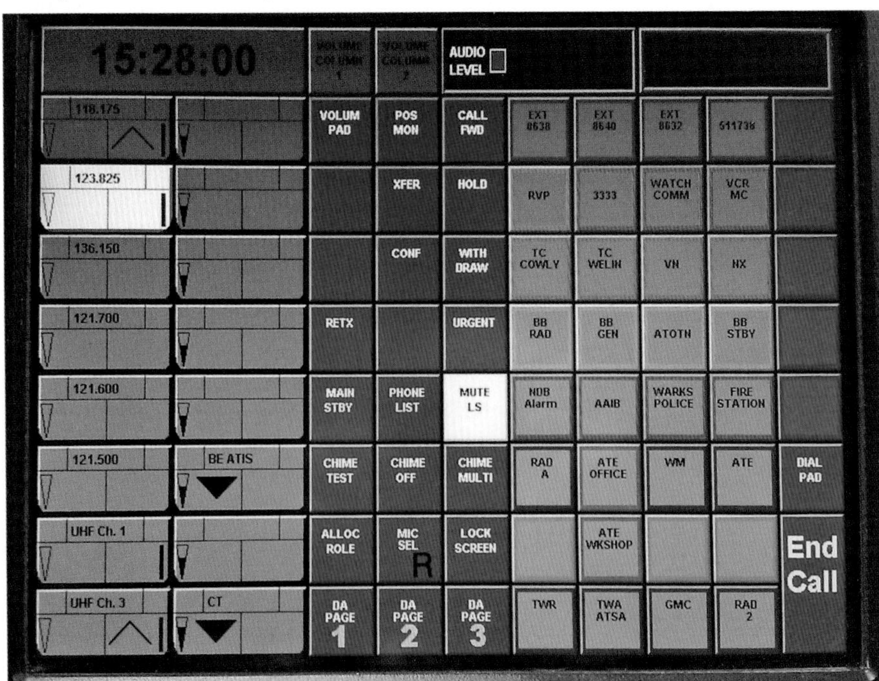

Secondary Surveillance Radar (SSR) Squawks

By agreement with the parent ACC, some towers with SSR capability validate the SSR code by checking it has been set correctly and verify the Mode C by asking for an altitude check on the initial climb out. If this is within 200ft either side of the height label on the controller's display, it is considered acceptable.

The SSR code, or 'squawk' as it is known, is allocated according to a predetermined system. The UK participates in the internationally agreed Centralised Code Assignment & Management System CCAMS). This was developed by Eurocontrol and endorsed by the ICAO. Since there are insufficient code blocks to develop a worldwide system it has been necessary to group certain countries into Participating Areas. The ICAO EUR region is divided into five of these areas, the United Kingdom falling into PA West.

CCAMS is designed to reduce R/T and cockpit workload by allocating an SSR code that will be retained by the aircraft from take-off to touchdown. This helps controllers in forward planning, particularly in areas of radar data processing. Each ACC is allocated two blocks of codes, one for internal flights (Domestic) and the other (CCAMS) for international flights. The ACC with jurisdiction over the airspace first entered by an aircraft will assign a discrete code from one of its blocks. The code will depend on the destination and will be retained throughout the flight within the Participating Area, being transferred from control centre to centre along the route.

SSR Mode S has solved the problem of the very limited number of codes available (there are 4,064). Mode S transponders employ a unique 'address' for each individual aircraft, 16 million being available worldwide. Approach Control units with SSR capability have their own small block of codes that they can allocate to traffic operating in their area, provided of course that the aircraft is transponder-equipped. Fortunately nowadays, most general aviation aircraft can comply with this.

Mention of the special squawk 7000 is often made on R/T. Pilots flying outside controlled airspace and Aerodrome Traffic Zones and who are not receiving a radar service are advised to set 7000, the Conspicuity Code, on the transponder. As the name implies, this makes the aircraft show up better on radar as well as indicating its altitude if Mode C is fitted. Above FL110, 7000 is mandatory.

Chapter 7

ATC at London's Airports

Bear in mind that at the time of writing, London's airports are a pale shadow of their former selves, but traffic is beginning to build again. It is assumed that in due course operations will resume normality and this chapter describes what will happen when they do.

The entire London area ATC operation is a very difficult and challenging one and the controllers who run it are, arguably, the world's best. Because of its intensity, traffic in the London TMA is handled rather differently from that of other British airports. The airports involved are Heathrow, Gatwick, Stansted, Luton, London City and Biggin Hill. Inbounds to RAF Northolt, because of its proximity and similar runway alignment, use the same standard arrival routes as Heathrow and are radar vectored by the latter's controllers.

Cross-Border Arrival Management (XMAN)

An innovative cross-border arrival management system, known as XMAN, is in operation for both Heathrow and Gatwick. The procedure's success relies on the sharing of information between NATS and surrounding Area Control Centres who work together to slow down aircraft that are up to 350 nautical miles from London. This ultimately reduces the holding times for aircraft approaching the two airports.

Departure queue at Heathrow. *NATS*

Once the forecast delay for Heathrow reaches seven minutes, NATS' Arrivals Management System (AMAN) automatically estimates the arrival time of incoming aircraft. The system sends this information to neighbouring centres, where the optimum speed can be shown in a label on the controller's radar display. The inbound flight can then be slowed down during the en route phase, at a higher altitude, where the aircraft operates more efficiently.

London Terminal Control Centre (LTCC)

Situated at Swanwick and usually referred to simply as 'TC', this is the hub of the operation, split into a number of important functions. These are (a) transition sectors that facilitate the interface between en route sectors of London and Scottish Controls and the London TMA; (b) TC London TMA sectors whose primary role involves tactical traffic deconfliction of arrivals and departures before transfer to Approach Control or transition to en route sectors; (c) further inbound sectors within the TMA share responsibility for the holding stacks with Approach Controllers; (d) Approach Control for Heathrow, Gatwick, Stansted (Essex Radar), Luton, and Thames Radar, which controls London City and Biggin Hill.

TC is responsible for a number of en route sectors in the lower levels of airspace immediately outside and on top of the TMA. These are controlled from TC because they mainly feed traffic into and out of the main London airports. They are grouped as TC East (four sectors), TC Midlands (four sectors) and TC Capital (two sectors). TC East's airspace adjoins the international boundary with Amsterdam and Brussels airspace.

The TMA itself is divided into sectors, each sector controller being responsible for a defined segment. Traffic flows predominantly in the same direction to minimise points of conflict and the need for co-ordination between controllers is kept to a minimum. TC TMA sectors are divided into two groups or banks along an east–west axis through Heathrow (TC North (five sectors) and TC South (six sectors)). London TMA inbound sectors share responsibility for the holding stacks with Approach controllers. Approach Control services for Heathrow, Gatwick, London City, Stansted and Luton are also carried out at Swanwick. TC's airspace extends up to FL155, above which are London Middle and Upper Sectors which mainly handle overflying traffic.

All sectors have the R/T callsign 'London Control'. Arrivals for the London airports are handed over from London Area Control or the TC en route sectors, following Standard Terminal Arrival Routes (STAR) and are descended against the departing traffic and sorted out into different levels They are then routed to various holds, where they will remain until the Approach Controllers are ready to position them into an approach sequence to land.

Arrivals are presented to TC Controllers by adjacent sectors from multiple directions. TC Controllers dictate the order aircraft arrive at the terminal holding stacks and ensure vertical separation therein. Prior to transfer of control to Approach, arrivals are normally directed to one of ten holding stacks, each of which is designated to a particular airfield or groups of airfields by the appropriate Tactical Controller.

At Heathrow, Gatwick, Stansted and Luton, aircraft are instructed to enter the holds at the lowest available level. The lowest level in these holding stacks is usually FL70 or FL80 depending on runway orientation and atmospheric pressure, as this maximises the efficiency of the operation. The terminal holding stacks are located relatively close to the airfields, enabling Approach Controllers to manage traffic efficiently enough to maintain runway capacity during peak times and accommodate requests for variable spacing on the ILS at short notice from the Tower Controller.

Heathrow departures all climb continuously to 6,000ft on Standard Instrument Departures (SIDs). SIDs from Heathrow, Gatwick, Stansted, Luton and London City are all separated from each other for the initial portion of their route. Except Heathrow, many SIDs contain step-climbs. This means that aircraft are required to level off for periods during their climb, rather than benefit from a continuous climb profile. Once the departure is clear of holding stacks and inbound conflicting aircraft, the pilots are issued further clearances dependent on prevailing traffic conditions and agreements with adjacent sectors.

When above the Noise Preferential Route (NPR), which follows the lower part of the SID, controllers have the flexibility to vector aircraft off their SID in order to facilitate climb earlier than would be possible if left to follow the SID profile. This is common practice and is indeed what TCs are trained to do until their workload becomes too high, at which point aircraft are left to follow the SID. However, aircraft cannot be left on all SID routes for their entirety due to other traffic interactions, therefore even during busy periods, tactical intervention may be required.

Aircraft inbound to Heathrow are directed by LATCC to one of four VORs – Ockham in Surrey to the south, Biggin Hill in Kent to the south-east, Lambourne in Essex to the north-east and Bovingdon in Hertfordshire to the north. If traffic is light they may not actually route overhead these beacons but are vectored by radar directly to intercept the ILS for the landing runway. As the traffic flow increases, aircraft may arrive at the beacons faster than the airport is able to receive them, allowing for the requisite separation on approach. Hence the term 'stacking' (in ATC more usually referred to as 'holding').

The incredible performance of enhanced Mode S transponders in aircraft enables the downlinking of flight information direct to a controller's radar display. Few UK ground units have this facility as yet and TC is one of them. The parameters include the current flight level or altitude from the autopilot, the current indicated airspeed from the airspeed indicator, the current heading, and the current rate of climb or descent. The information being visible on a separate vertical stack list. The controller can even monitor the altitude selections made by a pilot on his Flight Management Computer (FMC) and alert him if a wrong selection is made. It is no exaggeration to say that this is one of the most significant improvements in ATC safety since the introduction of SSR.

London Heathrow

Arrivals

During busy periods, when the flow of arriving traffic exceeds the immediate system capacity, the Terminal Holding Stacks form a 'reservoir' of queuing aircraft from which the approach radar controllers (known as Directors) arrange the optimum sequence. The radar technique is very deliberate, using upwind legs where possible so that the timing of the turn downwind can be controlled. This enables the length of the final approach to be fine-tuned so that it is kept at the optimum 15nm. Establishing on final at this distance enables rigid speed control to be applied to adjust any vectoring errors. The result is that the aircraft get as close as possible to minimum spacing (2.5nm) as they cross 4 miles DME from touchdown. Both the runways operate at saturation level for most of the day.

At the most busy times, six controllers work as a team. They consist of a North Intermediate Director and his support controller, a South Intermediate Director again with a support controller, a Final Director and a Special VFR Controller. Each Director controls the traffic from either Bovingdon and Lambourne in the north or from Ockham and Biggin in the south. As the aircraft nears one of these VOR beacons TC releases it to Heathrow Approach. On contact the pilot is told to enter the hold or, if there is no delay, vectored directly into the landing sequence.

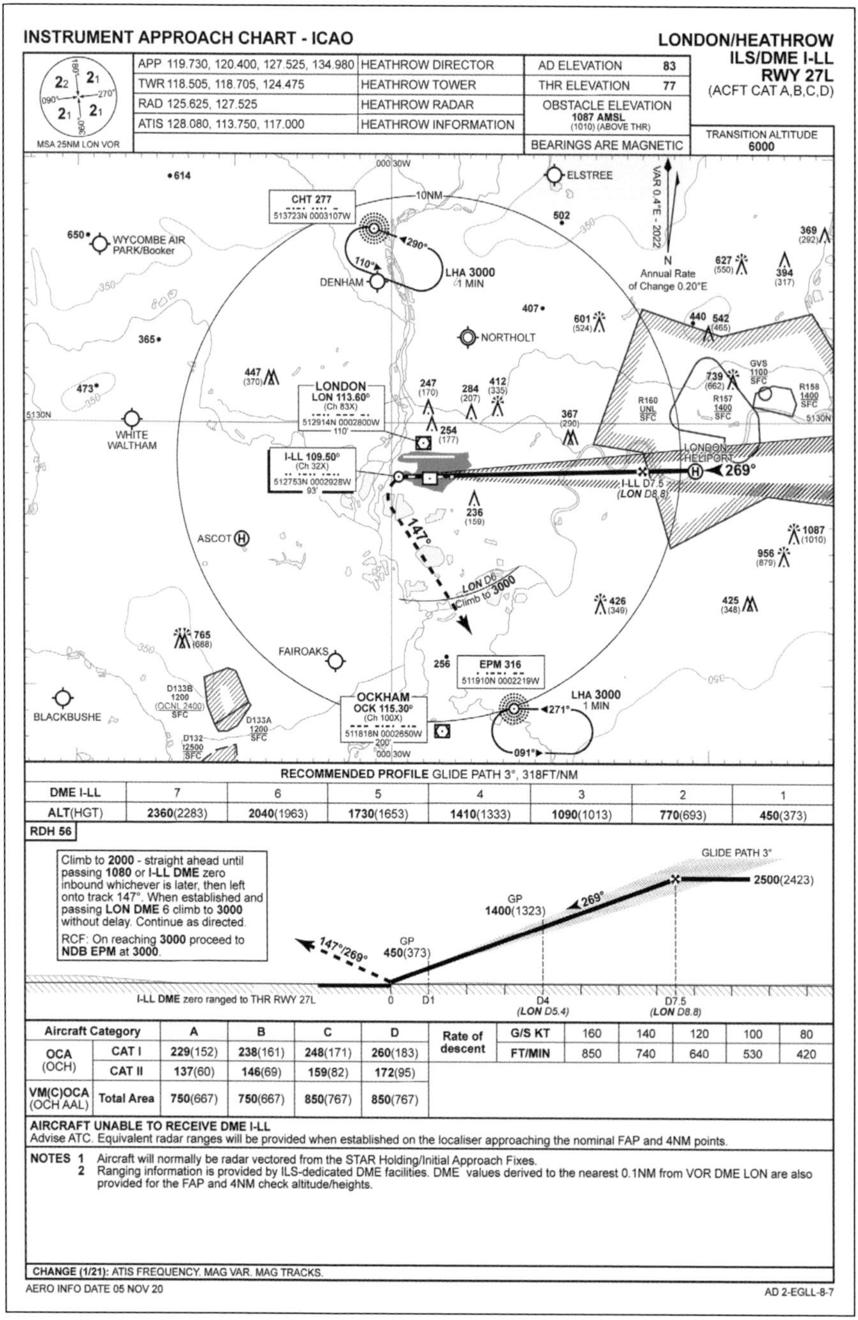

London Heathrow Runway 27 Left ILS approach chart. *NATS*

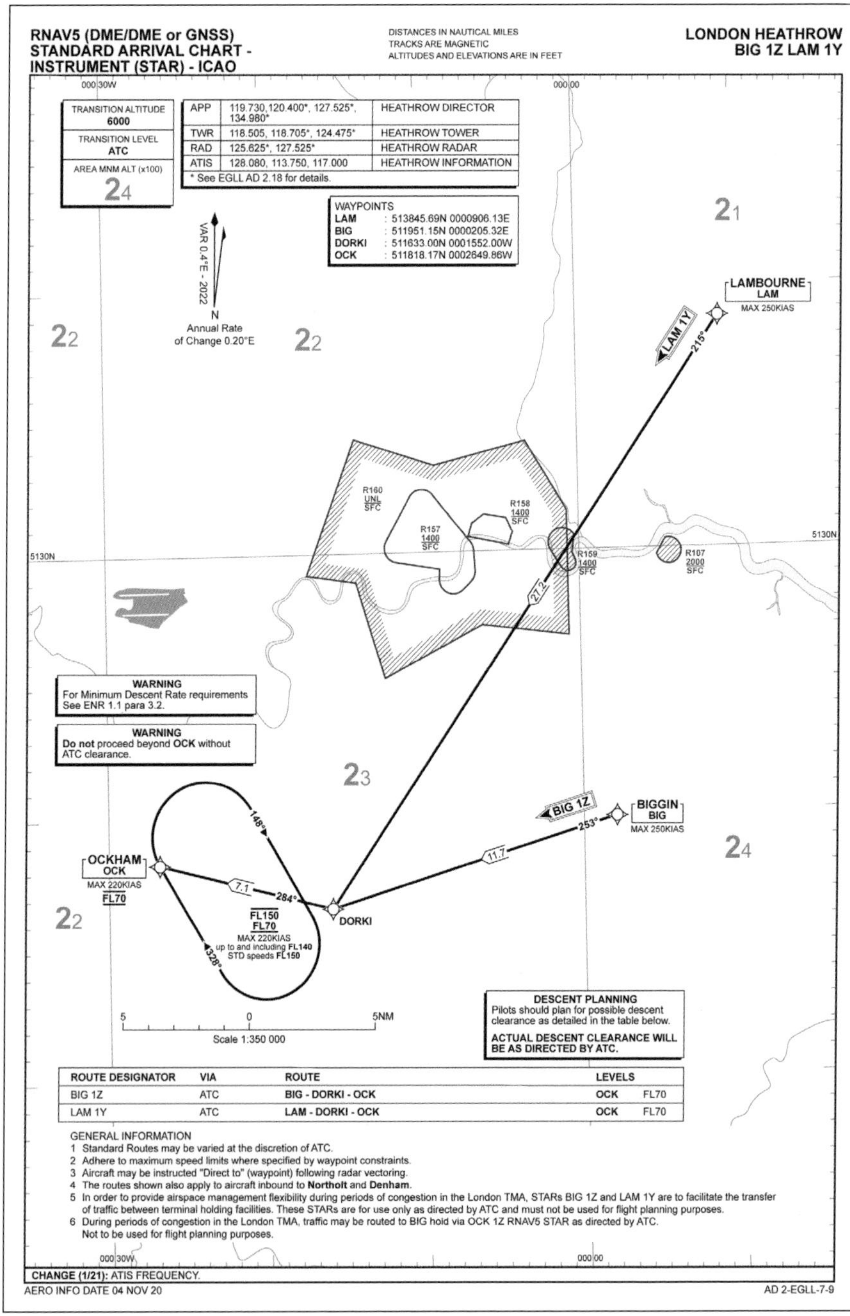

Heathrow STAR via Biggin and Lambourne. *NATS*

The Directors work closely together, instructing pilots to adjust their height, speed and heading so that two orderly streams of aircraft, one from the north, the other from the south, are brought onto the approach path. Aircraft in these two streams are handed over to the Final Director so that he can integrate them into a single stream of aircraft approaching the runway.

At this stage a correct landing interval must be established and the Final Director ensures that all aircraft are correctly separated, depending on the prevailing weather conditions and type of aircraft involved. The wake turbulence separations are explained in Chapter 12, but there are other considerations. For example, a Boeing 737 following a small turboprop will obviously have no problem with turbulence but will catch up rapidly if this is not allowed for. Similarly, if visibility is on limits an aircraft may be slow to clear the runway and the 'land after' procedure cannot be applied, resulting in a go-around if the next aircraft is too close behind.

When traffic is heavy and the holding stacks are filling up, the North Director takes on the title of Master Director and decides the overall landing order. Generally this will be on a first-come, first-served basis but as soon as traffic starts to build, the order will be manipulated at the earliest opportunity. The aim is to group similar aircraft types so as to maximise the landing rate. For example, if four Boeing 737s and four 747s arrived at the same time, the best landing rate would be achieved by positioning the 737s on final one behind another, followed by the 747s.

Another operational feature of London's airports, also adopted at other UK sites, is the Continuous Descent Approach Procedure (CDA). The aim is to provide pilots with the assistance necessary for them to achieve a continuous descent during intermediate and final approach, at speeds that require minimum use of flaps and speed brakes. This has significant benefits in terms of noise produced beneath the approach area and in reduction of fuel used. CDA requires ATC to apply specific or minimum speeds to inbound aircraft and to pass adequate 'range from touchdown' information. In a nutshell, low power, low drag, less noise.

When the two streams of approaching aircraft are satisfactorily merged into one, and as each aircraft is established on the ILS at a distance of 6 to 8 miles from touchdown, control is transferred to Air Arrivals Control in the tower. Like any other Tower Controller, he/she issues landing clearances, passes wind checks and details of surface conditions where appropriate. If there are no wake turbulence separation requirements, the spacing used on final approach is 3 nautical miles and under certain conditions this can be reduced to 2.5 miles. In Low-Visibility Procedures (LVP) conditions, the spacing will be increased to 6 miles, giving a landing rate of about twenty-eight per hour.

Before the pandemic, Heathrow handled about 1,300 movements per day, with a maximum declared hourly capacity of forty-five arrivals and forty-six departures.

During adverse weather with LVPs in force, a typical inbound flow rate is twenty-four to twenty-six per hour, matched by twenty-four to twenty-six outbounds. In ideal conditions the controllers can do up to forty-eight arrivals per hour. Departures are normally about forty-five per hour but if the traffic mix is good it can be up to fifty. All aircraft are instructed to fly at the same speeds. This is usually 220 knots off the stack, 180kts on base leg and, when correctly spaced on final approach, 160kts, which will be maintained until 4 miles from touchdown. Tactically Enhanced Arrival Mode (TEAM) is an agreement that during very busy periods, especially 0700–0900, Terminal Control may request the use of the departure runway for some inbound traffic in order to increase the overall landing rate and thus reduce inbound delays. This is the so-called mixed mode.

Ground Movement Control (GMC)

After the aircraft has landed and vacated the runway it will be transferred to the Ground Movement Controller, who directs it to the parking stand. He/she continues to monitor its progress and co-ordinates its movements with those of other aircraft and vehicles. Heathrow is split into three designated areas, each with its separate Ground Controller. GMC-1 is known as the 'master' position and provides bandboxed (combined frequency) coverage of GMC-2 and 3 when the latter are not open at quieter times.

Any airport has its quota of operational vehicles but Heathrow inevitably has more than most. There is, for example, a full-time mobile bird control unit, radio callsign 'Seagull'. 'Checker' is the airport surface and lighting inspection vehicle, 'Pixie' the ATC vehicle.

The maintenance of runways and taxiways and their associated lighting is one of the biggest problems for GMC. It seems that there is almost always some part of the airport being dug up or resurfaced. Each controller has an airport plan on which he notes the current unserviceable areas before taking over watch in the tower.

Heathrow has an A-SMGCS – Advanced Surface Movement Guidance and Control System. Without going into too much technical detail, A-SMGCS is a surface movement radar system that displays aircraft callsigns and allocated stand numbers on the ground radar display. When a pilot switches on his Mode S transponder with the Mode A code selected, the Mode A code is transmitted via Mode S, and a label is generated that is derived from the code/callsign database.

Supporting A-SMGCS is multilateration, which uses multiple ground stations to determine the position of aircraft, both on the ground and on approach, as well as providing altitude, identification and downlinked data. This information forms a vital part of NATS' 'Intelligent Approach' system for separating arriving aircraft. (See below). Another feature of the system is the RIMCAS – Runway Incursion Monitoring and Collision Avoidance System. It provides audible and visual warnings in the event of runway incursions.

Heathrow ATIS includes a request for pilots to leave their transponders on Mode S after landing, without appropriate Mode 3A set. The transponder is to be left on until parked on stand and selected with the allocated code during pushback. The aim is a marked improvement in the service pilots receive from tower and GMC in the dark and during LVPs. From what I understand, the Mode S 'squitter' transmits the aircraft's callsign once per second and it is this that the system uses.

Aircraft are assisted by green centreline and red stop bar lights set flush with the taxiways. These can be illuminated in sections to ensure that no two aircraft are in or crossing the same section at any one time. This complex lighting system is operated by Lighting Panel Operators, specialised support assistants who monitor their associated Ground Movement Controller's frequency and select the appropriate lighting. The lighting control panel is a mimic diagram, ie it is designed in the form of an airport plan with switches that directly operate the lighting in the corresponding section of the airport.

Departures

Prior to start-up, a flight crew will obtain their departure clearance from Clearance Delivery (callsign 'Delivery') either by voice or via datalink. When ready to start, the pilot, having previously noted the data on the continuous broadcast on the ATIS, informs Delivery that he is ready for pushback and start engines. If there are delays, an anticipated start time may be given to minimise ground delays and thus save fuel. Also taken into consideration are the number of other aircraft that have already started, air route congestion and Calculated Take-Off Time (CTOT), issued by NMOC.

When transferred to GMC, pushback and start-up clearance is issued and the crew will report ready to taxi. Guidance is then given to the runway-in-use and, as this is approached, the aircraft is handed over to the Air Departures Controller, who arranges the aircraft in a departure sequence to achieve the maximum use of the runway. Holding areas adjacent to the runway holding point provide sufficient space to 'shuffle' the order of departures. To make them more conspicuous, these holding areas are five-letter named rather than allocated complicated alphanumeric codes, examples for Runway 27 Right being 'PLUTO', 'TITAN' and 'SATUN'.

The basic rule of thumb is to alternate the departures between straight ahead, left and right. For example, when two aircraft of a similar type are departing in succession, one for a destination to the north followed by one to the south, they are allowed to leave one minute apart. However, due to the variety of aircraft types using Heathrow, this time interval may have to be increased depending on wake turbulence categories and specific departure route. To minimise runway occupancy time, on receipt of line-up clearance pilots are expected to taxi onto the runway as soon as the preceding aircraft has started its take-off roll. Again, once receiving take-off clearance, they are required to roll immediately. These procedures are known collectively as HIRO (pronounced Hero) – High Intensity Runway Operations.

Aircraft leaving Heathrow mostly depart on a free-flow principle. This means that the radar controllers do not release each individual flight for departure; they just receive a pre-note via computer that the flight is pending. This cuts down on inter-unit co-ordination and allows the Tower Controller at the airport to decide the most efficient departure order. In many cases the aircraft's Standard Instrument Departure (SID) routeing does not conflict with the approach sequence of aircraft arriving at the airport. Thus the airport's Approach Control does not need to handle the aircraft and it is transferred straight to the TMA Controller on departure. The TMA Controllers then climb the departures through the arrivals for the airports that they are also working.

The pair of westerly (27) runways at Heathrow tend to be used most frequently because of prevailing winds. One is normally used for landings and the other for departures, but a local agreement ensures a change from one to the other at around 1500 hours local time each day until after the last departure in order to spread the noise more evenly. When the tailwind component is no greater than 5 knots on Runways 27 Right and Left, they will be used in preference to Runways 09 Right and Left, provided the runway surface is dry.

Intelligent Approach (IA)

To increase runway capacity at Heathrow, NATS and Leidos, a leading technology provider, have developed tools to optimise arrival spacing in all conditions and for all runway configurations. It supplies capacity and safety benefits without the need for expensive changes to ground infrastructure. IA is operational at Heathrow Airport and designed in a modular way so that it can integrate with existing Air Traffic Management systems.

It is made up of the following three core modules: Distance Based Separation, which improves the consistency of approach spacing by providing controllers with a visual indication of the required separation between aircraft with optimised wake spacing rules; Time Based Separation (TBS), which provides resilience to headwinds by reducing the wake turbulence separation based on the live wind conditions and therefore improves operational and safety performance; and Optimised Mixed Mode, which has been specifically designed for mixed-mode runways to safely reduce inbound separation by taking account of departure runway occupancy.

TBS uses live data downlinked from the aircraft to dynamically calculate the actual winds on final approach to determine the optimal safe wake vortex spacing between aircraft. Real-time separation indicators are provided to controllers to assist with managing final approach separations. The result is an average tactical capacity gain of two aircraft landings per hour in all wind conditions. Not much perhaps, but significant at an airport that under normal conditions operates at 98 per cent capacity.

Under development is pairwise separation, which will allow Intelligent Approach to dynamically calculate the optimum spacing between more than 4,500 combinations of aircraft types. This would enable a new procedure called Independent Parallel Approaches (IPA), which has been identified as one way greater runway capacity can be achieved for the two runways.

Airport Collaborative Decision Making (A-CDM) and Target Start-Up Approval Time (TSAT)

In 2012 Heathrow joined Paris Charles de Gaulle, Frankfurt, Munich and Brussels as one of the first European airports to fully implement A-CDM. This concept enables Heathrow's partners, including airlines, ground handlers, ATC and airport staff, to share the latest and most accurate information about the status of inbound and outbound flights. This enables better-informed, more consistent decision making. As Heathrow is an airport operating at almost full capacity, operational efficiency is vital. By using A-CDM, the life cycle of each flight can be divided into sixteen stages, showing the progress of each aircraft as it comes in to land, throughout its turnaround and subsequent departure.

This means operational staff at the airport can calculate more realistic timings for each flight, reducing the duration of taxi times and potentially reducing delays. Alerts are generated automatically if an aircraft looks likely to miss its CTOT, so airport staff can react swiftly. Increased efficiency means that the number of minutes aircraft spend taxiing on the airfield is reduced, cutting the amount of fuel that is burnt. With 1,300 flights a day at Heathrow, that could mean a saving of up to 30,000 tonnes of CO_2 each year. As well as sharing data across Heathrow, A-CDM will also share information with airports across the European network. To achieve this, Heathrow has an automated data exchange in place for both departing and arriving flights. This helps to improve network predictability and reduce delays across Europe.

Aircraft held in a take-off queue with engines running are not only bad for the environment, but they also waste money due to excess use of fuel. To predict the delay an aircraft faces and thus absorb some of it at the stand, TSAT has been devised at Heathrow. It uses a variety of information sources, such as that from the air traffic controllers and airlines, to make more accurate predictions about running times. This allows the aircraft to leave the stand at the last possible moment, reducing fuel burn and allowing for a more efficient use of time. Improved efficiency leads to marked benefits that are not just economic and environmental. TSAT also enables better allocation of resources, such as pushback tugs, reduces taxi times and provides a much-improved passenger experience by providing them with more certainty of take-off times.

London Gatwick

Gatwick before the pandemic was recognised as the busiest single-runway airport in the world and has also now adopted A-CDM. Gatwick has two holding stacks known as WILLO and TIMBA, to the SW and SE of the airport respectively. WILLO takes traffic from the north, west and south-west plus all Atlantic and some Spanish traffic. TIMBA covers all other traffic from Europe. The parallel Runway 08 Left/26 Right is a non-instrument runway and is used only when 08 Right/26

Left is temporarily non-operational by reason of maintenance or accident. Simultaneous operations are not permitted as the runways are too close together. Gatwick is also working on the first introduction of permanent RNAV departure routes at any major UK airport.

Prior to the pandemic, the world's most efficient single runway at Gatwick had achieved the seemingly impossible declared capacity of fifty-five movements an hour at peak periods. The 'Drive for 55' programme involved implementing many different procedures and system improvements, both on the ground and in the air. Stabilising arrivals spacing on final approach was one improvement that produced a major increase in runway throughput. This provided much greater accuracy and predictability for launching a departure between two arrivals, while minimising the risk of an arrival going around. Gatwick controllers occasionally achieved sixty movements an hour on its single runway. This became another ambitious target to aim for, but the challenge for the airport was to find ways to deliver this rate consistently whenever needed, day in, day out. Over the last few years, Gatwick has been working on a major research effort to figure out how much more runway capacity can realistically be achieved. A rate of sixty movements an hour has never been reached at a commercial airport consistently, so ensuring it can be achieved regularly is a significant and complex project.

The airport's team has narrowed down the requirements to just two key things that Gatwick needs to do to achieve its ambitious objective. The first improvement involves integrating the latest technologies into a single operating system to achieve greater operational precision in the spacing and sequencing between aircraft. This builds upon some of the capabilities implemented during the 'Drive for 55' programme, including departures and arrivals spacing tools.

The second is far more radical and requires new tools and techniques to reduce the workload of the controllers to enable them to handle more aircraft. Currently, when Gatwick's tower requests the arrival spacing from London Terminal Control, it typically requests 6 or 5½-mile spacing. This distance gives the airport enough time between two arrivals to safely allow a departure. This system is not as efficient as it could be because, for example, it does not allow Gatwick to request a 5¾-mile separation. It is either a 6 or 5½-mile spacing. Translated into time, that means adding an extra six seconds of buffer to the spacing between the two arrivals. Adding all the six-second buffers up over the course of a day is equivalent to at least three more movements in an hour.

Operating at the equivalent of one aircraft per minute means that every second really does count. To achieve the required movement level, Time Based Separation (TBS) will be employed on approach, as opposed to the current system that measures the separation between aircraft by distance. TBS has already been proven at London Heathrow. Gatwick plans to adapt this work so that it fits in with the airport's mixed mode operation on a single runway. The plan is now on hold, of course, and it remains to be seen how long it will be before these measures can be put into effect. A fascinating prospect indeed.

London Stansted and London Luton

Stansted currently has two stacks at LOREL and ABBOT, to the north-west and north-east, respectively. LOREL also serves arrivals for London Luton. Stansted's Approach Control unit uses the callsign Essex Radar for initial vectoring, followed by handover to Stansted or Luton Directors. This sharing of holds and arrival routes is unique in the UK for two major airports. Any arrival delay or disruption at one airport can cause unnecessary arrival delay to the other.

At the time of writing, there is a proposal and resulting public consultation to separate Luton arrivals flight paths from Stansted's. It would also involve establishing a new hold exclusively for Luton traffic, to reduce delay and maximise efficiency of the airspace. The proposed new hold would be to the north of Luton.

Stansted tower controllers. *NATS*

Low Level Operations Within the London Control Zone

The management of low-level aircraft within the London and London City CTRs has evolved over more than forty years and, whilst there have been changes made as a result of both ATC and operator feedback, the fundamental principles of use have remained constant. The defined London Helicopter Routes have not undergone any significant changes since they were introduced, although the density and height of the urban environment has changed significantly since their introduction.

A re-evaluation of the route profiles (raising maximum altitudes), the conditions of availability and requirements associated with holding on the routes resulted in some changes in 2020. Until then, the London and London City Control Zones had minimal Visual Reference Points (VRPs) within them, although ATC and pilots routinely use many prominent ground features as unofficial VRPs. These include the London Eye and Wembley Stadium. Following consultation with operators, sixteen new VRPs were established. The intent of their use is to assist with existing traffic flows and not routinely introduce new areas to be overflown.

When an ATC clearance is issued to a pilot wishing to operate on the London Helicopter Routes the phrase 'Standard Operating Altitude' is used. This means a pilot may operate up to the maximum published altitude for the route. Pilots may fly at altitudes below the maximum published altitude for the route, but they are encouraged to operate at as high an altitude as possible to reduce the impact of noise.

Metropolitan Police helicopters obviously need to operate anywhere in the London area. Obtaining clearance to fly to any given location is relatively simple and relies upon a common reference source for mutual understanding. The pilot quotes a specific page and grid square

London City Airport from the air. *NATS*

reference in the Geographia Atlas for London. Using the same document, ATC clears him to this position.

London City Airport

Early in 2021, London City became the first major international airport in the world to be fully controlled by a remote digital ATC tower. This followed intensive testing and live trials of the revolutionary technology during the pandemic lockdown. All aircraft movements are now controlled from the London Area Control Centre at Swanwick, Hampshire. The controllers use an 'enhanced reality' view supplied by a state-of-the-art 50m tower sited at the airport.

This multi-million-pound investment in SAAB's remote digital technology was already proven at two Swedish airports. It uses sixteen high-definition cameras and sensors to capture a 360-degree view of the City Airport. This is relayed through a super-fast fibre connection to a control room at Swanwick. A team of controllers uses the live footage, an audio feed from the airfield and radar information to oversee aircraft movements in and out of the airport.

The live feed, transmitted through independent secure fibre networks, is displayed on fourteen HD screens at Swanwick to provide a panoramic moving image. This can be over-laid with digital data to provide an enhanced reality view. Information such as callsigns, altitude and speed of all aircraft approaching and leaving the airport, weather readings and the ability to track moving objects can all be included in this single visual display. Pan-tilt-zoom cameras can magnify images up to thirty times for close inspection. The tower has metal spikes on top to protect its cameras from birds, and each camera has a self-cleaning mechanism to stop insects and debris from blurring the lens.

London City's remote tower controller. *NATS*

The digital technology significantly improves controllers' situational awareness, enabling quick and informed decisions to improve safety and operational efficiency. The live sound of the airport is piped into the new control centre so that controllers still hear aircraft engines and the reverse thrust of touch down. One of the controllers is quoted as saying: 'Fundamentally, the job hasn't changed. It's still about the controller's eyes finding the aircraft and monitoring it visually. The difference is we're using screens instead of windows.' Once flying recovers after the pandemic, City will be able to handle forty-five movements per hour, up from forty in 2019.

In order to negotiate the limited space and large buildings nearby – the runway features the steepest glideslope in the UK (5.5 degrees), which together with a 1,500m runway creates a challenging approach for pilots of all aircraft. Neighbourhood pressures, together with the unique approach requirements, severely limit the aircraft types that can operate into the airport. It also requires specifically qualified crews in order to ensure safe operations. All of the stands face nose out, which negates the need for pushback from the terminal. Parking is a slick operation co-ordinated by two marshallers.

Traffic from and to London/City Airport is handled by a facility known as Thames Radar, which is co-located with Heathrow Approach. Because of its proximity to London City, Biggin Hill's IFR traffic is also co-ordinated by Thames Radar.

So far, the only use of Point Merge approach procedures in the UK has been at London City. Instead of flying over land, arrivals, including those for Biggin Hill, now join the Point Merge arc out over the North Sea before being peeled off in the optimum order for a continuous descent approach into the airport. It seems that Point Merge will not be adopted at Heathrow due to the limitations on the use of vectoring and also because some of the routes for Point Merge incorporate off-set approach. It would appear that Gatwick has no plans to utilise the system either, but for both locations this might change with radical airspace redesign at some future date.

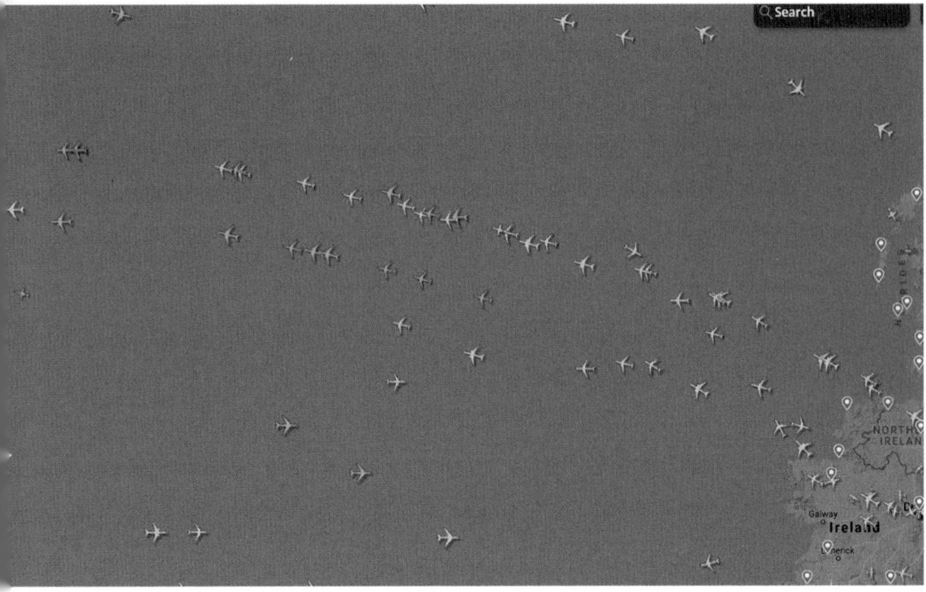

Chapter 8

Oceanic Control

ATC in the Shanwick Oceanic Control Area (OCA) – pre-pandemic, the world's busiest oceanic airspace – is provided by the Oceanic ACC at Prestwick, Scotland. It is supported by the communications station at Ballygireen, just north of Shannon Airport in Ireland, hence the composite callsign Shanwick Oceanic. The airspace between FL285 and FL420 over most of the North Atlantic is known as North Atlantic High Level Airspace (NAT HLA). As well as Shanwick, other controlling authorities in defined areas are Gander, Reykjavik, New York, Santa Maria in the Azores, and Bodø in Norway.

Aircraft flying within it are required to carry a certain scale of navigation equipment (Required Navigation Performance – RNP) so that they can be flown accurately within the parameters of the ATC clearance. This stipulates that an aircraft must be able to fly a specific path between two three-dimensionally defined points in space, with 95 per cent accuracy at all times.

Regardless of how sophisticated a navigation system is, it is still essential that stringent cross-checking procedures are maintained if Gross Navigational Errors (GNEs) are to be avoided. A GNE within NAT airspace is defined as a deviation from cleared track of 10 nautical miles or more. The North Atlantic Operations and Airspace Manual NAT007, prepared by the ICAO, covers this and every other aspect of crossing 'The Pond'.

North Atlantic traffic as seen on Flightradar24.

Organised Track System

There are currently no fixed air routes across the North Atlantic. Instead there is a procedure known as the Organised Track System (OTS) that is used for aircraft flying between North America and Europe between Flight Levels 290 and 410 inclusive. The system's periods of operation are westbound – 1130 to 1900 UTC and eastbound – 0100 to 0800 UTC. In the daytime, all traffic on the tracks operates in a westbound flow. At night, the tracks flow eastbound towards Europe. This is done to accommodate traditional airline schedules, with departures from North America to Europe scheduled for the evening, thereby allowing passengers to arrive at their destination in the morning. Westbound departures leave Europe at midday and arrive in North America in the late afternoon. The tracks are updated daily and their position may alter on the basis of a variety of variable factors, but predominantly due to weather systems that provide a tailwind where possible.

Prestwick OACC is responsible for the day track system and Gander in Newfoundland for the night ones. In each case, planners on both sides of the Atlantic consult with one another and co-ordinate as necessary with adjacent ATC agencies, both oceanic and domestic. This ensures that the system provides sufficient tracks and flight levels to satisfy anticipated traffic demand. Airlines that fly the North Atlantic regularly send a preferred route message (PRM) to Gander and Shanwick. On completion of negotiations, the OTS is sent out from the OACC concerned to all interested parties in Europe and North America. The daytime system is published by Prestwick around 2200 UTC and the night one by Gander around 1400 UTC. To ensure a smooth transition from night-time to daytime OTSs and vice versa, a period of several hours is interposed between the termination of one system and the commencement of the next. These periods are from 0801 UTC to 1129 UTC: and from 1901 UTC to 0059 UTC.

The tracks are known as Alpha, Bravo, Charlie and on to Mike, missing out 'I', the most northerly being Alpha. For night use the tracks are designated Zulu for the most southerly, Yankee for the next one to the north, ending at November, Oscar being missed out. Points along the route are identified by named waypoints (or fixes) and by the crossing of degrees of latitude and longitude (such as 54/40, indicating 54°N latitude, 40°W longitude).

Although the routes can change daily, they maintain a series of entrance and exit waypoints that link into the domestic airspace systems of North America and Europe. Standard route structures for use by westbound NAT traffic within UK and Irish upper airspace are specified in the UK AIP. Each NAT westbound oceanic entry point is related from UK airspace to the NAT organised track structure and to the originating area of the aircraft. In determining the UK track structure, account is taken of the expected traffic loading of the intended NAT tracks and the effect on domestic traffic densities.

For aircraft not equipped with HF radio, there are several routes known as 'Blue Spruce' that follow short hops between Iceland, Greenland and Canada within VHF radio and VOR/NDB coverage. However, the southerly Blue Spruce Route between Canada and Iceland runs south of this area. So, to fly on it between FL290–410 CPDLC (see page 39-40) and ADS-C are mandatory. Some aircraft may wish to operate outside the Organised Track System, for example on flights between Europe and the Caribbean. These so-called random tracks are also handled by Shanwick.

Prior to departure, airline flight dispatchers and flight operations officers will determine the best track based on destination, aircraft weight, aircraft type, prevailing winds and ATC route charges. Westbound aircraft operating within the UK UIR/FIR and the northern part of the France UIR are required to request oceanic clearance from Shanwick Oceanic on VHF R/T. UK departures are to request clearance as soon as possible after departure. Aircraft overflying the UK UIR/FIR and the northern part of the France UIR are to request clearance when they consider that they are within VHF R/T range of Shanwick Oceanic. Aircraft other than turbojets should request clearance at least forty minutes before the ETA for the Oceanic Control Area (OCA) entry point. Aircraft unable to contact 'Shanwick Oceanic' on VHF should request clearance on North Atlantic en route HF R/T Network (NARTEL) at least forty minutes before the ETA for the oceanic boundary and thereafter maintain a SelCal (Selective Call) watch for receipt of the oceanic clearance. Aircraft unable to contact Shanwick on VHF or NARTEL HF should request the ATC authority for the airspace in which they are operating to relay their request for oceanic clearance to Shanwick. Pilots of suitably equipped aircraft that will enter Shanwick airspace along the eastern boundary can obtain an oceanic clearance via VHF datalink, but voice read-back is required to confirm it.

Once the clearance is accepted by the pilot, the information is relayed to the relevant ACC and, where necessary, to adjacent OACCs. The clearance is then fed into Prestwick's computer, which prints the appropriate en route flight strips and relays the information to Gander's computer. These flight strips give all relevant flight details and computed times of arrival at specific reporting points along the track, normally at intervals of 10 degrees of longitude. The controller uses them to monitor the progress of the flight through the Oceanic Control Area. He is assisted in his task by the use of the Flight Data Processing System (FDPS), which carries out conflict prediction and detection, automatic update of flight profiles and data transfer to online adjacent ATC units.

Since the introduction of the Aireon Space Based ADS-B service in March 2019, NATS, Nav Canada and Nav Portugal have been trialling the use of reduced separations standards – known as ASEPS or Advanced Surveillance-Enhanced Procedural Separation standards – for aircraft flying through oceanic airspace. Having almost real-time surveillance over the ocean for the first time has made it possible for air traffic controllers to safely reduce the longitudinal spacing between aircraft from 40 nautical miles down to just 14 nautical miles, allowing more aircraft to share the fastest, most environmentally friendly routes. The success of the trial meant these separation standards were permanently adopted in November 2020, as well as published in worldwide ICAO documentation.

If an aircraft can no longer maintain the speed or altitude it was assigned, it can move off the track route and fly parallel to its track, but well away from other aircraft. Pilots on North Atlantic Tracks are required to inform ATC of any deviations in altitude or speed caused by avoiding weather, such as thunderstorms or turbulence. Aircraft must report in as they cross various waypoints along each track, their anticipated crossing time of the next waypoint and the waypoint after that. These reports enable the Oceanic Controllers to maintain separation between aircraft.

Operation in the NAT outside VHF coverage require two long-range communication systems, one of which must be HF. SATVOICE and CPDLC (appropriate to the route of flight) may satisfy the requirement for the second backup system. SATVOICE refers to the Aeronautical Mobile Satellite (Route) Service.

In the case of HF reports, each aircraft operates using SelCal: Selective Calling. SelCal can be muted so it only needs to wake up when there are incoming communications for that aircraft. This means that pilots do not need to keep a constant listening watch on HF with all its atmospheric noises.

The mandatory carriage of Automatic Dependent Surveillance (ADS-C & ADS-B), means that voice position reports on HF are no longer necessary, as automatic reports are downlinked to the Oceanic Control Centre. In this case, a SelCal check only has to be performed when entering the oceanic area and with any change in radio frequency, to ensure a working backup system in the event of a datalink failure.

Strategic Lateral Offset Procedure (SLOP)

Satellite navigation technology allows modern aircraft to fly very accurately, sometimes too accurately it seems. This is known as the navigation paradox, with research showing that increases in navigation precision actually increase the collision risk! Aircraft are now able to fly *exactly* over an airway or oceanic track, ie with a lateral error of less than 0.05 of a nautical mile. SLOP was devised as a mitigation strategy to increase the lateral separation between aircraft in case of crew error or operational errors involving the ATC clearance. SLOP requires the aircraft to fly either the centreline, 1 nautical mile or 2nm right of centreline. No left offsets are permissible. Aircraft that do not have an automatic offset capability (ie one that can be programmed in the Long Range Navigation System (LRNS) should fly the centreline only. Pilots must return to the centreline by the Oceanic exit point. Using TCAS, aircraft travelling along these tracks can monitor the relative position of other aircraft, thereby further increasing the safety margin of all track users.

Aircraft are not necessarily required to maintain their lateral offset but may switch between the centreline and the offsets at any time from entry point to exit point. For the operator, SLOP costs nothing but is priceless in terms of safety. Contingency plans also exist within the North Atlantic Track system to account for any operational issues that occur. For example, if an aircraft can no longer maintain the speed or altitude it was assigned, the aircraft can move off the track route and fly parallel to its track, but well away from other aircraft. Also, pilots on North Atlantic Tracks are required to inform ATC of any deviations in altitude or speed necessitated by avoiding weather, such as thunderstorms or turbulence.

SLOP also reduces the probability of high altitude wake turbulence encounters. During periods of low wind velocity aloft, aircraft that are spaced 1,000ft vertically but pass directly overhead in opposite directions can generate wake turbulence that may cause either injury to passengers/crew, or undue structural airframe stress. This hazard is an unintended consequence of RVSM vertical spacing reductions that are designed to increase allowable air traffic density. Rates of closure for typical jet aircraft at cruise speed routinely exceed 900 knots.

Flight Director over the Baltic.

Where HF radio is in use, the Oceanic Controllers at Prestwick do not talk to the aircraft directly but teletype their instructions to specialised, usually ex-marine, radio operators at Ballygireen just north of Shannon Airport. The latter talk to the aircraft and teletype the responses back to Prestwick. This is not as inefficient as it sounds because HF communications can be so distorted that experienced radio operators do better than the controllers themselves, and the short delay in reply is insignificant with such long distances between aircraft.

Suspending the North Atlantic Organised Track Structure

Capacity on the most efficient routes has always been limited by the huge separation distances required. That changed in 2019, when NATS and Nav Canada became the first air traffic service providers in the world to start using Aireon's real-time satellite-based ADS-B surveillance system to monitor North Atlantic air traffic. As well as the obvious safety benefit that having real-time surveillance brings, it has also allowed the safe reduction in separation distances down to as low as 14 nautical miles, which in turn offers aircraft more flexibility in terms of their speed and trajectory. That has meant more flights have been able to take advantage of the best routes, but have still been flying within an OTS environment.

A reduction in the OTS has long been part of NATS and Nav Canada's vision for the North Atlantic. The dramatic fall to around 500 flights a day instead of the usual 1,300 during the pandemic has fortuitously provided an opportunity to do things differently, and to introduce things more quickly than otherwise might have been possible. So, on days where ATC supervisors don't believe it is necessary, the Organised Track Structure will be suspended. Therefore, no tracks will be published either west or eastbound and the airlines will be asked to flight plan based entirely on their optimum route, speed and trajectory. It is hoped that analysis of these flights, together with other tabletop exercises, will provide the evidence needed to decide on the value of more permanent changes.

Emirates Airbus A380 at Manchester.

Chapter 9

Flight Information Service and Aerodrome Air/Ground Service

An ATC service can be provided only by licensed controllers, but at certain small airfields an Aerodrome Flight Information Service is in operation. The AFIS Officers, or AFISOs for short, are also required to be licensed, and many of them are flying instructors doing this ground job on a part-time basis. Airband listeners will notice considerable differences in the R/T phraseology used by AFISOs, reflecting the fact that their instructions are of an advisory nature only. The service provided by an AFISO is to give information useful for the safe and efficient conduct of flights in the Aerodrome Traffic Zone. From the information received, pilots will be able to decide the appropriate course of action to be taken to ensure the safety of flight. Generally, the AFISO is not permitted to issue instructions or advice to pilots of his own volition.

However, AFISOs are allowed to pass instructions to vehicles and personnel operating on the manoeuvring area and information and instructions to aircraft moving on the apron and specific parts of the manoeuvring area. Elsewhere on the manoeuvring area and at all times in the air, information only is passed to pilots. Further details on the passing of instructions by AFISOs at aerodromes are contained in CAP 797 Aerodrome Flight Information Service Officer Manual, available online.

Wolverhampton-Halfpenny Green tower provides an FIS.

AFISOs are also permitted to pass messages on behalf of other agencies and instructions from the aerodrome operator. If they do so, they will include the name of the agency so that pilots will be aware that the message comes from a legitimate source, eg 'London Control clears you to join …' AFISOs must ensure that the information given to pilots is distinct and unambiguous, as pilots will use this information for the safe and efficient conduct of their flights. An AFISO may request pilots to make position reports, eg 'downwind', 'final' etc. These requests do not have the status of instructions, although it is expected that most pilots will comply.

At the time of writing, AFISOs at North Weald, Manchester Barton and Goodwood aerodromes are involved in a CAA-authorised trial of Electronic Conspicuity at general aviation airfields. A specific element of this project is an ADS-B trial to demonstrate the possibilities for small airfields to improve situational awareness for FIS/ATC staff and pilots. Although web-based virtual radar (see Chapter 25) has been shown to have its uses in maintaining situational awareness, it is definitely not approved by CAA because of time lag and data unreliability.

Phraseology Examples

AFISO: 'G-CD, Traffic is a Cessna 172 base leg, take off at your discretion, surface wind 270 15.'

Or:

'G-CD, Via C2 take-off at your discretion, surface wind 270 15.'

Aircraft: 'G-CD, Taking off.'

AFISO: 'G-CD, Land at your discretion, surface wind 050 10 knots.'

The Aerodrome Air/Ground service is a rudimentary one, but persons providing it must possess a CAA Certificate of Competence, gained after passing an examination and an RT practical test. It is often encountered at club and private aerodromes, Haverfordwest in south-west Wales and North Weald in Essex being examples. Basic information is passed to pilots, including wind direction and confirmation that the runway is clear. The callsigns for AFIS and A/G are 'Information' and 'Radio' respectively. It should be noted that the phraseology used by Air/Ground Communication Service (AGCS) operators is different from that used by controllers and AFISOs. An AGCS radio station operator is not necessarily able to view any part of the aerodrome or surrounding airspace. Traffic information provided by an AGCS radio station operator is therefore based primarily on reports made by other pilots. Information provided by an AGCS radio station operator may be used to assist a pilot in making decisions, but the safe conduct of the flight remains the pilot's responsibility.

Radio operators must ensure that the full callsign, including the suffix 'Radio', is used in response to the initial call from an aircraft and on any other occasion that there is doubt. Personnel providing an Air/Ground service must ensure that they do not pass a message that could be construed to be either an air traffic control instruction or an instruction issued by AFISOs for specific situations. Air/Ground operators must not use the expression 'at your discretion' as this is associated with the service provided by AFISOs and is likely to cause confusion to pilots.

'G-CD downwind.'

'GCD roger no reported traffic.'

'-CD final.'

'G-CD roger surface wind 220 15. Traffic is a Cessna 172 reported lining up to depart.'

'G-CD ready for departure.'

'G-CD roger. No reported traffic, surface wind 230 degrees 10 knots.'
'Roger, taking off G-CD.'

Or:

'G-CD traffic is a Cherokee reported final, surface wind 230 degrees 10.'
'Roger, taking off G-CD.'

Or:

'Roger holding position G-CD.'
Once the Cherokee has landed and vacated:
'G-CD lining-up and taking off.'
'G-CD roger surface wind 230 degrees 10 knots.'

A common frequency (135.475MHz) known as SAFETYCOM is made available at airfields where no other frequency is allocated, to enable pilots to broadcast their intentions to other aircraft that may be operating on, or in the vicinity of, the aerodrome. At some UK airfields, aircraft movements may take place outside the published hours of watch of the ATC unit. In the interests of safety, pilots should broadcast their intentions to other aircraft that may be operating on or around the airfield. All transmissions in these circumstances are addressed to '(Aerodrome name) Traffic'. Since this is a common frequency, use of the airfield location is essential to avoid confusion.

Aeronautical radio stations located offshore on oil rigs, platforms and vessels provide an Offshore Communication Service (OCS) to helicopters operating in the vicinity. The radio operator must be able to volunteer information that may affect the safety of helicopter operations, for example: 'Caution flare venting,' or: 'I am shipping light/heavy spray on deck.'

A Flight Information service is provided by licensed controllers at Area Control Centres on a twenty-four-hour basis. The London FIR outside controlled airspace is divided into three, with a separate radio frequency for each. The Scottish FIR is covered by a number of frequencies, as noted in Appendix 3. FISOs do not use radar-based surveillance, they rely on the information pilots give them to help form a traffic 'picture' and utilise a 1:500,000 VFR chart.

Pilots do not have to call and use the service, but there are numerous reasons why they should. The FIR controller is able to offer the following services: weather information, changes of serviceability of radio navigation aids, aerodrome conditions, proximity to other aircraft warnings and much other information pertinent to flight safety. Because of the multiplicity of possible reporting points in the FIR, ranging from disused airfields to towns and coastal features, it is difficult to assess the possibility of collision and therefore no positive control or separation can be provided. The other problem is that of civil and military aircraft flying random tracks and for whom there is no requirement to contact the FIR controller.

When he/she receives a service from London or Scottish Information, a pilot will be asked for aircraft type, position, altitude and routeing, and then asked to squawk 'conspicuity 1177' for London or '7401' for Scottish. As a non-radar service, this squawk is not primarily for the benefit of the FISOs; it informs all the radar units across the London and Scottish FIR that you are talking to Flight Information. Quite often, a radar unit will contact Flight Information to ask for a transfer of the 1177 or 7401 squawk on their frequency to provide local traffic information. Sometimes, if an aircraft is flying close to controlled airspace, radar units can quickly contact Flight Information to confirm that your routeing is not going to interfere with other traffic.

Air Traffic Services Outside Controlled Airspace (ATSOCAS)

Outside controlled airspace, ie within Class G Airspace, it is not mandatory for a pilot to be in receipt of an air traffic service. This principle generates an unknown traffic environment, where pilots are ultimately responsible for collision avoidance and terrain/obstacle clearance. Radar-equipped ATC units form an overlapping network of radar coverage that is made available to aircraft operating either VFR or IFR and either inside or outside controlled airspace. The service covers most of England and Wales and limited parts of eastern Scotland. Controllers should make all reasonable endeavours to provide the service that a pilot requests, although this obviously depends on existing workload.

The **Basic Service** is intended to offer the pilot maximum autonomy and the avoidance of other traffic is solely his responsibility. It is essential that a pilot receiving this service remains alert to the fact that, unlike the Traffic Service and Deconfliction Service described below, the provider of a Basic Service is not required to monitor the flight, nor provide any traffic information. However, where a controller/FISO has information that indicates that there is aerial activity in a particular location that may affect a flight, in so far as it is practical, they should provide traffic information in general terms to assist with the pilot's situational awareness.

A pilot who considers that he requires a regular flow of specific traffic information must request a **Traffic Service**. This provides the pilot with radar-derived traffic information on conflicting aircraft. No deconfliction advice is passed and the pilot remains responsible for collision avoidance. If a pilot requires deconfliction advice outside controlled airspace, **Deconfliction Service** must be requested. A controller should make all reasonable endeavours to accommodate this request as soon as practicable. This service provides the pilot with traffic information and deconfliction advice on conflicting traffic. However, the avoidance of other aircraft is ultimately the pilot's responsibility.

The above is merely a summary of complex procedures. See CAP 774 UK Flight Information Services for the full details.

Military ATC radar units provide a Lower Airspace Radar Advisory Service (LARS) to any aircraft outside controlled airspace that requests it. The lower limit is 3,000ft and the upper limit is, with certain exceptions, FL95, the service being given within about 30 miles of each participating unit. From FL95 up to FL245 a similar Middle Airspace Advisory Service is provided. Whenever possible aircraft will be handed over from one controller to the next and pilots told to contact the adjacent unit.

Sleap tower provides an Air/Ground Service.

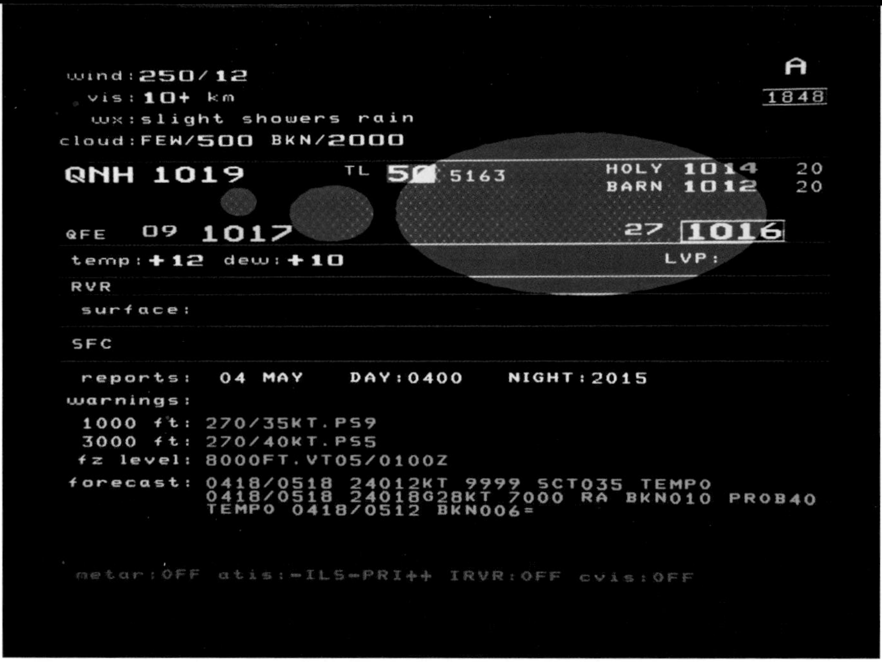

Chapter 10

Weather and Air Traffic Control

METARs (Met Actual Reports) at the larger airports are created from observations every thirty minutes; at twenty minutes past and ten minutes to each hour. At the less busy airports they are made once in each hour. Special observations, known as SPECIs (pronounced 'Spessys') must be made within these times if certain changes are observed, eg at the onset or cessation of hail or thunderstorms. If there is a Met Office available, the observations will be made by met staff who are all government employees. Otherwise, they are made by ATC personnel who are required to hold a Met Observer Certificate, gained after a short course at the Met College in Exeter. Many airports are now equipped with automated weather observing systems that provide continuous, real-time information and reports on airport weather conditions.

The code word 'Auto' or 'Automatic' in an ATIS broadcast (see below) indicates that the report has been generated using data from an automated observing system.

There is a standard format that is passed to aircraft, consisting of the wind direction in degrees True and its average speed in knots, with a note of any significant gusts. This is, however, always read by the controller in degrees Magnetic direct from the instruments in front of him so that it can be related by the pilot to the magnetic heading of the runway. The wind speed is normally presented by the anemometer as an average over two minutes but this can be switched to a so-called 'instant wind' when the pilot requests instantaneous surface wind read-outs in difficult conditions. The word 'instant' is then inserted into the controller's transmissions.

Tower controller's weather display.

The prevailing visibility is passed in increments of 50m when the visibility is less than 800m; in increments of 100m when it is 800m or more, but less than 5km. It is passed in kilometre steps when the visibility is 5km or more but less than 10km. When the visibility is 10km or more, it is given as 10km. Visibility values are rounded down to the nearest lower step. Where the visibility in any direction is less than the prevailing visibility and less than 1,500m, or less than 50 per cent of the prevailing visibility, the lowest visibility observed will also be reported in the increments described above. The distance is determined from the known ranges of conspicuous landmarks visible in the locality. Runway Visual Range (RVR) will be included when measured.

The next item is the weather, eg drizzle, fog, rain and so on, followed by cloud heights and amounts. Cloud base is measured by means of a cloud base recorder, which scans the sky overhead with a laser beam. At less well-equipped airfields, cloud base is found by estimation, with experience a surprisingly accurate method. Pilot reports can be requested to confirm the base. Cloud amount is measured in oktas, ie eighths, and height in feet up to and including 5,000ft. Cloud above this level in the UK is of academic interest only to aircrew so is not reported. Not more than three layers are reported, the exception being when cumulo-nimbus cloud, referred to as Cb or Charlie Bravo, is present. If necessary this can be reported as a fourth group. Cloud amounts are now referred to simply as scattered (1–4 oktas), broken (5–7oktas) or overcast (8 oktas). When cloud base is not discernible due to fog, snow, etc, 'sky obscured' is reported.

Air temperature is passed in degrees Celsius, together with the dew point if the two figures are significantly close, indicating that fog may be about to form. The QNH and QFE (Threshold QFE at certain airfields) is given in hectopascals, the terminology that has now replaced millibars in European ATC.

Where the weather conditions meet particular criteria – visibility of 10km or more, no precipitation, no thunderstorm or shallow fog, no cloud below a level of 5,000ft above aerodrome elevation and no Cb at any level – the visibility and cloud groups are omitted and the word 'CAVOK' (pronounced 'Cav OK') is passed.

Digital barometer. *RW*

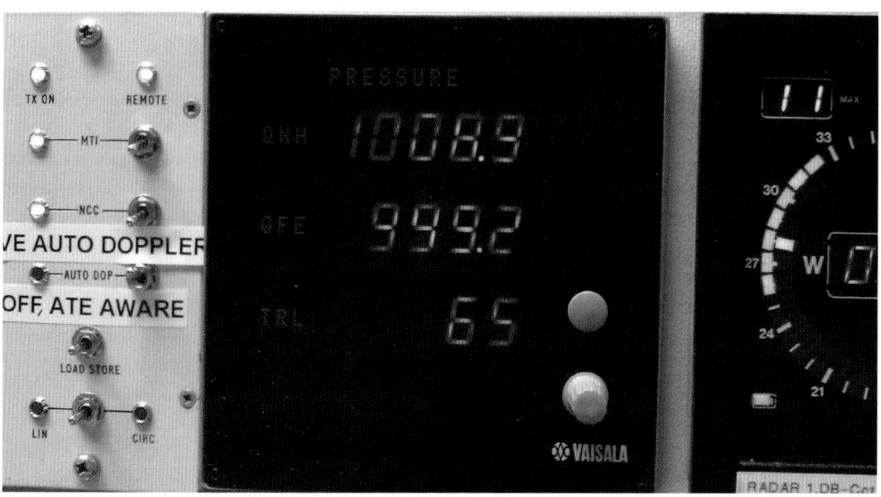

At most UK airports the current met observation is transmitted continuously on the appropriate Terminal VOR or ATIS (Aerodrome Terminal Information Service) frequency. The information is typed in and software converts it into a synthesised voice message. A transcript of a typical broadcast for Manchester is as follows:

> 'This is Manchester Arrival Information Juliet 0855 hours weather. Landing Runway 23 Right 250 degrees 12 knots. Slight rain, scattered at 800ft, overcast at 2,500ft. Temperature plus 10 Dew Point plus 6, QNH 1002. Report aircraft type and acknowledge information Juliet on first contact with Manchester.'

The significance of Juliet is that each observation is given a code letter, beginning with Alpha and working through the alphabet, starting once more when Zulu is reached. The controller is thus sure that the pilot has copied the latest observation. If, while directing an aircraft, the code changes, a controller will pass the new one and alert the pilot to any significant changes.

Datalink-ATIS (D-ATIS) enables a crew to download a copy of the current weather. Airports at which D-ATIS is available include Heathrow, Gatwick, Manchester and Aberdeen. An example of a flight deck printout at Manchester is:

EGCC ARR ATIS M 0850Z
LANDING RWY 23R
28010KT 20KM FEW020 09/07 Q1017
QFE1008
RWY SFC WET WET WET
LINK G IS CLOSED
LINK JB IS CLOSED
ACKNOWLEDGE RECEIPT OF INFORMATION M
AND ADVISE AIRCRAFT TYPE ON FIRST CONTACT

Runway Visual Range

RVR, as it is normally referred to, makes available a more localised assessment of how far the pilot is likely to be able to see along the runway. Measurement only begins when the official met report gives a general visibility less than 1,500m. The figure is essential to enable the pilot to decide whether or not it is within the limits of what are known as 'company minima' for landing or take-off. RVR is measured in 25m steps from zero up to 400m, then 50m from 400m to 800m, and 100m from 800m to 1,500m.

RVR is calculated by either the human observer method or by means of electronic equipment. The former requires a person, usually an airport fireman, to stand on a vehicle adjacent to the runway threshold at a specified height to simulate the pilot's eye level. He then counts the number of lights or, at some locations, marker boards, he can see down one side of the runway. The total is passed by radio to the tower and the RVR read off a pre-computed table.

The Instrumented RVR system, called IRVR, measures the opacity of the atmosphere and gives a constant read-out in the tower of the RVR at three fixed transmissometers along the runway, referred to as 'touchdown', 'mid-point' and 'stop end'. If the runway lights are switched to the opposite end, the IRVR will switch automatically.

SIGMET

The term SIGMET (Significant Meteorological Conditions) is a warning of such hazardous phenomena as thunderstorms, severe turbulence and severe airframe icing. Another jargon word is NOSIG, short for No Significant Change, and sometimes appended to aerodrome forecasts when passed on the radio. The term 'trend' is employed to indicate the way the weather is likely to go, codes such as 'tempo' for a temporary change being added as appropriate.

Wind Shear

Wind shear can be a very serious hazard to aircraft and pilots can often be heard reporting its presence to the tower so that following aircraft can be warned. Briefly, wind shear is a change of windspeed and/or direction between two points in the atmosphere. By such a definition it is almost always present and normally does not cause undue difficulty to pilots. However, on take-off and especially landing, what amounts to an instantaneous change in headwind can be dangerous. A sudden decrease in headwind on the approach will tend to increase the rate of descent and an instantaneous increase in headwind will tend to decrease it. In both cases the pilot is faced with a rapid change in airspeed, coupled with a departure from the glide path and either a 'hot and long' landing or an undershoot become likely. A flight deck automatic voice warning 'Wind shear, wind shear' will almost certainly result in a go around.

Modern airliners carry on-board wind shear detection systems that, as in the example above, will audibly warn the crew of its presence. Such audible alerts can be either predictive, occurring before the aircraft enters the wind shear, or reactive after penetration of the wind shear. Pilots will continue to fly the wind shear recovery manoeuvre until the on-board system ceases to annunciate the alert, and may therefore require deviation from their clearance. The priority of the crew during wind shear recovery is to keep the aircraft under control while ensuring terrain clearance. Rates of climb during such recovery manoeuvres, which employ the use of maximum thrust, will significantly exceed those during missed approaches executed for routine reasons such as an occupied runway or lack of visual contact in poor visibility. Controllers are aware that these high rates of climb can result in pilots exceeding their cleared level and eroding separation from other aircraft.

Horizontal wind shears are generally outflows from the bases of Cb clouds or are caused by the passage of active weather fronts. Local topographical features, both natural and artificial, can also cause shear. Buildings and other large structures close to runways can spark off turbulence and rotor effects, with marked differences in wind direction. Since wind shear is obviously invisible, much experimental work has been carried out with Doppler radar, acoustic Dopplers and optical lasers in order to detect and measure it. Currently, no UK aerodrome is equipped with automated ground-based remote-sensing equipment for the detection of wind shear. Heathrow is unique in the UK in having a wind shear alerting service. Certain weather criteria are used to assess its possible presence and this is backed up by pilot reports. The alert message is inserted in the arrival and departure ATIS broadcasts.

Runway Condition Reports

'Excursions' off the paved area remain one of the ICAO's top aviation safety concerns, with the most common landing excursion risk factor ineffective braking action due to runway contamination, such as snow, ice, slush or water. This trend is also confirmed by the main aircraft manufacturers. Shortfalls in the accuracy and timeliness of runway assessment and reporting methods by aerodromes have contributed to the problem, despite many decades of research effort to harmonise various friction measurement devices and their linkage to aircraft performance.

While friction measurement equipment is useful for runway maintenance purposes, it is misleading to pilots due to the disconnect between the friction measurement and actual aircraft performance. To help mitigate the risk of excursion, ICAO has developed a new harmonised methodology for assessing and reporting runway surface conditions.

The Global Reporting Format (GRF) harmonisation enables runway surface conditions to be reported in a standardised manner, such that flight crew can determine accurately aircraft take-off and landing performance. It also incorporates the potential to communicate actual runway surface conditions to flight crew in real time and in terms that relate directly to aircraft performance data.

The GRF comprises an assessment by airport operations staff, who assign a Runway Condition Code (RWYCC) ranging from 6 to 0. This code is complemented by a description of the surface contaminant based on type, depth and percentage coverage for each third of the runway. The code is based on the effect of the runway conditions on aircraft braking.

The outcome of the assessment and associated RWYCC are forwarded to ATC for communication to pilots, either by speech or ATIS. The pilots will use the code to determine their aircraft's performance by correlating the code with performance data provided by their aircraft's manufacturer. This will help pilots to carry out their landing and take-off performance calculations correctly for wet or contaminated runways.

Briefly, the codes run from 6, a dry runway, to 0, wet ice, water on top of compacted snow or snow on top of ice. The numbers in between indicate steadily deteriorating conditions with factors such as standing water, dry snow or slush. The GRF also allows pilots to report their own observations of runway conditions, thereby confirming the RWYCC or providing an alert to any changing conditions. The other key attributes to the GRF are its relative simplicity of use and the fact that it is globally applicable.

The word 'Snowtam' refers to an ingenious system of describing and tabulating runway conditions under snow, slush or ice and the degree to which they are cleared or about to be cleared. Braking action as determined above is also included. A series of letters and figures, each referring to a specific detail, can easily be decoded on receipt. The word 'SNOCLO' used on R/T and in Snowtams means that the airfield is closed because of runway contamination. In the meantime, attempts will be made to clear the snow.

Each airport has a Snow Plan detailing the priorities for snow clearance, the runways obviously taking first place, followed by taxiways and apron. As a general guide, the object is to clear the snow to a 'black top' surface. This can be achieved on most occasions by using snow sweepers, as long as clearing is commenced as soon as snow or slush begins to lie. Aircraft operations may continue but may be delayed while the sweeper finishes a run. Backup, if required, is provided by snow ploughs and snow blowers. For best effect, sweepers work in echelon, sweeping one full length of the runway, working outwards from the centreline. If conditions continue to deteriorate beyond those acceptable for aircraft operations, the runway will be closed to afford maximum priority to snow clearance. Salt-free chemicals are sprayed on runways and taxiways for anti-icing or de-icing in response to frost and/or snow warnings.

In normal conditions, runway state messages on ATIS will divide the runway into three sequential sections, hence 'Runway damp/damp/damp' or 'Runway wet/wet/wet or 'Runway wet/damp/wet'. The reports are originated by the aerodrome authority based on regular runway inspections. Definitions are:

Damp: The surface shows a change of colour due to moisture. If there is sufficient moisture to produce a surface film or the surface appears reflective, the runway will be reported as wet

Wet: The surface is soaked but no significant patches of standing water are visible. Standing water is considered to exist when water on the runway surface is deeper than 3mm. Patches of standing water covering more than 25 per cent of the assessed area will be reported as water patches

Water patches: Significant patches of standing water are visible. Water patches will be reported when more than 25 per cent of the assessed area is covered by water more than 3mm deep

Flooded: Extensive patches of standing water are visible. Flooded will be reported when more than 50 per cent of the assessed area is covered by water more than 3mm deep

Volmet

These are the broadcasts of the London and Scottish Volmet Services, the 'Vol' part of the title being derived from the French word for flight. Weather conditions in a standardised form are transmitted continuously for the main UK and selected European airports. Pilots can thus monitor Volmet while en route and note the current conditions at their destination and suitable alternatives, without having to make specific calls for the information. If their destination is a smaller airfield not on the Volmet they can either call it direct or request the information via London or Scottish Flight Information, who will obtain it by telephone.

There are four separate broadcasts on different VHF frequencies:

London Volmet North, broadcast from Great Dun Fell in Cumbria on 126.6MHz;
London Volmet South: 128.6MHz;
London Volmet Main: 135.375MHz;
Scottish Volmet: 125.725MHz

Using synthesised speech, the message is made up from a store of individual words and short phrases, which are selected by a computer and then joined to form the required sentences. (ATIS is usually broadcast in this form as well.)

The presentation of the information is as described above but where significant changes are expected, one of the following will be heard:

Gradu	The change is expected at a constant rate
Rapid	The change is expected in a short period of less than thirty minutes
Tempo	The change is expected to last for less than one hour
Inter	Frequent changes are expected, fluctuating almost constantly
Trend	A change is anticipated but it is expected to occur slowly throughout the period

As with ATIS described above, pilots can download Volmet via datalink.

ATIS via telephone, examples:

Birmingham: 0121 767 1260
Carlisle: 01228 574123
Edinburgh: 0131 333 6216

Manchester: 0161 209 2860
Jersey: 01534 446301
Stansted: 01279 669 325
Wick: 01955 607596

Area and Aerodrome Forecasts

Area forecasts (AIRMET) and coded aerodrome forecasts (TAFs and TRENDs) are prepared and issued by the Met Office. They are updated routinely and may be amended as necessary. AIRMET regional and area forecast texts are prepared every six hours covering a period of eight hours with an outlook for a further six hours. They comprise: Meteorological (synoptic) situation; Upper winds and temperatures – at 1,000ft, 3,000ft and 6,000ft; Height of 0°C isotherm; Weather conditions – surface visibility, weather and cloud (amount, type, height of base and top); Weather warnings – strong winds and gales, turbulence, icing, mountain waves or thunderstorms.

For those aerodromes providing regular coded aerodrome weather reports (METARs) undertaken by certificated meteorological observers, TAFs can also be prepared covering a period of nine hours (or the period flying is expected to take place, if less), twenty-four hours or thirty hours. All TAFs are issued approximately one hour before the start of validity time. The update periods of the TAF will be every three hours for aerodromes that are provided with a nine-hour TAF, and every six hours for aerodromes that are provided with a twenty-four- or thirty-hour TAF. Additionally, for selected aerodromes, landing forecasts (TRENDs) are added to each routine METAR to indicate significant changes expected from the current weather conditions over the next two hours.

Aerodrome Warnings

An ATC unit may be provided with warnings of any of the following weather hazards that could affect the safety of aircraft operations and parked aircraft: gales, squalls, snow, frost, thunderstorm, freezing precipitation and fog. Once the service has been approved by the meteorological authority, the procedure for the issue of warnings is arranged locally between the aerodrome management and the designated liaising meteorological forecast unit and is reviewed annually. A warning usually remains in force until the end of the quoted period of validity but may be extended or cancelled as necessary and amended if the conditions change.

Much more information can be found on the Met Office website GETMET, including how to decode aviation weather reports and forecasts.

Anemometer display showing maximum gusts. *RW*

Chapter 11

Airfield Visual Aids

Airfield lighting ranges from the basic edge lights found at many smaller locations to the complex and impressive systems to be seen at major airports. The paraffin flares from an earlier era, known as 'goosenecks', were retained at a few small airfields as emergency lighting, but have almost certainly been replaced by now with portable battery lamps, which are easier to handle but no more effective.

On certain instrument runways the caution zone, ie the last 600m, may have yellow rather than white lights. In addition, the centreline is usually delineated by flush-fitting lights for the whole length. These are colour-coded to give an indication of the distance remaining in poor visibility. The lights are coloured red over the final 300m and alternately red and white between 900m and 300m from the runway end.

As well as centreline lighting, all runways that comply with Precision Approach Category II and III lighting standard are provided with Touchdown Zone lights (TDZs). These consist of many flush-fitting white lights set into each side of the centreline in the first 900m of the runway. A row of green threshold lights marks the beginning of the paved surface and a similar line of red ones marks the stop end. Approach lighting is usually non-existent at small aerodromes and at others varies in standard, depending upon the approach aids and type of traffic handled.

Lined up on Runway 27 at Liverpool. TDZs, centreline lights and edge lights with PAPI to left.

The approach lights at major airports begin at an average distance of 300m out from the threshold and extend for a further 900m out on the approach. They consist of a centreline and up to five cross-bars in white lights. Where Category II and III lighting standard is required, red supplementary approach lighting is provided within the basic system for the inner 300m as an extra aid for landing in marginal weather conditions. All lighting is controlled in intensity from the tower, the criteria being laid down clearly for differing met conditions.

The lights are displayed all the time at busy airports, but for other locations the normal requirement is for high-intensity systems – where installed – to be on in daylight hours whenever the visibility is less than 5km and/or the cloud base less than 700ft. At night for less busy airfields, all lighting will be switched on prior to an aircraft's ETA and left on after a departure to allow for a possible emergency return. The actual times will be specified in local ATC orders.

Taxiway lights are standardised as green for the centreline and blue for the edges. The latter are used only to delineate apron edges and as an extra guide for bends in taxiways. The lights are 15m apart, which is reduced to 7m for ILS Category III systems. Red stop bars mark holding points, mainly those at runway entrances. There may also be traffic lights for airfield vehicles. Both can be operated from the tower and the stop bars normally have a short time delay so that they revert to red after an aircraft has passed. London Heathrow has a particularly elaborate system of lighting for the control of taxiways. Taxiways at all airports are now designated by a letter of the alphabet, excluding Oscar, India and X-Ray. Where there are more taxiways than letters of the alphabet, double letters are used to designate some of them. Double letters may also be used to identify short taxiway stubs – known as links – between a runway and an adjacent taxiway.

Rapid Exit Taxiways only have their centreline lights lit from the runway direction. The lights in the opposite direction are blanked off to prevent inadvertent infringement of an active runway. This was yet another result of the enquiry into the 1977 Tenerife collision. Rapid Exit Taxiway Indicator Lights (RETILs) may be provided to indicate the distance to go to the nearest RET. In low-visibility conditions, RETILs provide useful situational awareness cues to assist in appropriate rates of deceleration and to allow flight crew to concentrate on keeping the aircraft on the runway centreline during the landing roll. They usually consist of six yellow lights adjacent to the runway centreline, configured as a three–two–one sequence spaced 100m apart, with the single light positioned at 100m from the start of the turn for the rapid exit taxiway.

Runway guard lights, consisting of a pair of alternately flashing lights and known colloquially as 'wig-wags', may be located on both sides of holding positions. The purpose of these yellow lights is to improve the conspicuity of holding points and to warn pilots of the proximity of an active runway.

Once a pilot on approach is within sight of the runway, visual guidance is provided by the Precision Approach Path Indicator (PAPI). Four PAPI lights are placed in line to the left of the runway threshold. They are arranged so that when the pilot is on the correct approach path two appear white and the other two are red. When a third light shows red, the aircraft is getting slightly low; when all four are red it is significantly below the glide path. Conversely, four whites indicate it is too high.

A number of smaller airfields have an installation called LITAS (Low Intensity Two Colour Slope System). It has lights of lower intensity placed generally on the left-hand side of the runway only. Although designed for use at night, the system has been found to give assistance by day in anything other than bright sunlight. There are some visual aids that are peculiar to helicopter operations. One is the Helicopter Approach Path Indicator (HAPI), which provides helicopter pilots with guidance similar to that provided by PAPI, although with a different format of display and signal interpretation.

Another is the Helicopter Aiming Point Marker placed on an area designated as a helicopter arriving point at a heliport or aerodrome. It is used to mark the point at which a helicopter will arrive at a low hover on completion of an approach. The marker consists of a white equilateral triangle lit at night.

The other major visual aids on airports are the painted markings on the manoeuvring area. All runways in regular use will have centreline and threshold markings, the latter varying from the designator number alone to separate 'piano keys' and designator, depending upon the importance of the runway and its associated instrument aids. While threshold markings are usually at the end of the runway, they sometimes need to be displaced upwind if, for example, there are obstacles such as a public road on the approach. Arrows then indicate that the first portion of the runway is sterile for landing.

All runways more than 1,600m long without PAPI, and all precision instrument runways, will have an additional symbol 300m from the landing threshold known as the 'fixed distance marker'. The apparent distance between this and the threshold marking, seen from the approach, should aid pilots in judging their angle of descent and the two markings also bracket the optimum Touchdown Zone on the runway.

Touchdown Zone markings, extending for a distance of at least 600m from the threshold, will be provided on precision approach runways equipped with such aids as ILS. These are intended to give added texture by day and, except in fog, added texture by night in the light of landing lamps. Yellow lines delineate the centres of taxiways and at certain airports self-manoeuvring stand markings enable aircraft to be taxied to the correct parking position without the aid of a marshaller. There are several systems, including AGNIS (Azimuth Guidance for Nose-in Stand) and Safegate, all coming under the collective title of Visual Docking Guidance Systems. They use ingenious systems of coloured lights and words on a dot matrix display to align the aircraft and enable the pilot to stop in the correct position.

At airfields that accept non-radio equipped aircraft, ground signals will be displayed for guidance. They are normally to be found in front of the control tower, but not always, which gives rise to a funny story. One day many years ago a pilot who had suffered a radio failure landed at Blackpool. On reporting to the tower, he complained that he could not make any sense from the ground signals. Further conversation revealed that he had been trying to interpret the strange shapes on the crazy golf course adjacent to the airport's public viewing area!

Obviously not all the following ground signals can be seen at any one airfield but they cover all those to be seen at UK civil locations. This list does not include signs peculiar to military airfields.

(a) Direction for landing or take-off: A large white 'T' signifies that aircraft will land or take off in a direction parallel to the 'T' and towards the cross-arm. A white disc above the cross-arm of the 'T' indicates that the direction of landing and take-off do not necessarily coincide.

(b) A white 'dumb-bell' means that aircraft movement on the airfield is confined to paved surfaces only. A black strip across each disc of the dumb-bell at right angles to the shaft signifies that aircraft taking off and landing shall do so on a runway but that ground movement is not confined to paved surfaces. A red letter 'L' superimposed on the dumb-bell signifies that light aircraft are permitted to take off and land either on a runway or on the area designated by a further 'L' (painted white) elsewhere on the aerodrome. A red-and-yellow-striped arrow indicates that a right-hand circuit is in force. This can also be shown by a rectangular green flag flown from a mast.

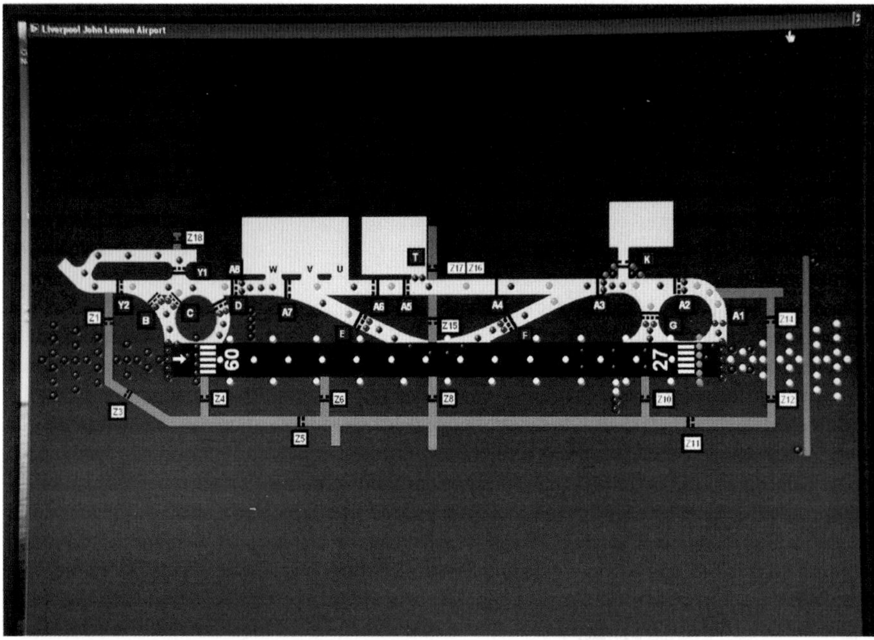

Airfield lighting mimic panel showing the settings selected.

(c) A red square with one yellow diagonal bar warns that the state of the manoeuvring area is poor and pilots must exercise special care.

(d) A red square with a yellow cross superimposed along the diagonals declares that the airfield is unsafe for the movement of aircraft and that landing is prohibited. (Usually found at grass airfields that are waterlogged in the winter months!)

(e) A white letter 'H' marks the helicopter landing area.

(f) A double white cross signifies that glider flying is in progress. (A yellow cross indicates the tow-rope dropping area on the airfield.)

(g) 'Aerodrome Control in operation' is shown by a red and yellow chequered flag or board. (Aircraft may only move on the manoeuvring area with ATC permission.) A black letter 'C' on a yellow board indicates the position at which a pilot can report to the ATC unit or to the person in charge of the aerodrome.

(h) On grass aerodromes areas of 'bad ground' are marked by triangular orange and white markers (colloquially known as 'Toblerones'), alternating with orange and white flags. Similar coloured markers outline the aerodrome boundary.

Chapter 12

Airport Operations and Procedures

Wake Turbulence

Behind each wingtip of an aircraft in flight and, in the case of a helicopter, the tip of each rotor blade, a trailing cylinder of rapidly rotating air is created, known as a vortex. The heavier the aircraft, the more intense the effect, which is quite capable of throwing a following aircraft out of control if it gets too close. These hazardous wake vortices begin to be generated when the nosewheel lifts off the runway on take-off and continue until it touches down on landing. To minimise the danger, controllers apply a system of spacing that is outlined below.

In the United Kingdom, aircraft types are divided into five categories for approach and four categories for departure, according to their MTOM (Maximum Total Mass) in kg at take-off:

Birmingham Radar suite. *RW*

Heavy	Greater than 136,000kg;	
Medium	40,000kg to 136,000kg;	
Upper Medium	104,000 to 136,000kg	Arrivals only
Lower Medium	40,000kg to 104,000kg	Arrivals only
Small	17,000kg to 40,000kg	
Light	17,000kg or less	

There are, however, a few exceptions to this. Helicopters generate more intense vortices from their rotors than fixed-wing aircraft of the same weight, therefore AS-332 Super Pumas and larger types are included in the Small category. The Medium category embraces aircraft in the Airbus A320/Boeing 737 class, together with propeller aircraft such as the Hercules. The Small category includes the ATR-72 and Dash 8, and Light anything from executive jets downwards. The Airbus A380, while falling within the Heavy category, has some additional spacing applied as shown below.

The heavier the aircraft, the greater the turbulence it generates. In layman's terms, the cause of wake turbulence is really quite simple: the higher pressure under the wing results in the air spilling over the wingtip. This forms a spiral flow, or vortex. In order for this to happen, lift needs to be generated to create the pressure difference. Thus, during the take-off roll, turbulence gradually increases and becomes significant once the nosewheel lifts from the ground. In flight, the slower the speed, or higher the angle of attack, ie the angle at which the wing enters the airflow, the more severe the vortex.

The behaviour of the vortices after they have left the wingtips depends on several factors. They are separated by approximately three-quarters of the aircraft's wingspan and will gradually descend below its flight path, typically for a height of 900ft. However, when the aircraft is close to the ground, the vortices will descend, then move outwards from the aircraft's track at a speed of around 5 knots. In completely calm conditions, this should leave a funnel through which, at a reasonable distance, it is safe to fly. Unfortunately, it is rarely completely calm and therefore, if there is a crosswind of just a few knots, it will quickly move the downwind vortex away from the runway but will hold the upwind vortex on, or near to, the runway.

A groundcrewman in intercom contact with an Airbus A319 flight deck gives the 'aircraft brakes off' signal to the tug driver.

Arriving Flights

Where flights are operating visually (IFR flights operating under the reduced minima in the vicinity of aerodromes, VFR flights, or a mixture of the two), pilots are to be informed of the recommended spacing.

For other flights the spacing listed below is to be applied between successive aircraft on final approach.

Signifies that separation for wake turbulence reasons alone is not necessary.

Leading aircraft	Following aircraft	Minimum distance
A380-800	A380-800	#
A380-800	Heavy	6 miles
A380-800	Upper and Lower Medium	7 miles
A380-800	Small	7 miles
A380-800	Light	8 miles
Heavy	A380-800	#
Heavy	Heavy	4 miles
Heavy	Upper and Lower Medium	5 miles
Heavy	Small	6 miles
Heavy	Light	7 miles
Upper Medium	A380-800	#
Upper Medium	Heavy	#
Upper Medium	Upper Medium	3 miles
Upper Medium	Lower Medium	4 miles
Upper Medium	Small	4 miles
Upper Medium	Light	6 miles
Lower Medium	A380-800	#
Lower Medium	Heavy	#
Lower Medium	Upper and Lower Medium	#
Lower Medium	Small	3 miles
Lower Medium	Light	5 miles
Small	A380-800	#
Small	Heavy	#
Small	Upper and Lower Medium	#
Small	Small	3 miles
Small	Light	4 miles

Departures

The minimum spacing listed below is applied between successive aircraft, both IFR and VFR flights.

Aircraft departing from the same runway or from parallel runways less than 760m apart (including grass strips).

Leading aircraft	Following aircraft	Minimum wake turbulence spacing at time aircraft are airborne
A380-800	A380-800	No wake turbulence separation required
A380-800	Heavy (including A380-800)	2 minutes
A380-800	Medium (Upper and Lower)	3 minutes
A380-800	Small or Light	3 minutes
Heavy	Medium (Upper and Lower)	3 minutes
Heavy	Small or Light	2 minutes
Medium (Upper and Lower or Small)	Light	2 minutes

Aircraft departing from an intermediate point on the same runway or a parallel runway separated by less than 760m

Leading aircraft	Following aircraft	Minimum wake turbulence spacing at time aircraft are airborne
A380-800	Heavy (including A380-800)	3 minutes
Heavy	Medium (Upper and Lower), Small and Light	3 minutes
Medium or Small	Light	3 minutes

Note that controllers do not have any discretion to reduce wake turbulence separation even when requested by a pilot

Departure Flow Regulation

Calculated Take-Off Times or CTOTs were known previously as 'slot times' and often still referred to as such. During peak times some countries are unable, for a number of reasons, to cope with the extra traffic. For instance, prior to the pandemic, over fifty European and thirty UK airports were sending aircraft to the Mediterranean. Spain has about nine airports to receive the majority of them, with Palma the most popular destination. When the number of aircraft wishing to fly outstrips the capacity of the control centres along the route or that of the destination airport, the flow of traffic has to be regulated to ensure safe separation both nationally and internationally. This means that aircraft have to be held on the ground at the departure airports until such time as they can be accepted.

Declared Capacity is a measure of the ability of the ATC system or any of its sub-systems or operating positions to provide service to aircraft during normal activities. It is expressed as the number of aircraft entering a specified portion of airspace in a given period of time, taking due account of weather, ATC unit configuration, staff and equipment available, and any other factors that may affect the workload of the controller responsible for the airspace.

Europe's Network Manager Operations Centre (NMOC), formerly known as the Central Flow Management Unit (CFMU), is located at Brussels and provides departure times about two hours ahead for every aircraft flying on a regulated route. This ensures an organised system of queuing for all flights, as well as enabling airlines to plan aircraft and crew utilisation. The prime objective of Air Traffic Flow Management (ATFM) is to ensure that ATC sectors do not receive more traffic than they can handle. This first objective is therefore entirely safety related. The second is to ensure that the available ATC capacity is used efficiently to the benefit of all aircraft operators. NMOC at Brussels achieves these targets in a variety of ways but ultimately where, despite all other efforts, an over-delivery is still anticipated to occur, a 'regulation' will be implemented and CTOTs issued. The principle of first come, first served is applied strictly in calculating the slot. All flights – apart from hospital ones – are therefore treated equally, regardless of aircraft size, passenger numbers, scheduled, unscheduled or private.

A flight that has been allocated a CTOT by NMOC is expected to present itself for push-back, start-up and taxi to the active runway in time to comply with the CTOT. A window of fifteen minutes (-five to +ten) is available round the CTOT to provide GMC and the Tower Controller with the flexibility needed to integrate the deporting traffic with other aircraft movements. This window is the average for smaller regional airports but is longer for the bigger and more complex ones. It is vital that the CTOT is complied with to avoid an over-delivery of aircraft into an ATC sector. An over-delivery is defined as a situation where the actual number of aircraft that enter a sector is more than 100 per cent of the regulated capacity. A five-minute extension to the slot window is usually available on request to NMOC.

The Traffic Orientation Scheme (TOS) forms the basis for the routeing of aircraft on the major traffic flows during the summer peak season. The aim is to balance the demand on Europe's air route system by confining traffic for a specified destination to a particular route with an alternative in the event of unforeseen en route congestion. Getting an aircraft airborne within its CTOT window can cause GMC or the Tower Controller something of a headache as extra-careful planning is often necessary to make sure that the aircraft gets away on time.

During busy periods, some airports may become short of parking stands so an aircraft may be required to taxi well before its CTOT and shut down on a remote holding bay. Certain airlines may request to pushback early onto an adjacent stand so that they can start later and taxi straight out. This is a ploy to enable them to claim that they left the stand at the scheduled time even though they subsequently went nowhere! In the meantime, a 'Ready message' will be sent by ATC or airline ops in the hope of bringing the slot forward.

Airport-Collaborative Decision Making (A-CDM)

A-CDM is about partners working together and making decisions based on more accurate and higher-quality information, where every bit of information has exactly the same meaning for every partner involved. More efficient use of resources, and improved event punctuality as well as predictability are the target results. Put simply, it ensures that aircraft operators, ground handlers, de-icing companies, ATC, the Network Manager at Brussels, and support services (Police, Customs and Immigration etc) are all singing from the same hymn book!

Definitions of Commonly Used A-CDM Terms are: Calculated Take-Off Time (CTOT) – Assigned by Eurocontrol's NMOC when flow restrictions are in place. Aircraft must depart within -five to +ten minutes of its CTOT. Target Off-Blocks Time (TOBT) – The time an aircraft is expected, and agreed by the Ground Handling Agent and flight deck, to be ready to leave the stand (in the case of normal operations), or ready for on stand de-icing to commence (where appropriate, in the case of winter operations). This must be updated to an accuracy of plus or minus five minutes by the Ground Handling Agent. Accurate and stable TOBTs enhance operations on the ground as they provide all airport partners with a clear picture of the intentions of aircraft on the ground.

Target Start Approval Time (TSAT) – The time provided by ATC that an aircraft can expect to receive start approval. TSAT will be displayed on Stand entry Guidance System (SEGS). Aircraft on stands with no active SEGS will have TSAT confirmed by ATC on initial call-up. Alternatively, TSAT can be advised by the Company Dispatcher. TSAT should reduce queuing times at the runway hold, while maintaining a high runway utilisation. Calculated automatically by the Departure Sequencer by taking into account TOBT, CTOT, wake vortex, SID routeing, Variable Taxi Time (VTT), demand and any capacity constraints, eg Low-Visibility Procedures.

Target Take-Off Time (TTOT) – The time that an aircraft is expected to take off. TTOT is calculated by adding a VTT to the TSAT. TTOT is updated in line with any updates to the TSAT. It is also noted that the requirement for an aircraft to be airborne within a time window only applies to flights with a CTOT.

The Flight Deck must comply with the following A-CDM procedure. They should ensure that their flight is ready to push at TOBT plus or minus five minutes: ground activities completed, doors closed, push-back tug connected, cockpit ready for start-up. They must maintain regular communication with their handling agent, who is responsible for updating their TOBT. If the crew identify any delays or believe they will be able to depart earlier, they must notify the agent immediately.

Noise abatement

In an effort to minimise noise nuisance to local residents, most airports have their own noise abatement procedures. These are devised by the aerodrome operating authority in conjunction with airlines and local airport consultative committees. Over built-up areas Noise Preferential Routes have been defined, which carefully route aircraft away from the more densely populated areas. Engine climb power is also reduced for the period when the aircraft must fly over certain conurbations.

At Heathrow different parallel runways are used for take-off and landing and these are alternated regularly so that noise is spread more equitably over the areas beneath the flight paths. Runways 27 Left and 27 Right are the preferred ones, provided the tailwind component does not exceed a certain figure and, in addition, flights are severely restricted at night. At Manchester the direction of approach is changed at regular intervals and at both locations noise levels are monitored. Operators whose aircraft exceed the permitted values are penalised.

Noise Preferential Routes are integrated with the lower end of Standard Instrument Departures, which are themselves designed to cause the least disturbance to those living below. Similarly, Continuous Descent Approaches have been brought into operation to reduce noise and, as a bonus, to speed up the arrival rate. On receipt of descent clearance the pilot descends at the rate he judges to be best suited to achieve continuous descent. The object is to join the glide path at the appropriate height for the distance without recourse to level flight.

The procedure requires that aircraft fly at 210kt during the intermediate approach phase. ATC may request speed reductions to within the band 160kt to 180kt on, or shortly before, the closing heading to the ILS, and 160kt when established on the ILS. Aircraft unable to conform to these speeds are expected to inform ATC and state which speeds they are able to use. Since wheels and flaps remain retracted until the final stages, less engine power is needed, which results in a much quieter approach.

Aircraft type and airfield designators

For flight planning and flight progress strip presentation, aircraft types have been allocated a designator of not more than four characters, by the ICAO. Where possible this conforms to the manufacturer's designation, or at least to part of it. For example, Boeing 737-800, 747-400 are represented by B738 and B744, the Fokker 100 is the F100 and the Airbus family are represented by the individual number prefixed by 'A' – A319, A330 and A388 (A380-800) for example. More are listed in Appendix 5.

Four-letter designators for airfields are often heard on HF R/T but rarely on VHF. They are allocated by the ICAO on a worldwide basis for flight planning and telex purposes. British airfields are prefixed 'EG,' hence EGLL for Heathrow, EGKK for Gatwick and EGCC for Manchester. A few European examples are EDDH (Hamburg), LFPO (Paris Orly), EBOS (Ostend), LSZH (Zurich) and LEMD (Madrid). American airports are prefixed 'K', as in KJFK (Kennedy) and KLAX (Los Angeles). The full list is available in ICAO Doc 7910 Location Indicators.

Low-Visibility Procedures (LVPs)

Many commercial transport aircraft are now fitted with automatic landing equipment and thus, in theory, can land in the poorest visibility. However, lengthy gaps are required between arrivals, both to ensure that the first landing aircraft has vacated the runway and also to allow departures. A further consideration is that critical areas near ILS aerials must not be infringed by taxiing and departing aircraft when an arriving flight is within a certain distance – usually 4 miles – from the runway threshold on final. The result is that runway capacity is drastically reduced and inbound aircraft may be required to hold for long periods, perhaps having to divert elsewhere when fuel approaches the statutory minima.

The weather minima associated with the different categories of ILS are defined by the ICAO as follows:

Cat I: A decision height not lower than 60m (200ft) and with either a visibility not less than 800m, or a Runway Visual Range (RVR) not less than 550m.

Cat II: A decision height lower than 60m (200ft) but not lower than 30m (100ft) and an RVR not less than 350m.

Cm IIIA: Either a decision height lower than 30m (100ft), or with no decision height and an RVR not less than 200m.

Cut IIIB: Either a decision height lower than 15m (50ft), or with no decision height and an RVR less than 200m but not less than 50m.

Cat IIIC: No decision height and no RVR limitations.

Decision height is referenced to the runway threshold elevation and is defined as the height at which the pilot on a precision approach must carry out a missed approach if he/she fails to achieve the required visual reference to continue the approach to a landing. Note that a precision approach must have an electronic glide path. Localiser/DME ILS approaches have higher limits because they are not deemed to be precision approach aids and hence no category is published for them.

Cat I, as the most basic, requires little more safeguarding than keeping ground vehicles away from the aerials while the ILS is in use for an approach. They may only cause a momentary blip on the aircraft instruments but sometimes can make the ILS 'trip', in other words switch off automatically. It can normally be reset quite quickly in the tower but in the meantime the aircraft may have wandered off the centreline and be forced to make a missed approach. All Localiser and glide path signals are monitored continuously by a receiver aerial sited in their radiation path. This is known as the far field monitor. If there is a failure or change in parameters, a warning light and tone is activated on the control panel in the tower.

When we enter the realms of Cat II and III there are a number of vital conditions. First, the ILS, approach and runway lights must be run directly from a standby generator so that in the event of a failure the system will revert instantaneously to mains power. Since the generator is a diesel truck engine, it takes several seconds to start and run up after a mains failure, and a landing aircraft could be left with no outside indications for an unacceptable period. Protection of ILS signals during Cat II and III operations may dictate that pre-take-off holding positions are more distant from the runway than the holding points used during good weather. Such holding points will display signs reading 'CAT II/III HOLD' on one or both sides of the taxiway and there will also be a stop bar of red lights. For aircraft taxiing off the runway during LVPs, white flashing lights are sometimes provided at designated runway exits to enable the aircraft to report that it has vacated the runway. They are located at the boundary of the ILS sensitive area, the Obstacle Free Zone or OFZ. For practice Cat II or III approaches in good weather the safeguarding procedures are not normally imposed in order to avoid undue disruption to other traffic and essential ground vehicle movement.

Although most modern ILSs are Cat II and III capable, they will not be approved for anything other than Cat I ops unless the airfield lighting is upgraded. The extra lights required include high-intensity centreline, colour-coded to warn the pilot he is approaching the end of the runway. White centreline lights extend from the threshold to 900m from the end of the runway, the following 600m are lit with alternate red and white lights and the final 300m have red only. Touchdown Zone lighting (TDZ) is embedded in the runway in order to give 'texture' to the surface in the landing area. The additional lights extend from the threshold for 900m along the runway. Other important visual clues are given by supplementary approach lights. One system is known as SHINGALS – Supplementary High Intensity Narrow Gauge Approach Lighting System – and is superimposed on the normal approach light pattern and only switched on when RVR and/or cloud base go below specified limits.

Landing in zero conditions is not much use if you then can't find your way to the apron. At major UK airports, the exits from the runway have colour-coded alternate yellow/green centre-lines. When established on the normal green centreline the pilot must report 'Runway vacated'. ATC rely heavily on these ground position reports when visibility is bad and ground movement radar is not available. The utmost care is necessary on the part of all involved and this is a further reason why operations are slowed down so much in foggy conditions.

As another aid to ground movement in fog, a taxiway guidance system may be installed. It operates by selective switching of the taxiway centreline lights so that individual sections or routes, each terminating at a lighted stop bar, are illuminated in order to show the way ahead. The stop bar is extinguished as the next section of centreline lights is selected, indicating to the pilot that he may continue taxiing. At some less well-equipped airports a vehicle with an illuminated 'FOLLOW ME' sign is often used to lead aircraft to and from the runway in fog. It is a piece of Second World War technology that is just as effective today. A further precaution is the runway guard light, colloquially known as a 'wig-wag'. They are pairs of alternately flashing yellow lights located on each side of the taxiway outboard of the holding sign.

The other major element in Low-Visibility Procedures is, of course, RVR measurement. RVR is the distance the pilot of an aircraft on the runway centreline can expect to see along it. For Cat I and II the automatic or human observer systems are acceptable but for Cat III only the automatic is authorised. The manned system requires an observer near the runway threshold to count the number of runway edge lights he can see along the far side. The figure is passed to the tower by radio and a table is used to convert it into metres. The automatic IRVR (Instrumented RVR) method provides a continuous read-out of the RVR at three points on the runway, known as the Touchdown. Mid-Point and Stop End.

Changes in the RVR must be passed to pilots immediately to avoid them infringing their company minima. In the case of IRVR the readings are recorded automatically on paper and, by regulation, sent to the CAA for checking against aircraft movement records. Any 'busting' of minima is picked up rapidly, to the embarrassment or worse of those concerned.

An additional procedure at Heathrow is intended to sequence aircraft ground movements for take-offs in low visibility (RVR minima also apply to departures). For example, if the aircraft's take-off minimum is 200m, the pilot is asked not to request start-up until the actual RVR is reported as equal to or greater than 150m. There is then a reasonable chance that the extra 50m may be achieved by the time the runway holding point is reached. Most of the UK's regional airports have at least Cat II ILS. Those Cat III capable include Belfast/Aldergrove, Birmingham, Doncaster Sheffield, East Midlands, Edinburgh, Gatwick, Glasgow, Heathrow, Leeds-Bradford, Liverpool, Luton, Manchester, Newcastle, Norwich and Stansted.

Before LVPs actually come into force, a number of conditions have to be met. They may vary with the complexity of the airport but the following are typical of the requirements: All non-essential vehicles are removed from the runways and taxiways, work in progress will be suspended, standby generators powering the ILS, airfield lighting and other vital services will be switched on, airfield and approach lighting will be checked for serviceability, a perimeter security check will be carried out and barriers placed where necessary at points where vehicles may inadvertently enter the manoeuvring area. The Airport Fire Service is also placed on Weather Standby. Once these conditions are met, the phrase 'Low-Visibility Procedures are in force' will be added to the ATIS broadcast and the airport is ready to handle traffic again. LVPs are imposed in two or more phases, depending on the current touchdown RVR. When it is apparent that the visibility is dropping below, say 2,000m and forecast to get worse, airport ops are warned and everyone concerned can begin their duties.

Surface Movement Radars (SMR) at major airports are specifically designed to detect all principal features on the surface of an airport, including aircraft and vehicular traffic, and to present the entire image on a display in the tower. Some, including Manchester's, are augmented by RIMCAS – Runway Incursion Monitor and Conflict Alert System. A-SMGCS (Advanced Surface Movement Guidance and Control System) is currently the ultimate SMR and is operational at London Heathrow, Gatwick and Edinburgh.

Apron Control

Totally separate from ATC, they allocate parking stands (gates) for aircraft and communicate this information to tower or GMC, as well as the airline handling agents. Usually this happens in advance but it is often a dynamic situation with aircraft late to taxi, meaning last-minute stand changes. It is not unknown at busier airports for arriving aircraft to hold on taxiways for quite long periods waiting for a stand to become vacant. Apron Control is also responsible for authorising vehicle movement on the apron areas where it is likely to conflict with taxiing aircraft, outside painted roadway markings for example.

Pushback Operations

To maximise apron space and connect with air bridges, aircraft are usually parked nose in to the terminal building. This makes it necessary to push them backwards onto what is known as the taxi-lane for engine start. The tug crew also monitor ATC instructions to the pilot, as a safety backup to ensure that the instructions passed to them by the crew are the same as those given by ATC. At Gatwick, to cite one example, there is a series of 'standard' pushback manoeuvres, unique to each parking position, which the tug drivers have to know off by heart. This saves time on the radio for normal operations. However, sometimes these are varied by ATC, if, for instance, they want the aircraft to push far enough back to allow an inbound aircraft on to the same gate.

Occasionally, visiting crews whose first language is not English don't fully relay all this information to the tug crews, which is where the crew listening to ATC comes in very useful. One of the tug crew plugs a headset on a long lead into a socket under the aircraft's nose so that he can talk directly to the flight crew. A steel pin is inserted into the nosewheel steering mechanism to override the aircraft's steering system and allow the tug to turn the aircraft. After the pushback is completed the ground crewman will wave this pin and its attached red flag at the pilots to indicate that they have control over the steering once more.

Pushback is actually quite a complex process. The ground crew not only carry out a comprehensive final walk-round to ensure all hatches are secure and that nothing looks damaged or out of alignment, but they also monitor engine start, to make sure that nothing is going to get jet blasted and that fuel doesn't start leaking out. Correct setting of brakes at all stages is another major issue and the ground crew are firmly in charge here. Being a part of the pushback crew is a highly responsible position and a major contribution to flight safety. Conversely, when an aircraft parks on stand the rules say that no one is to approach it until all engines are shut down and the anti-collision lights are switched off.

Hot Spots

The ICAO defines a hot spot as 'a location on an aerodrome movement area with a history or potential risk of collision or runway incursion, and where heightened attention by pilots and drivers is necessary'. Amsterdam and Brussels Airports seem to have pioneered the concept and it soon spread to the UK. Heathrow has two Hot Spots added in the customary red lettering on the Aerodrome Chart. One is at the SATUN holding area for Runway 27 Right. The ICAO's officially published Aerodrome Chart says: 'Pilots are to maintain a good lookout at all times and are responsible for wingtip clearance.' At Coventry Airport's Charlie One holding point there is a Hot Spot with the note: 'Pilots caution when entering runway, entire length not visible.'

Bird Scaring and Grass Cutting

Most airports now have a dedicated bird control unit to make regular patrols, broadcasting bird distress call recordings, and firing crackers to chase them away from the runways. Radio contact is maintained constantly with ATC to enable speedy reaction to any perceived hazard. Pilots must also be warned of the presence of birds when considered necessary. It has been discovered that birds prefer shortish grass because they can see predators approaching more easily. Thus most airfields keep the grass rather longer than your average lawn. The grass still needs cutting, of course, and the operation requires much liaison with ATC. An airport is divided into numbered areas for ease of reference and the grass cutter will request permission to operate in them. The cleared and graded strip each side of runways is a problem and the cutter may have to move off frequently when there is an aircraft movement. For light aircraft movements, by agreement, the runway length may be reduced using side markers to show the touchdown area. Grass cutting can then continue adjacent to the sterile portion. It may even have to be done at night at some busy locations.

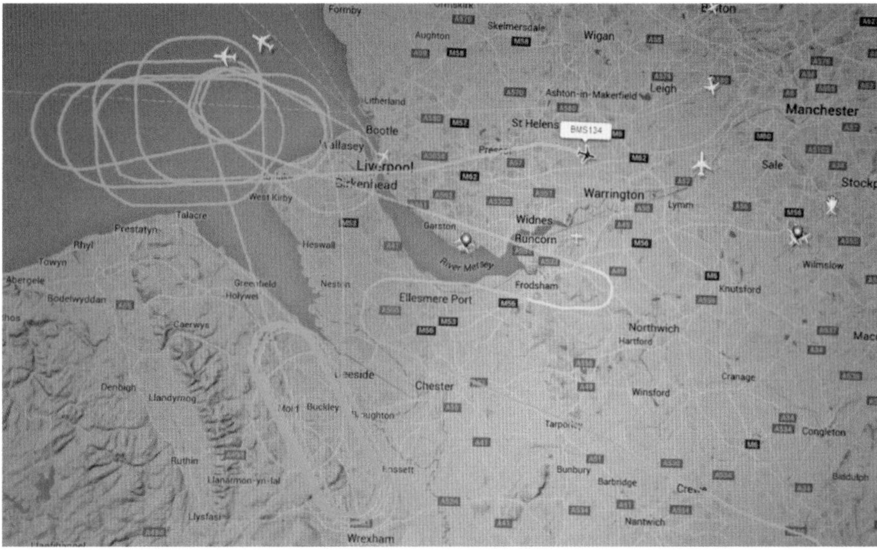

Chapter 13

Emergencies and Unusual Circumstances

Emergency situations with aircraft are fairly common, and although the word conjures up images of catastrophic failure or fire in the air, few are very dramatic, even though they may give the pilot(s) some anxious moments. The air traffic controller is a very significant team member in the safe and successful resolution of most emergencies and the CAA's Safety Regulation Group has circulated a well-thought-out booklet entitled *Aircraft Emergencies – Considerations for Controllers*. It has been distributed to all UK controllers with the aim of increasing awareness of the effect of different types of emergencies on aircraft performance and to give guidance on ways they can assist pilots faced with emergency situations.

When flight crew are confronted with an abnormal situation while in flight, they will normally prioritise their immediate actions in the following order: AVIATE, NAVIGATE, COMMUNICATE. The immediate workload is likely to be high, so ATC may get nothing more than a '(Callsign) we've got a problem, standby'. The crew then follow checklists, try to diagnose the problem, discuss options and decide what to do next. A diversion or rapid descent may be necessary.

For ATC, it is vital to establish basic information as soon as possible without hassling a crew who will already be extremely busy. The facts needed are: nature of the emergency, intentions of the crew, time available, additional information. The actual degree of emergency must be established, as pilots are sometimes reluctant to use the prefix 'Pan' or 'Mayday'.

Radar24 picture when a Blue Air Boeing 737 had a bird strike on departure from Liverpool and performed multiple holds while monitoring the problem and burning off fuel.

What controllers really require is a brief, preferably non-technical, description of the problem and its possible effect on the handling and performance of the aircraft. Also essential is the number of persons on board so that rescue services can account for everyone in the event of an accident.

In a critical situation such as an engine fire, an immediate landing will be required. In some incidents – an undercarriage malfunction, for example – the aircraft may have to enter a holding pattern while drills are carried out. Sometimes it may be necessary to jettison fuel to bring the aircraft down to minimum landing weight.

Types of emergency are tabulated in the booklet, including fire, loss of pressurisation, engine, failure, hydraulic failure, landing gear problems, fuel shortage, control problems and icing. Crew responses and options are listed, along with controller priorities and actions. The following list attempts to highlight some of the factors that may affect the progression and outcome of particular types of emergency.

Fire: Location – engine, cabin, cargo, wheel well, extinguishable? There may be no way of using aircraft systems. Time is critical – flight crew will want to land the aircraft as quickly as possible. ATC will alert them to the nearest airfield and offer radar vectors to it. Crosswinds may cause complication on landing due to the location of the fire. Evacuation is likely.

Smoke in cockpit: Emergency descent may be necessary. Instruments may be difficult to read. Frequency changes may be impossible. Type of approach may be critical. Crew incapacitation possible.

Loss of all engines: Range (height)/endurance (electrical power reserves) available. ATC vectors to nearest airfield, maybe orbit overhead to assist in planning the glide approach. When giving turns, the rate of descent may double.

Total (or nearly total) electrics failure: Immediate diversion essential. Limited instrumentation. High cockpit workload. Navigation may be difficult. Only one radio may be available. Minimise communication to conserve batteries. Abnormal approach configuration likely. May be caused by lightning strike.

Loss of pressurisation: Emergency descent to 10,000ft or lower. Rate of descent 8,000 to 9,000ft for jet but may be much lower for turboprop. Descent may already be established before controller can be contacted. Possible spiral descent. Communication difficult because of high ambient noise and use of oxygen mask. Immediate diversion likely. Explosive decompression – additional technical and medical problems likely to follow.

Hydraulic failure: Very high workload with multiple system failures. Severely reduced deceleration on landing. Limited directional control. Possible runway blockage on landing, unable to manoeuvre off runway. Longer runway than normal may be required, minimum crosswind for landing. Possibility of fire from leaking hydraulic fluid.

Engine failure on take-off: Very high workload initially – control problems and cockpit drills. Major loss of performance, larger radius of turn. Emergency return or diversion likely. The aircraft may not follow initial departure clearance – it may continue straight ahead or follow its own emergency turn procedure. Degradation of other systems can result.

Engine failure, climb, cruise or descent: Aircraft likely to drift down, crew will advise height that can be maintained. Increased turn radii. Diversion likely.

Control problems: Likely to be most serious with smaller, less-sophisticated aircraft. Approach and landing possibly high speed with straight-in required. Problem may clear in warmer air if due to icing. Handling checks may be required before an approach is attempted.

Fuel shortage: Crew often reluctant to declare emergency. Either range (low quantity) or endurance (weather or traffic delays) may be a critical factor.

Icing: Predominantly a turboprop, piston and helicopter problem. Little or no warning – descent may already be established before controller can be contacted. Flight controls can jam. Performance of propellers, rotors and engines severely reduced, can cause engine flame-out. Descent or turn to warmer air may resolve situation.

Radio failure: Crew may be unaware of the failure. Crew may be unfamiliar with local radio failure procedures and unsure of action to take. Crew may be distracted while finding procedure. Crew may be confused initially. Other methods such as company frequency, SELCAL or ACARS can be used to contact aircraft.

Additional Considerations

As the booklet comments, there is rarely a single correct way to deal with an aircraft emergency because each one is different. For example, on an occasion that I hope will remain unique, I was in the tower at Halfpenny Green airfield, near Wolverhampton, when a skydiver jumped from an Islander at 10,000ft and crashed through the roof of an accompanying Dragon Rapide. The idea was a sixteen-man link-up but something went very wrong.

The Rapide, with an unserviceable radio, made a rapid descent trailing torn fabric and, after it landed safely, the unexpected passenger was found to have sustained only broken wrists. The Islander pilot was moonlighting from the RAF and was anxious to keep a low profile. It was, as I remarked at the time, rather like referring to the *Titanic* as a boating accident, but we concocted a very deadpan report to the CAA and I never heard anything more about it. That was many years ago; nowadays there would be a major investigation!

In many parts of the world a pilot has formally to declare an emergency before the safety services are alerted. A UK controller uses their judgment and almost always puts them on a Local Standby at the very least, working on the saying 'better safe than sorry'. A Local Standby brings aerodrome services to a state of readiness to respond immediately in the event of an incident. There is also the possibility that a minor problem with the aircraft may distract an inexperienced pilot enough to make him misjudge the landing. For Royal Flights, a Local Standby is standard procedure in all circumstances.

The scale of rescue and firefighting services at a particular airport is determined by the overall length and maximum fuselage width of the largest aircraft handled on a regular basis. The lowest is the Special Category licensed solely for flying instruction to take place. Then follow Categories 1 to 10, rising from an overall length of 9m progressively up to – but not including – 90m. Bristol, a typical regional airport, is Cat 7, Heathrow Cat 10. Up to Cat 9, the category may be increased by one to cover the occasional larger aircraft, provided this does not occur more than a permitted number of times per year. At most airports much larger aircraft can be accommodated by pre-arrangement simply by calling in off-duty personnel.

There are six standard categories of emergency, beginning with the self-explanatory 'Aircraft Accident'. A 'Full Emergency' is declared when it is known that an aircraft is, or is suspected to be, in such trouble that there is a danger of an accident. The problems include the thankfully rare fire in the air, fuel shortage and the not uncommon engine failure on multi-engined aircraft. In the latter case an experienced and properly trained pilot should have no difficulty in making a safe landing as he is required to practise asymmetric flying at regular intervals and pass a check. The safety services are alerted, however, and at larger airports this usually means the outside fire services will be summoned automatically as a backup.

Next comes the 'Local Standby', which I have already mentioned, and the 'Aircraft Ground Incident', which covers occurrences other than accidents. These include burst tyres, fuel spillages and bomb scares on parked aircraft. A 'Weather Standby' is instituted when 'weather conditions are such as to render a landing difficult or difficult to observe'. Bad visibility is one obvious instance, a significant crosswind component is another. The final category is 'Domestic Fire', which, as its title implies, covers such things as grass fires on and adjacent to the airfield and fires in its buildings. At major airports the rescue services have the use of a common frequency of 121.6MHz – callsign '(Location) Fire' – to talk directly with the flight crew when necessary.

Emergencies can include the situation where a passenger on board becomes seriously ill – the Medical Emergency. A pilot is then expected to make formal declaration of this fact to ATC using the distress ('Mayday') or urgency ('Pan') prefix, depending on whether the passenger requires immediate assistance. The nature of the passenger's medical condition, diagnosed or otherwise, is included in the message. Controllers then provide the appropriate priority to such flights and inform the emergency services.

A pilot requiring immediate assistance is expected to transmit a Distress Message with the prefix 'Mayday, Mayday, Mayday'. If the situation is less serious, an Urgency Message with the prefix 'Pan, Pan, Pan' is used. Unfortunately, pilots, particularly phlegmatic British ones, are unwilling to make too much of a fuss, so if you hear a 'Mayday' call, things have really reached the critical stage! The announcement of the loss of one engine – provided there are more than one – is usually delivered in a matter-of-fact tone, together with a request for diversion. This calm approach is sometimes self-defeating – a controller who would be sparked into instant action to clear a path for an aircraft that has abruptly turned into a glider in the circuit may think he has misheard if the magic word 'Mayday' is not used, and waste time asking for a repeat.

Transmissions from an aircraft in distress have priority over all other messages. When a pilot is already in contact with an ATC unit, assistance should be sought on the frequency in use, otherwise a call should be made on 121.5MHz. On hearing a distress call, all stations must maintain radio silence on that frequency unless they themselves are required to render assistance and should continue to listen on the frequency concerned until it is evident that assistance is being provided.

Ballistic Recovery Systems

Ballistic recovery systems, which take the form of a parachute, are fitted to some general aviation aircraft, notably the Cirrus SR22, for use in situations where a pilot considers continued safe flight is no longer possible. Such situations could include engine failure and loss of control. Where time permits, the phrase 'Ballistic recovery system deployed' should be used by pilots as part of the emergency message.

Fuel Shortage

A pilot's declaration of 'Minimum Fuel' indicates that no further fuel diversion options are available where the aircraft is committed to land at the pilot's nominated aerodrome of landing, with not less than 'final reserve fuel'. However, 'Minimum Fuel' R/T phraseology is not universally used by every aircraft operator and pilot. Controllers are not required to provide priority to pilots of aircraft that have declared 'Minimum Fuel' or that have indicated that they are becoming short of fuel.

Therefore, controllers will respond by confirming the estimated delay he can expect to receive, expressed in minutes if the aircraft is en route to, is joining, or is established in an airborne hold; or by expressing the remaining track mileage from touchdown if the aircraft is being vectored to an approach. They will also ask the pilot if they wish to declare an emergency. If so, they are expected to make a Mayday call, after which they will be given Category A priority.

The Distress Frequency 121.5MHz

The UK has two Distress and Diversion (D&D) Sections, located at Swanwick and Prestwick. D&D is manned by RAF control staff, who are assisted in the provision of an emergency service on the VHF International Aeronautical Emergency Frequency of 121.5MHz and its military UHF counterpart of 243.0MHz by suitably equipped civil and military units and certain HM Coastguard stations.

The emergency service is available on a twenty-four-hour basis to pilots flying within UK airspace who are in distress are or experiencing difficulties that could lead to a state of emergency. Provided the aircraft is above 3,000ft over most of the landmass to the east and south of Manchester or down to 2,000ft in the south of England, D&D has a truly amazing ability to fix an aircraft's position. This is known as Auto-Triangulation and uses sixteen outstations that automatically process its radio signals and display the location to the controller on a huge map.

For pilots flying at lower altitudes, position fixing can be carried out manually using bearings from various airfields around the country, although this takes several minutes to achieve. If the aircraft is equipped with a transponder, the code 7700 can be selected to indicate an emergency. This activates an alarm at every radar station able to receive the signal and also makes the radar position symbol pulsate to attract the controller's attention. It also breaks through any height filters applied.

Airband listeners monitoring 121.5 will find very little activity; the odds against hitting on anything interesting are very high. Aircraft on transatlantic flights are required to monitor 121.5 at all times, which is why it is often referred to as the Guard Frequency. There have been many occasions when a high-flying airliner has relayed messages from a much lower light aircraft on a delivery flight and alerted the rescue services. It is also used as an unofficial means of communication between crews of the same operator. Having made contact, a terse 'Go to company' (frequency) follows, so that they can have a chat.

Careless use of 121.5 is frowned upon and the following story is claimed to be true. Above the Arabian Gulf, two young American voices are discussing baseball results on 121.5. Suddenly, a typical British voice is heard, 'I say chaps, do you realise this is 121.5, the emergency channel, reserved for emergency use only?'

Silence ...

Then one American voice says: 'Gee! Ed, do you think it was God talking to us?'

In the UK, pilots are encouraged to make practice 'Pan' calls on 121.5, having first asked permission in case there is a real emergency in progress. The usual scenario is to simulate getting lost and request homing to destination or the nearest airfield. It is very impressive to hear how quickly D&D can fix the aircraft's position even when it is not fitted with a transponder. Not everyone agrees with this use of 121.5 for practice fixes, American airline captains especially. They can sometimes be heard complaining to the D&D controller about what they see as misuse of the frequency.

Often to be heard on 121.5 are broadcasts to alert pilots, especially military ones, to the setting up of a Temporary Danger Area around Search and Rescue (SAR) Operations. The message is usually prefixed, 'Securité, Securité: Temporary Danger Area D399 established at (position in lat and long), geographical position, radius 5 miles, up to (X) thousand feet, SAROPS on.' The aim is to exclude all aircraft other than SAR or those police-operated, thus reducing the chance of a mid-air collision.

Also associated with the Distress Frequencies are those used by the Aeronautical Rescue Co-ordination Centre based at the National Maritime Operations Centre (NMOC) at Fareham in Hampshire. Scene of search frequencies in use are as follows: HF – 3023kHz (civil/military night), 5680 (civil/military day), 5695 (military/day), 3085 (military night), 8364 (international intercommunication); VHF/UHF – 123.1 (civil), 156.3 (Channel 6 FM Marine), 156.8 (Channel 16 FM Marine), 282.8 (NATO). Other HF frequencies may be used as directed by the RCC controller.

The centre is responsible for co-ordinating all Maritime & Coastguard Agency Search and Rescue (SAR) helicopters. It monitors rescues in the United Kingdom Search and Rescue Region (UK SRR), which extends to 30° west in longitude, and from 45 to 61° north latitude (as far north as just south of the Danish Faroe Islands), excluding the Republic of Ireland (Ireland SRR). Sikorsky S-92 helicopters can operate in excess of 250 miles from their base, with an endurance of over four hours. AgustaWestland AW189 helicopters can operate in excess of 200 miles from their base, also with an endurance of over four hours.

Fareham controls HM Coastguard rescue helicopters at: Stornoway Airport on the Isle of Lewis in the Outer Hebrides, Sumburgh Airport, south of Lerwick in the Shetland Islands; Lee-on-Solent, 4 miles west of Portsmouth in Hampshire; Portland, within Portland Harbour; Humberside Airport; Inverness Airport; Caernarfon Airport; Lydd Airport; St Athan; Prestwick Airport; and Newquay Airport.

The NMOC is also home to the UK Cospas-Sarsat Mission Control Centre (UKMCC). This is the centre that detects emergency beacons within the UK Search and Rescue Region (SRR) using an advanced computer system. Maritime distress beacon information is passed to the Coastguard authorities but terrestrial alerts are investigated by the UKMCC, often requiring the use of SAR helicopters to pinpoint the beacon's position.

Fuel Jettisoning

Pilots of aircraft in flight are permitted to dump fuel in emergency and may request guidance from ATC. The recommendations are that it should be carried out over the sea if at all possible or above 10,000ft above ground level. Exceptionally, if neither option is available, or inconsistent with safety, fuel may be jettisoned above 7,000ft in winter and above 4,000ft in summer. For fuel to be dumped below these levels the situation must be unavoidable. A vertical separation of at least 1,000ft should be maintained between aircraft. As a rough rule of thumb, aircraft dump fuel at up to 2 tonnes per minute, so a 747 could take anything up to an hour. Note that not all jet transport aircraft have fuel dumping capability, so may have to burn off fuel to get down to allowable landing weight.

An Air India aircraft dumping fuel at FL150 over north-west England prior to a diversionary landing at Heathrow with a seriously ill passenger. It had been en-route from New York to Mumbai. *John Locker*

Flight Plans and Overdue Action

When an aircraft is operating on a flight plan (see page 32-33) and fails to turn up within thirty minutes of its ETA, the controller at the destination airfield is required to confirm the ATD (actual time of departure) from the departure airfield. Other set procedures known as Preliminary Overdue Action are put into effect. After one hour, or sooner in certain cases, Full Overdue Action is taken by the parent ATCC and a search launched for the missing aircraft.

Aircraft on a flight for which a plan has not been filed have no such protection, although they are required to 'book out' with the ATC unit at the departure aerodrome, assuming one exists. The departure details – destination, time en route, fuel endurance and persons on board (sometimes referred to as 'souls on board') are recorded but no further action need be taken. If an aircraft goes missing, it is often some time before people start asking questions, usually sparked off by anxious relatives.

Flight plans must be filed at least thirty minutes before requesting taxi clearance or start-up approval. A pilot may file one for any flight and for certain categories they are mandatory. These include all IFR flights within controlled airspace, those that cross an international boundary, and for any flight where the destination is more than 40km from the aerodrome of departure and the aircraft's maximum take-off weight exceeds 5,700kg. In addition, a pilot is advised to file a flight plan if he intends to fly over the sea more than 10 miles from the coast or over sparsely populated areas where search and rescue operations would be difficult.

For scheduled airline routes and other regularly recurring IFR flights with identical basic features, a repetitive flight plan saves operators and crews the chore of filing a separate plan each time. Often referred to as a 'stored plan', it is submitted by an operator for computer storage and repetitive use by ATC units for each individual flight.

Airprox

An Airprox Report should be made whenever a pilot or controller considers that the distance between aircraft as well as their relative positions and speeds have been such that the safety of the aircraft was or may have been compromised. A sense of proportion is required for this, however, as light aircraft in traffic circuits occasionally get very close to one another, usually through inexperience and/or not keeping a good lookout.

Pilots flying under IFR in controlled airspace may well file a report if they see another aircraft that they believe is closer to them than required by the separation rules. In a radar-controlled environment this may be 4 instead of 5 miles, which a pilot flying under VFR would consider ludicrous.

All Airprox Reports are investigated, not so much to allot blame as to try to prevent a recurrence by examining the circumstances. The degree of actual risk of collision is assessed and regular summaries of the most serious ones are published for all to read. In the past, when circulation was restricted, the press had to rely on leaked reports. One they never heard about unfortunately was the large pink pig that an Army helicopter nearly rammed one hazy day over the River Thames. It was an advertising balloon that had broken away from its moorings and drifted away! Most make very dull reading, an exception being the celebrated 737/UFO near Manchester in 1994! (See page 111-112)

Level Busts

A level bust is defined as an unauthorised vertical deviation of more than 300ft from an assigned level or altitude. Within RVSM airspace, this limit is reduced to 200ft. Records show that most level busts occur below FL120 in busy terminal airspace. Some level busts have been traced to the misinterpretation of flight profiles, typically Standard Instrument Departure (SID) and Standard Arrival (STAR) procedures, published in charts provided by commercial organisations. The CAA recommends that flight crew training should include in-depth familiarisation for crews with the presentation of contents and layout of charts used by the operator. This should ensure that the layout of check altitudes, tracks etc. become second nature to pilots.

Radio Failure

If an aircraft suffers a radio failure there are published procedures to which the pilot is expected to adhere. A squawk of 7600 set on the transponder will alert SSR-equipped ATC to his problem. If the transponder and/or essential navigation equipment has also failed, pilots are advised as a last resort to carry out a special procedure to catch the controller's attention. The aircraft is to fly at least two triangular patterns before resuming course, as follows:

Aircraft speed	Length of leg	Transmitter failure only	Complete failure
300kt or less	2 minutes	Right-hand turns	Left-hand turns
More than 300kt	1 minute		

If the controller should notice such a manoeuvre (and RAF experiments show that they often do not!) he is advised to inform D&D of the position and track and continue to plot the aircraft while it is within his radar cover. A shepherd aircraft of similar performance will then be sent out to lead it, hopefully, to a safe landing.

Quite often the failure is of the transmitter only and the controller can instruct the aircraft to make one or more turns and check if the pilot is complying. If it becomes obvious that the receiver is working, normal radar service is resumed. There are some subtle ways by which the aircraft's altitude and other information can be ascertained, such as, 'After passing FL50 turn left heading 270 degrees.'

There are occasions when an aircraft receiver is working correctly but the reply transmitted is unintelligible at the ground station because the speech is badly distorted or non-existent, perhaps because the microphone is unserviceable. Military pilots are briefed on a special code that makes use of the carrier wave only. The pilot presses his transmitter button a certain number of times according to the following code:

One short transmission – Yes (or an acknowledgment)

Two short transmissions – No

Three short transmissions – Say again

Four short transmissions – Request homing

One long transmission (two seconds) – Manoeuvre complete (eg, steady on heading)

One long, two short, one long – The aircraft has developed another emergency

A controller will be alerted to the presence of an aircraft with this kind of failure if he hears, or sees on the VDF, four short carrier wave transmissions. The controller should then interrogate the pilot, using the callsign 'Speechless Aircraft', unless he is already aware of its identity, to find out what assistance is required. He must be careful to ask questions that can be answered with a direct yes or no. The code is also recommended for use by civilian pilots as it can easily be explained by the controller in the first few transmissions.

Summary

As the CAA's *Aircraft Emergencies* booklet says: 'The controller is a very significant team member in the safe and successful resolution of most aircraft emergencies. Likewise, the controller has a variety of resources that he or she can call on to assist an aircraft. Flight crews look to the controller for direct assistance and to act as intermediaries with other ground-based services. Crews rely on controllers to provide timely and useful assistance, but not to interfere with the completion of vital checks and drills. Co-operation and co-ordination to minimise crew workload are the keys to success. Keeping procedures as close as possible to normal will assist greatly. Crews will normally want to give ATC as much information as they can, but it can take time to ascertain the full extent of the problems they face. In modern aircraft, single failures are rarely significant once cockpit drills have been completed. However, some drills can be complicated and lengthy. Patience can be a virtue!'

Boeing 737 at Coventry having a 'wet start' with raw fuel igniting. Not a major emergency but the crew needs to be informed immediately! *RW*

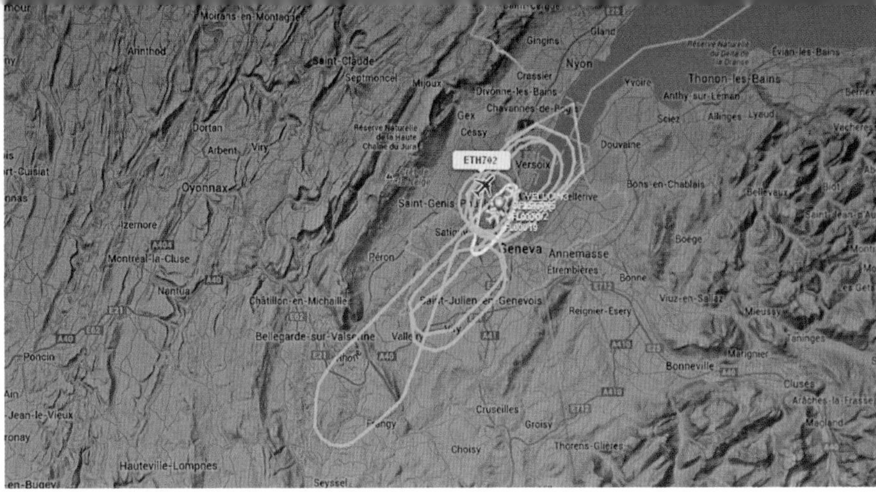

Chapter 14

Unlawful Interference (Hijacking) and Other Exceptional Events

The continuing possibility of airborne terrorism means that fighter aircraft are always ready to counter it. Each state enjoys exclusive sovereignty over the airspace above its territory and territorial waters. Consequently, no aircraft may enter its airspace without prior permission or authorisation. Each state will react to an intruder according to its own interpretation of the risk being faced. A trigger could be a single event or a combination of small errors. Historically, actions resulting in a scramble of QRA (Quick Reaction Alert) aircraft have been: unauthorised deviation from the cleared flight profile; loss of radio contact, particularly if associated with a flight profile deviation; unauthorised SSR transponder code changes or extended use of the Ident feature (the aircraft position symbol will pulse on the radar display); use of non-standard phraseology by the crew or other actions that could be construed as a covert attempt to alert agencies to a situation on board; notification of a threat from official or non-official sources.

Some nations, such as France, have a very overt reaction policy. For example, fighters are scrambled against any aircraft failing to establish two-way communication as it enters their airspace. Having scrambled, they will often complete the interception, even though communications may subsequently have been re-established. In contrast, the UK has adopted a slightly less conspicuous threat-based Air Defence posture, which is changed constantly to meet the perceived threat to UK airspace and the homeland. Consequently, over the UK it is highly unlikely that civil aircrew will see RAF QRA Typhoons at close quarters unless all other methods of confirming the integrity of the flight deck have been exhausted. Standard procedure for so-called 'hot intercepts' is for the interceptor to follow in trail about a mile behind with transponder inactivated to avoid a TCAS alert.

The Ethiopian Airlines Boeing 767 hi-jacked in 2014 by its co-pilot while the captain was out of the cockpit. En route Addis Ababa to Rome, it was eventually landed at Geneva where the co-pilot gave himself up to police. None of its occupants was harmed.

Some years ago, it was realised that TCAS evasion recommendations, called Resolution Advisories (RAs), have to be followed within five seconds to avoid an intruder aircraft. It would thus be possible that during an Air Policing Mission civil aircraft might perform evasive manoeuvres that could then be interpreted by the interceptor pilot as a non-friendly action, with maybe negative consequences. Procedural arrangements were applied so that when closing in on an intercept target, the military pilot disables Mode C and Mode S. (Some nations switch the transponder to Standby, which means no Reply in any Mode). In both procedures, the lack of altitude information will prevent an RA.

If the airline crew are aware of the presence of an interceptor, they must, if able to do so, inform ATC and try to contact it on 121.5MHz and/or 243.0MHz, the VHF and UHF international distress frequencies, respectively. They must then comply with all instructions. Non-compliance will obviously give the agencies on the ground cause for greater concern. If radio contact between the two aircraft is established, but communication in a common language is not possible, the following internationally agreed phrases are used to convey instructions and obtain acknowledgements:

Intercepting aircraft

Phrase	**Meaning**
Callsign	What is your callsign?
Follow	Follow me
Descend	Descend for landing
You land	Land at this aerodrome
Proceed	You may proceed

Intercepted aircraft

Phrase	**Meaning**
Callsign	My callsign is ...
Wilco	Understood, will comply
Cannot	Unable to comply
Repeat	Repeat your instruction
Am lost	Position unknown
Mayday	Mayday
Hijack	I have been hijacked
Land (place name)	I request to land at (place name)
Descent	I require descent

The key recommendations for pilots and aircraft operating in UK airspace to ensure that any event is handled in the most appropriate manner are: be aware of potential situations such as loss of two-way communications or inadvertent selection of the hijack transponder code that may indicate to ATC a potential security threat to the aircraft; communicate clearly when in your opinion there is an actual security threat; volunteer information regarding the integrity of the flight deck to ATC in a timely manner; use appropriate R/T phraseology and special-purpose SSR codes; comply with government instructions whether given by radio or through visual intercept signals.

The following examples are situations that may represent an unusual event: unauthorised deviation from cleared flight profile; refusal or inability to comply with ATC instructions (including vectoring) with no good reason; loss of R/T contact, particularly associated with flight profile deviation; unauthorised SSR code changes or extended use of IDENT; use of non-standard phraseology by the crew, or other covert attempt to highlight the situation (marked change in voice characteristics, etc.); Non-ATC related R/T transmission (eg political statement).

Depending upon circumstances, controllers might be heard to use one or both of the following standard phraseologies: (a) 'I am instructed by Her Majesty's Government to refuse entry into United Kingdom airspace' or 'to inform you that landing clearance has been refused for any airfield within the United Kingdom. What are your intentions?' (b) 'I am instructed by Her Majesty's Government that you are to hold at (exact reporting point or latitude/longitude) at (level). Acknowledge.'

Distinctly different procedures may have to be adopted for situations involving an element of uncertainty, such as attempted or suspected hijacking. These principles would concern situations where a flight crew is still in control, or thought to be still in control, and one where the hijackers appear to be in control of the aircraft. Consideration may also need to be given to the manner in which controllers respond to circumstances of lost radio or transponder contact. While many of these situations will arise because of equipment or operational error, there is always the possibility that a communication lapse is caused by an act of unlawful interference. Either circumstance may give rise to deviation from assigned routes and levels, followed by an interception that may itself lead to a violent outcome.

Controllers, therefore, must have a means to readily differentiate between incidents attributable to genuine operational or technical causes and those potentially related to hijacking. Any delay in determining the reason for loss of radio or transponder contact should be minimised by the use of procedures that isolate the cause or by utilising technology that would resolve doubt, or by both. In the course of a normal flight, significant periods may elapse between R/T exchanges, but one possibility for a timely alert involves the development of a transponder that cannot be reset after the emergency mode has been activated. This may involve use of a 'panic button' that, once activated, automatically transfers selection of the transponder signal to the avionics and out of reach of personnel in the cabin and on the flight deck.

Due Regard

Press reports of Russian Air Force Bear and other aircraft close to the UK have, predictably, been exaggerated. The facts are that the flights take place in international airspace where military aircraft, including those of NATO and European air arms, can and do operate as they wish. The procedure is called 'Due Regard' and is employed for situations when military aircraft are not able to accomplish the mission while complying with ICAO procedures for point-to-point and navigation flights. There are operational situations that do not lend themselves to ICAO flight procedures. They may include politically sensitive missions, military contingencies, classified missions or routine aircraft carrier operations. When operations of this type are not conducted under ICAO flight procedures, they are operated under the 'Due Regard' prerogative of military aircraft. Due Regard means that the aircraft commander of a state aircraft will operate that aircraft with 'due regard' for the safety of all air and surface traffic. Before an aircraft commander can declare due regard, there are certain conditions that must be met:

(1) Aircraft shall be operated in Visual Met Conditions (VMC); or

(2) Aircraft shall be operated within radar surveillance and radio communications of a surface radar facility; or

(3) Aircraft shall be equipped with airborne radar that is sufficient to provide separation between themselves, aircraft they may be controlling, and other aircraft; or

(4) Aircraft shall be operated outside controlled airspace and, when possible, away from high density traffic areas

(5) Currently, no specific language is published for notifying a controlling agency that you are exercising the Due Regard option. Aircraft commanders must ensure that the affected controlling agency understands his intentions. Prior co-ordination can help limit potential communication problems

Essentially, flight under the Due Regard option obligates the aircraft commander to be his own ATC agency and to separate his aircraft from all other aircraft.

However, for civilian controllers Due Regard is unsatisfactory and poses a perceived danger to civil operations, despite its legality. UK sovereign airspace is not being breached, only the airspace for which the UK has civil ATC responsibility. Middle East civil air routes are being infringed continuously by USAF and RAF aircraft operating under Due Regard. The Bear infringements are no worse but in fact a lot less dangerous because the Russian bombers are tracked initially by the Norwegians and the radar picture is shared.

As they cross the Kola peninsula around 30° East, a penetration time for the UK Air Defence Region is calculated on the assumption that they will continue south-west. This will be more than two hours ahead and the RAF's QRA takes one hour to get there, so there is no necessity for a Battle of Britain-type scramble as sometimes claimed by the press! The Bears tend to cruise at around Flight Level 360 and routinely do not talk to ATC or file a flight plan. They stay in international airspace over international waters, do not infringe the 12-mile limit and therefore contravene no laws.

UFOs and Air Traffic Control

Note that Unidentified Flying Objects are now redesignated by the Pentagon as UAPs (Unidentified Aerial Phenomena), but the old title is unlikely to drop from popular usage. Having been an aircraft enthusiast for well over fifty years and an air traffic controller for nearly forty, I have spent much of my time gazing up at the sky. In all that time I regret that I have never seen anything that I considered extra-terrestrial but I keep an open mind and live in hope! The world of ATC is a small one and gossip soon goes the rounds. According to the grapevine, there were several incidents involving lights in the sky around Manchester Airport in the early 1990s. Nothing was seen on radar and no official reports were made, as far as I am aware. That was until January 1995, when a near miss was reported between a Boeing 737 and a UFO about 9 miles south-east of the airport. The 737 was at 4,000ft over the Pennines being radar vectored for an ILS approach by Manchester Radar. Although it was dark, visibility was good. While flying just above the tops of some ragged cumulus cloud, the crew saw a lighted object fly down the right-hand side of the aircraft at high speed from the opposite direction. The captain was able to track the object through the right-hand windscreen and side window, having it in sight for a total of about two seconds. There was no apparent sound or wake and the first officer instinctively ducked as it went by.

A brief exchange followed on the radio between pilot and controller but, as the latter could not see anything else on radar, it was inconclusive. In subsequent telephone conversations, the captain was convinced that the object was itself lit. 'Although he could not determine a definite pattern, he described it as having a number of small lights, rather like a Christmas tree.' The first officer, however, felt that the object was illuminated by their landing lights ... he was unable to assess its distance, other than to say that he involuntarily ducked, so it must have appeared to him to have been very close.

He was entirely convinced, as was the captain, that what they had seen was a solid object and not a met phenomenon, balloon or any other craft with which they were familiar, or an F-117 stealth aircraft, which he had himself seen and which he feels he would have recognised.

Recordings of the radar data showed only the 737 and other aircraft being radar sequenced in the Manchester Terminal Area. There was no evidence of military activity 'from any official source'. The possibility that the object might have been a hang glider, paraglider or microlight was investigated but dismissed as extremely unlikely on a dark, windy night. Sensibly, the investigators refused to speculate on extra-terrestrial activity, preferring to leave this 'to those whose interest lies in this field'.

UFO sightings tend to be made by well-meaning members of the public rather than oddballs but, having handled many queries to ATC over the years, I know that it is very difficult to convince them that what they saw was almost certainly the planet Venus, or aircraft lights on final approach just above the horizon on a clear night.

The CAA's Manual of Air Traffic Services Part One (available online) has a section on UFO reporting. A controller observing a UFO or receiving a report from aircrew should consider if the sighting has any flight safety significance. If it does, a report should be compiled in the following format:

> (A) Date, Time and Duration of Sighting (Local times to be quoted) (B) Description of Object (Number of objects, size, shape, colours, brightness, sound, smell, etc) (C) Exact Position of Observer (Geographical location, indoors or outdoors, stationary or moving) (D) How observed (Naked eye, binoculars, other optical device, still or movie camera)
>
> (E) Direction in which Object was First Seen (A landmark may be more useful than a badly estimated bearing) (F) Angular Elevation of Object (Estimated heights are unreliable) (G) Distance of Object from Observer (By reference to a known landmark wherever possible) (H) Movements of Object (Changes in E, F and G may be of more use than estimates of course and speed. (J) Meteorological Conditions During Observations (Moving clouds, haze, mist, etc) (K) Nearby Objects (Telephone or high-voltage lines; reservoir, lake or dam; swamp or marsh; river; high buildings, tall chimneys, steeples, spires, TV or radio masts; airfields, generating plant; factories; pits or other sites with floodlights or other lighting) (L) To Whom Reported (Police, military organisations, the press etc) (M) Name and Address of Informant (N) Any Background Information on the Informant that may be volunteered (O) Other witnesses (P) Date and Time of Receipt of Report.

In practice, many of the sightings can be explained immediately to the satisfaction of ATC, even if the person reporting it is not always convinced. MoD now seems to be of the opinion that as UFOs do not appear to pose a threat to national security, there is no point in serious investigation. Very sensible, unlike another story that emerged some years ago. Just after an incident where the captain declared a full emergency due to a problem with the aircraft's ailerons, ATC received a telephone call from a local radio station. The caller asked if it could confirm or deny that an aircraft had recently declared an emergency, having been forced to land at an aerodrome because of aliens!

Despite my scepticism, there are definitely a number of incidents on record that defy explanation, particularly where credible witnesses were involved. One has to keep an open mind on the subject.

Chapter 15

UK Military Air Traffic Control

Military aviation in Britain is organised much the same as its civil counterpart, although the ultimate purpose of a considerable amount of military ATC is to bring aircraft together (formation join-ups, air-to-air refuelling, interceptions etc) rather than to keep them apart. Most airfields have a Ground Movements Controller as well as a Tower Controller, who is known also as the 'local' controller. The controller who sequences traffic onto final approach is the Director, the next stage being the Talkdown Controller, who uses Precision Approach Radar (PAR) to bring the aircraft down to visual contact with the runway. PAR, discontinued in UK civil ATC decades ago in favour of ILS, uses two radar displays. One shows the aircraft and final approach in plan view, the other the picture from the side that monitors deviations above and below the glide path. The pilot can thus be given height as well as heading corrections.

It should be noted that official RAF documents now refer to 'Air Systems' rather than aircraft. This all-inclusive terminology is defined as 'fixed or rotary wing aircraft, piloted or remotely piloted, and the ground-based systems vital to their safe operation'. Another radical development at the time of writing is that RAF Lossiemouth in north-east Scotland is well on the way to having what is claimed to be the world's first military digital ATC capability. Defence contractor Saab UK Ltd is creating an experimental digital control tower. The technology would be similar to that used for some civilian airports to control them from a remote location.

Hawks at RAF Valley.

Under the plan for digital capability, controllers will remain at Lossiemouth but they would have access to a series of wide angle and zoom lens cameras. These would give the controllers a 360-degree view of the airfield, allowing them to monitor it through a series of communication links. The MoD is also tendering for remote control tower services for Royal Naval Air Station Predannack in Cornwall. The requirement is for services to be performed from nearby RNAS Culdrose. The tender includes options for similar operations at other unspecified locations.

RAF rules governing runway occupancy, separation and other procedures are similar to those in civil ATC. Considerable use is made of ILS installations, but few are rated more accurate than the minimum civil Category 1 (minimum of 200ft cloud base and 600m RVR). Efforts are being made to improve this situation to counter the planned demise of PAR.

London Air Traffic Control Centre (Military), normally referred to as 'London Mil', is co-located with the civil ATCC at Swanwick. To meet the requirements of all airspace users, the civil controllers provide air traffic services to en route GAT (General Air Traffic) flights usually within the airways system and within fixed geographical sectors. The military controllers give a service in a more flexible fashion to OAT (Operational Air Traffic) flights. OAT flights are generally those that cannot conform to the requirements of flights within airways and other regulated airspace. Within the airways system GAT, including military traffic operating as GAT, is normally given priority over OAT. Exceptions are made, however, for such operations as military aircraft engaged in the calibration of a radar system. Conversely, outside the airways and upper route structures OAT generally gets priority over off-route GAT.

Flight Plans are vitally important for the efficient operation of the system. GAT Plans are processed in the normal way by the civil computer, while those for OAT are fed into the military computer by RAF personnel. If any of the flight plans affect Swanwick airspace, the relevant flight details are distributed to the appropriate sectors.

As one military controller working at London Mil remarked, it soon becomes obvious that most of the aircraft based in the east of England want to exercise in the west, and those from the west want to exercise in the east! The problem is that to get to those areas the aircraft need to cross one of the busiest air route complexes in the world. In most cases the crossing is achieved with very little fuss due to constant co-ordination with the civil controllers on the spot.

Radar Corridors

The standard method of crossing controlled airspace is via the Radar Corridors that have been established at the points most frequently required to be crossed by military flights. The Dean Cross RC permits airways crossing over Cumbria at FL190, the TILNI RC at FL190 is in the vicinity of Newcastle, and the Lynas RC is over Anglesey at FL170, the Lichfield RC in the north-west Midlands facilitates crossings at FL140, while the Gamston RC runs through airway LIMA 975 at FL190. The Daventry RC allows crossings at FL110, and the Westcott RC takes military traffic across the airways system just north of London at FL230 or FL240. Brize Radar at Brize Norton in Oxfordshire provides a service for the Swindon RC at FL230 and FL240. These 'blocks' of airspace simplify crossing procedures, but the pilot must still request a prior clearance from the controlling authority.

Swanwick Mil is split into eight sectors to cover the whole of the UK and surrounding areas. The sectors are simply named after the geographical area covered, for example North West and North over Scotland; West; East and Central. They surround the Central Sector, which covers much of England.

TACAN Routes

Delineated by TACAN (TACtical Air Navigation) beacons equivalent to civilian VOR/DMEs, and often used for upper airspace transits.

The military TACAN route system. *NATS*

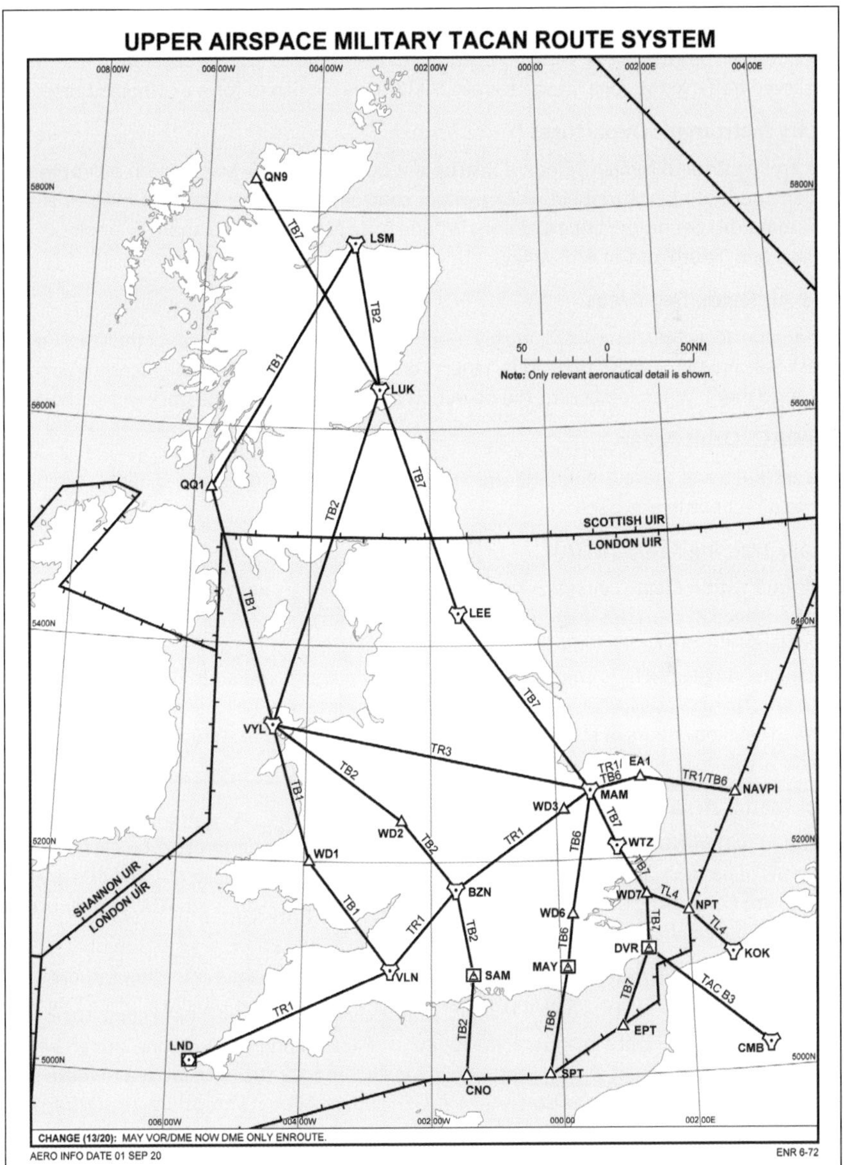

Military Aerodrome Traffic Zones

The purpose of a MATZ is to provide a volume of airspace within which increased protection may be given to aircraft in the critical stages of circuit, approach and climb out. It normally comprises the airspace within 5 nautical miles of the airfield from the surface up to 3,000ft. In addition, a 'stub' out to 5 miles protects the final approach path of the most used instrument runway. Although it is not mandatory for civil pilots to request permission to penetrate a MATZ, it is obviously highly desirable for them to do so. A MATZ Penetration Service is provided to civil aircraft. Traffic information will be given along with any instructions necessary to achieve separation from known or observed traffic in the zone. In some areas MATZs may overlap to form a combined zone.

Military Instrument Departures

These are identical to civilian Standard Instrument Departures (see page 53-54) except that the latter ensure that aircraft remain wholly within controlled airspace. Most UK military airfields do not meet this definition, but exceptions include Brize Norton and Northolt. Examples of MIDs are 'East' and 'South' out of RAF Valley.

Air-to-Air Refuelling Areas

There are fourteen Refuelling Areas, mostly over the North Sea, with others over the West Country, the Irish Sea and the Scottish Highlands. Tankers orbit in the ARA to allow the receiving aircraft to home onto them. When 'on boom', the operation begins along a specific track within the AARA.

E-3 AWACS Orbit Areas

There are twelve of these around the UK, mainly off the coast, where an E-3 Sentry can hold in order to direct battle exercises.

Military Training Areas (MTA)

Established within Class C airspace to provide military aircraft with freedom of operation for aircraft engaged in exercises incompatible with radar control.

The largest is the North Wales MTA, with a vertical extent of FL245 up to FL450.

The East Anglian MTA is co-ordinated by RAF Waddington and stretches from FL245 up to FL350. The North Wales MTA, under RAF Valley, has limits of FL245 and FL450. Outside the published weekday hours of training activity, MTAs revert to normal status. Occasional weekend operations will be given prior notice.

Aerial Tactics Areas (ATA)

Embedded within MTAs, they enable high-energy combat manoeuvres to be carried out by formations of up to six aircraft. Current examples are Valley ATA; the Wash ATA, the primary users of which are Coningsby, Cottesmore, and Wittering; and the Lakenheath ATA, mainly used by Lakenheath-based aircraft.

Areas of Intense Air Activity

Defined as 'an airspace within which military and/or civil aircraft, singly or in combination with others, regularly participate in unusual manoeuvres'. Pilots of non-participating aircraft who are unable to avoid these areas should keep a good lookout and are strongly advised to make use of a radar service. Examples are the Cotswold AIAA, Shawbury AIAA in Shropshire, the Oxford AIAA, and Yeovilton AIAA in Somerset.

Quick Reaction Alert (QRA)

Typhoons are kept on standby in an air defence role at two QRA stations, North at RAF Lossiemouth and South at RAF Coningsby. They will be supported by a tanker and sometimes an E-3 Sentry if the situation requires it.

Low Flying

The UK Military Low Flying System (UKLFS) extends across the whole of the UK and surrounding sea areas, from the surface to 2,000ft. This permits a wide distribution of activity, which contributes to flight safety and reduces the environmental impact of low flying. Military pilots are directed to avoid major conurbations, built-up areas, controlled airspace, aerodrome traffic zones and other sensitive locations. Inevitably, the protection given to these areas creates unavoidable concentrations of military low-flying activity where corridors are formed between them. Where necessary, military pilots follow uni-directional flows below 2,000ft to reduce the risk of collision.

For administrative purposes, the UKLFS is divided geographically into low-flying areas (LFA). Certain LFAs nominated as Dedicated User Areas (DUA) are allocated for special use, such as concentrated helicopter training, and are managed under local arrangements. Civil pilots should be aware that what is known as Unusual Air Activity and night exercises are frequently conducted in DUAs. These exercises can include aircraft operating without, or with restricted, navigation lights. In the north of Scotland, the Highlands Restricted Area (HRA) is used for special training, often in Instrument Met Conditions (IMC). To ensure safety, entry by civil and non-participating military aircraft is normally prohibited during published operating hours.

Red Arrows Hawk on short final at Hawarden.

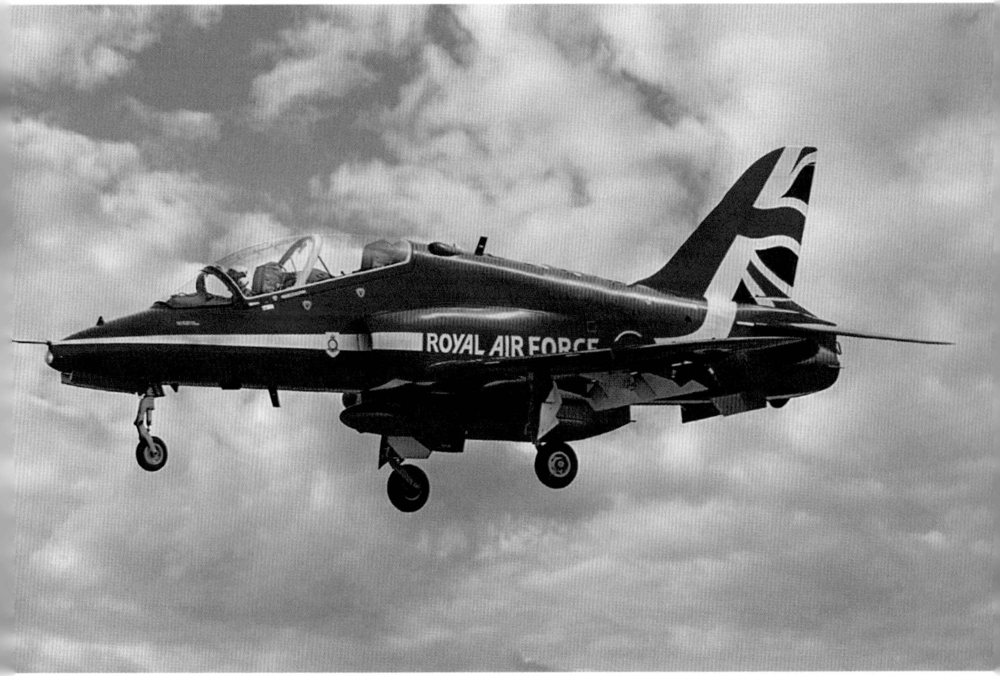

Military fixed-wing aircraft (except light aircraft) are considered to be low flying when less than 2,000ft Minimum Separation Distance (MSD), which is the authorised minimum separation, in all directions, between an aircraft and the ground, water or any obstacle. The lowest height at which military aircraft normally fly is 250ft MSD. However, in three specially designated areas, known as Tactical Training Areas (TTAs), located in Mid Wales, the Borders of Scotland and the North of Scotland, a small number of flights may be authorised to fly down to 100ft MSD. Military light propeller aircraft and helicopters are considered to be low flying when operating below 500ft. In practice, most military low flying takes place between 250 and 600ft MSD, decreasing in intensity up to 1,000ft MSD and reducing further in the 1,000–2,000ft height band. Occasionally, however, military aircraft perform high-energy manoeuvres between 250ft and 2,000ft, during which rapid changes in height, speed and direction will occur.

Lower Airspace Radar Service (LARS)

Military units also offer a LARS outside controlled airspace up to FL100 for both military and civil aircraft, and a similar service up to FL245 within what is termed 'Middle Airspace'. Its availability is subject to the range and cover of the particular radar in use as well as controller workload. The procedure when within approximately 30 miles of the radar unit is to establish R/T contact on the appropriate frequency using the phraseology '(ATC unit) this is ... (aircraft callsign) request Lower Airspace Radar Service.' Pilots may be asked to 'standby for controller'. When asked, they are to pass aircraft type, position and heading, flight level or altitude, intentions and type of service required.

Distress and Diversion

The RAF Distress and Diversion Cell at Swanwick has already been described in detail in Chapter 13. Briefly to recap, 'London Centre', as it is known by its callsign, has a computer-based facility that can calculate and display the position of any aircraft transmitting on the military distress frequency of 243.0MHz. If a crash or ditching occurs, Search and Rescue (SAR) is co-ordinated by the Aeronautical Rescue Co-ordination Centre based at the National Maritime Operations Centre (NMOC) at Fareham in Hampshire.

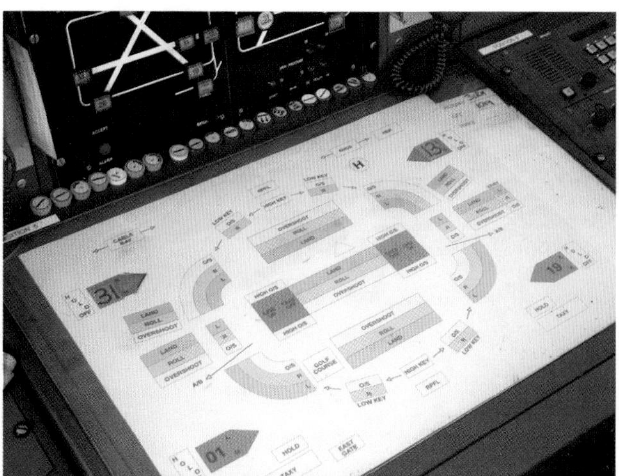

Valley tower controller's magnetic board to indicate aircraft positions.

Of course, the emergencies do not just involve aircraft; they may be ships in distress, climbing accidents, floods and a variety of other incidents. A Temporary Danger Area is established around the site so that SAR ops can be continued without interference from press aircraft and other non-essential intruders. When an aircraft is fitted with an ELT (Emergency Locator Transmitter) or a downed pilot activates a SARBE (SAR Beacon), the signals will be picked up by SARSAT (Search and Rescue Satellite Aided Tracking). The system is highly sensitive in detecting transmissions on 121.5, 243 and 406MHz and thus alerting the rescue services.

Royal Flights

Operational control of No. 32 (The Royal) Squadron is vested in the RAF. Royal Flight status is often extended to other reigning sovereigns, prime ministers and other heads of state as a courtesy. Contrary to popular opinion, there are no special increased separations for Royal flights; they are treated exactly the same as any other aircraft in controlled airspace, although a higher priority is given because the Royal personage usually has to meet a tight schedule. Royal flights in fixed-wing aircraft are always provided with controlled airspace to cover the entire flight path when it is within UK airspace. This coverage is obtained by the establishment of temporary controlled airspace where the route runs outside existing Class A and C airspace, and special Control Zones at the departure and destination airfields if these are not already in existence. The vertical dimensions, relevant radio frequencies, times and any other pertinent information will be detailed in the NOTAM concerning the flight.

The NOTAM is prepared by the Airspace Utilisation Section whenever a Royal flight is arranged. It is distributed to the ATCCs and airfields concerned, normally providing at least forty-eight hours' warning. The airspace concerned is notified as Class A, ie any aircraft within it must fly under IFR at all times. In the case of temporary Control Zones, ATC may issue Special VFR clearances to pilots unable to comply with the IFR requirements and thus ensure positive separation.

Controlled airspace is not normally established for Royal helicopter flights but a Royal Low Level Corridor, marked by a series of checkpoints, is promulgated. These checkpoints will be approximately 20 miles apart and will usually coincide with turning points on the route. Pilots flying near the Corridor are expected to keep a good lookout and maintain adequate separation from the Royal helicopter. The NOTAM will incorporate a list of nominated aerodromes from which pilots may obtain information on the progress of the flight.

USAF Bases

US Air Force operations from their two British bases are handled in a similar way to those of their RAF opposite numbers. They have their own controllers in the airfield towers, but Approach Control at Lakenheath and nearby Mildenhall is centralised and co-ordinated. Similar arrangements can be found at various RAF stations where a Centralised Approach Control service may be operated. There is a network of military upper airspace TACAN (Tactical Air Navigation) Routes across Britain and Europe linking TACANs, the military equivalent of the civil VOR/DME.

UK Aerospace Surveillance and Control System (ASACS)

Parented by RAF Air Command, ASACS is tasked with providing early warning of air attack against the UK air defence region, fighter and missile defences and the associated ground control system, fighter co-ordination with Royal Navy ships and to maintain the integrity of UK airspace in war. The organisation's hub is at RAF Boulmer in Northumberland, the elements under its control comprising:

Control and Reporting Centre – Boulmer

No. 1 Air Control Centre – RAF Scampton, Lincolnshire

Remote Radar Head (RRH) – Benbecula in the Outer Hebrides

RRH – Buchan, Aberdeenshire

RRH – Brizlee Wood, Northumberland

RRH – Staxton Wold, Yorkshire

RRH – Neatishead, Norfolk

RRH – Portreath, Cornwall

Weather Colour Codes

In addition to a normal TAF or METAR, RAF aerodromes use a colour code, which is a form of shorthand for their crews to reinforce the information in the main message. The meaning of each colour is listed below. Civilian PPL holders without instrument qualifications are advised that any code except 'blue' or 'white' may indicate serious problems, and even 'white' is no guarantee that the weather is good, even at the time of the report.

Colour	Minimum base of lowest cloud (Scattered or more)	Minimum reported visibility at aerodrome level
Blue	2,500ft	8km
White	1,500ft	5km
Green	700ft	3,700m
Yellow 1	500ft	2,500m
Yellow 2	300ft	1,600m
Amber	200ft	800m
Red	below 200ft (or sky obscured)	Below 800m
Black	Aerodrome unavailable for reasons other than cloud or visibility	

Chapter 16

Drones and Air Traffic Control

Remotely Piloted Aircraft Systems (RPAS) – better known as drones – have made great progress in a civilian context since the last edition of this book. Plans to integrate them safely with normal traffic in UK skies are already in motion. NATS and UK-based drone traffic management solutions company Altitude Angel have entered a long-term partnership. It aims to lay the foundation for a future whereby drones and manned aircraft can safely co-exist in the UK's busy skies.

Drones offer huge potential benefits to public services and the economy, with a growing number of organisations, from online retailers through to emergency services, expecting to increase their use of drones in their everyday operations, However, reports of incidents involving drones flying dangerously close to manned aircraft are on the rise, with drone incidents now accounting for more than half of all Airprox (near miss) reports received by NATS.

Schiebel Camcopter S-100 as used in UK Coast Guard trials. *Schiebel*

As the number of unmanned aircraft grows, increasing the visibility of drone flights is crucial to keep the skies safe. The partnership between NATS and Altitude Angel will enable the integration of drone flight and operational data with information and systems involved in managing manned aviation. Merging the two information streams will increase situational awareness among all legitimate airspace users and provide the digital foundations necessary to allow air traffic controllers to engage with drone operators. This partnership lays the foundation for a future whereby access to lower-level airspace could increasingly be granted digitally. It links knowledge of an operator's aircraft, qualifications and mission, pioneering a new form of airspace management suited to the changing use of our skies.

During 2020, a search and rescue (SAR) drone underwent a successful trial from Caernarfon Airport in North Wales. Drones then began operational missions for the first time in the UK to assist SAR helicopters. Initially, the drones flew at weekends only, allowing coastguard teams to watch live incidents from the air. They are flown by a pilot using digital control and imaging technology to allow them to see through the eyes of its on-board cameras. They can operate theoretically up to 18,000ft, staying airborne for about ten hours and can beam live video back to their control room day or night, even in adverse weather conditions.

These operations enable the helicopter crew at Caernarfon to remain on standby for lifesaving events, while the unmanned aircraft are tasked with providing safety over watch and monitoring, which those manned aircraft would otherwise have been sent to carry out. It is expected that unmanned aircraft will fulfil an increasingly important role in SAR.

At the time of writing, the delivery of mail and medical supplies by drone was being trialled between the mainland and the Isles of Scilly. These Beyond Visual Line of Sight (BVLOS) flights authorised by the CAA are also being trialled in a number of areas, including the Scottish Highlands and Islands, where deliveries to remote areas can be made in a fraction of the time it takes on the surface.

That drones are capable of flying great distances was proved in July 2018 when an MQ-9B SkyGuardian RPAS landed at RAF Fairford for an airshow. This transatlantic proving flight began at Grand Forks Air Force Base in North Dakota. A number of Temporary Danger Areas (TDAs) were established to facilitate its safe transit within the London Flight Information Region, routeing via Strumble VOR in south-west Wales direct to Fairford. In the event of it being unable to complete the flight to Fairford for any reason, the contingency plan was a diversion to either Culdrose or Predannack in Cornwall or to Llanbedr in North Wales. TDAs would have been established at the chosen destinations.

Although these pilotless aircraft, whatever size, are generally referred to as drones, the ICAO has defined an RPAS as: 'An unmanned aircraft which is piloted from a remote pilot station and is expected to be integrated into the air traffic management system equally as manned aircraft' with real-time piloting control provided by a licensed remote pilot.' The terms Unmanned Aircraft System (UAS) and Unmanned Aerial Vehicle (UAV) are also in use for sub-categories of RPAS. All very confusing!

The rapid growth in civil and military drones has increased the demand for access to non-segregated airspace. Technical solutions and procedures are being developed to integrate them into non-segregated airspace. Manned aviation is able to manage dangerous situations such as potential collisions with other airspace users, obstacles and ground operations at aerodromes, through the ability of a pilot to see and avoid these hazards. The absence of a pilot on a drone brings the challenge of replicating this ability, a concept known as 'detect and avoid'.

A serious concern is that introducing more and more drones equipped with ADS-B will flood the 1090MHz band with messages. This will degrade all systems working on 1090MHz, such as

Mode A and C, Mode S and TCAS. Interference is likely and in congested airspace the frequency is already congested without adding drone traffic. The ICAO is already urging member states to consider new surveillance technology for drones operating in uncontrolled airspace. They have concluded that continuing to use existing ADS-B technology would be disastrous.

Even if all drones were equipped with Mode-S transponders, the pool of 24-bit addresses (hex codes) is not large enough to cover potentially tens of millions of individual drones. The theoretical limit is 16,777,214 unique ICAO hex codes. The net effect of multiple drones flying at low level near airports could blind the surveillance system to the existence of manned aircraft operating at altitude.

For legal guidance on private small drone use, the essential Drone and Model Aircraft Code can be viewed on the Civil Aviation Authority's website.

The Lighter Side

Over Afghanistan, ABC123 is a drone and the link between the ground station and the aircraft has gone down.

Control: 'ABC123 you are leaving your assigned airspace. Having problems?'

ABC123: 'We have lost the link, the aircraft will maintain speed and heading until it is re-established.'

Control: 'Well get new batteries in your remote and get it back in your airspace before it hits a real airplane!'

Chapter 17

A Career in Air Traffic Control

Be aware that at the time of writing, the pandemic has put many aspects of recruiting and training on hold. However, this could all change very quickly, with traffic getting back to normal levels. Hence the outline of career opportunities given below will again become valid.

An interest in aviation and a basic familiarity with ATC gained from airband monitoring may spur younger readers into the thought of taking it up as a career. Like most jobs in aviation, Air Traffic Control is very demanding and requires the highest standards. It is also a job that is associated with high levels of stress, although this depends on location and experience. In high levels of traffic, bad weather, or emergencies, it can indeed be stressful, but controllers are highly trained to deal with these types of situations. Not only are they trained at the start of their career, but they are given continuous training to keep them current and prepared for infrequent scenarios.

You may ask what are the basic qualities required by a controller? Difficult to answer; many psychologists and other medical people have attempted to analyse the pressures of the job, so far be it for me to comment further. One source did say that controllers often speak, listen, write and think all at the same time!

Tower simulator.

To summarise the ATC system, the Tower Controller works at airports and aerodromes, co-ordinating the traffic on the runways and taxiways by using radio instructions, issuing the necessary clearances to the cockpit crew before and after landing and take-off. At very busy airports, Ground Movement and Clearance Delivery will share the tower's workload. Most of the time, the Tower Controller works from visual reference, by keeping the aircraft in sight. Soon after take-off and for a period prior to landing, the pilot communicates with an Approach Controller or a Terminal Controller, depending on the configuration of the airspace. The Approach or Terminal Controller, using radar, directs arriving flights to the point where they are handed over to the tower. He/she also directs departing flights to the point where control is assumed by an Area Control unit (sometimes called an En Route unit). When 'en route', the aircraft may transit several control areas. It maintains course with the help of radio beacons and modern airborne navigation systems, but remains under constant control from controllers in an Area Control Centre.

To act as a civilian air traffic controller in the UK, a full UK Air Traffic Controller's licence is required. Before obtaining the licence you will need to complete a course of training successfully at a CAA-approved ATC training establishment and obtain a first Certificate of Competence. Once you have successfully completed the first rating course (in most cases this will be the Aerodrome Control rating) you will be issued with a Student Air Traffic Controller's licence. This will allow you to undertake on-the-job training at a UK ATC unit. The training will form the minimum experience requirement (MER) or approved unit training plan (UTP) and should lead to the grant of a first Certificate of Competence and the issue of a full ATC licence. The MER or UTP must commence within twelve months of completing the rating course.

Global ATS Ltd at Gloucestershire Airport (global.ats.com), as well as a complete range of advanced ATC courses, offers ab initio controller training courses, an expensive option if sponsorship is not available. The alternative route is to apply to NATS for a trainee controller position. Application forms can be downloaded from the NATS website, the basic entry requirements being: you must be at least 18 at date of application and eligible to work in the UK, have five GCSEs at Grade 4 or Scottish National 5s Grade A-C, including English and Maths, and be eligible to work in the UK. If successful, you must pass a European Class 3 medical examination and have security clearance. Wearing glasses is acceptable if your eyesight reaches certain standards, but colour blindness will bar you. ATCOs also have to pass a thorough medical examination every two years until they are 40, then every year after that.

Candidates will first register their details and complete an online application form. After this, if the minimum requirements have been met, they will be invited to sit some online tests. These are designed to test cognitive and decision-making skills that are important to controllers. If they are deemed successful in the test, they will be invited to take an online Situational Judgment Test and Personality Questionnaire.

The third stage is attendance at a one-day assessment centre to take part in some further ATC-related tests, have an interview and take part in a group exercise. If accepted by NATS as a Trainee Air Traffic Controller, attendance at one of its colleges in either Hampshire, Gloucester or Jerez in Spain is the first step. The length of college-based training varies depending on a host of factors, including the specialism you take and how quickly you can complete different phases. Most college-based training is completed within a year to eighteen months and includes a combination of practical and theory-based sessions.

This is merely a summary and the whole procedure is explained in detail on the NATS website. The ATC section of the Professional Pilots' Rumour Network website (www.pprune.org) contains a wealth of advice from and for candidates for NATS interviews and training.

The college course lasts approximately eleven months for Area Trainees and Terminal Control Trainees, and between six and nine months for Aerodrome and Approach Trainees. This is not the end of the training as there is a period of validation training at the posted operational unit. The validation period is dependent on the unit and the individual's ability to reach the desired competency. The number of trainees allocated to each discipline is determined by the NATS business need. The biggest requirement is for Area Controllers, so normally the majority of trainees are streamed to the area discipline. During the basic course, a decision will be made on which discipline you will follow, primarily based on the skills you have demonstrated in your training. Your personal preference on which discipline you would like to pursue will be taken into account as a secondary factor in the decision.

Your progress through training is assessed continually by means of theoretical examinations, practical assessments and oral tests, and successful completion of these assessments will be required for the continuation of training. The course of action following failure of an assessment is determined on a case-by-case basis taking account of all relevant factors including regulatory requirements, and it could result in training being terminated. Obviously as you come towards the end of your college course you will be asked where you would prefer to be posted. While NATS tries to take personal circumstances into account, its operational needs must come first. You therefore must be prepared to work anywhere in the UK.

Unfortunately, the failure rate in ATC training is high, somewhere around the level of 40 per cent it has been said. It is important to understand that a student may be dismissed at any stage of training if their results are unsatisfactory. NATS does not have to reimburse any of the costs incurred. This negative aspect should nevertheless not stop you applying. Other job and education opportunities will also carry a certain amount of difficulty and risk of failure in examinations or tests. Having said that, many of my colleagues fell by the wayside for various reasons and, with a little less pressure, became competent controllers at regional airports. Some have even returned to NATS at a later date, having proved themselves in the meantime.

New technology, new airspace, new regulations all combine to produce an ever-increasing level of complexity for controllers to cope with. There will shortly come a time – indeed many believe it has already arrived – when controllers will have to specialise, not just when they go operational but from day one of their training. The current controller training tends to follow a well-worn path of theory leading to aerodrome training, approach training (procedural followed by radar) and then finally onto area training. In today's complex airspace, the Area Controller rarely, if ever, draws on his aerodrome skills, so it could be argued that there is no point in learning them.

NATS' College of Air Traffic Control is at Whiteley, Fareham, Hampshire, about 3 miles from the Swanwick Area Control Centre. Those destined for NATS operational units will be part of a team that handles a combined total of 6,000 movements per day in complex and crowded airspace. In order to achieve a skill level commensurate with such a demanding control environment, today's students must have access to the very best teaching aids. These comprise modern classroom facilities and teaching techniques, along with simulators that accurately represent the airspace and traffic they will experience in real life. The lessons and training exercises are designed to fully prepare them for all eventualities they will experience in the 'real world'.

The career of an operational controller in NATS is clearly structured and will depend on your progress in attaining and maintaining the necessary levels of proficiency and experience. If you wish, you may spend your whole career as an operational controller. As you acquire more experience and follow technical and operational developments, your progress could lead to the attainment of the grade of Principal Controller. You would continue to benefit from the advantages of shift-work, including flexibility of working patterns and shift-work payments on top of an already good salary. Different career development opportunities exist for those with the right abilities (operational training officer, supervisor, centre supervisor) and those who wish to progress to management responsibilities. An operational (shift-working) controller will cease active operational service at the age of 55 (which could be extended to a maximum of 57) and will receive a retirement pension calculated according to the pension rights acquired at that date. NATS currently provides the ATC service at the following airports: Heathrow, Stansted, Luton, London City, Manchester, Cardiff and nearby St Athan, Bristol, Glasgow, Aberdeen, Belfast City, Belfast International, Southampton and Farnborough, as well as the Control Centres at Swanwick and Prestwick.

There are opportunities to work in Europe because Eurocontrol, responsible for the Maastricht Upper Area Control Centre, is actively recruiting trainee controllers. This site in the Netherlands houses a multi-national team of controllers, supported by engineers, technicians and other specialists and controls traffic operating above 24,500ft in the skies of Belgium, Luxembourg, the Netherlands and northern Germany.

Eurocontrol training lasts about 2½ years, including courses with theoretical and simulator lessons at the Eurocontrol Institute of Air Navigation Services in Luxembourg and intensive on-the-job and simulator training at the Maastricht UAC. Current entry requirements are: you must be at least 18 and less than 25 years of age. Be a national of one of the Eurocontrol Member States (the latter includes the UK). Have successfully completed secondary education at an advanced level. Have a good command of English and be medically fit. Air Traffic Control is traditionally seen as a stressful occupation, but much depends on training, experience and temperament.

A Eurocontrol document has this to say about it: 'Stress is a physiological syndrome. You feel it when put under mental or physical constraint. Stress can be a positive and necessary stimulator of action to help you work out a difficult situation. Due to its multivariate pattern, stress might also be inappropriate to solve the problems with which you are faced. Obviously, some aspects of the ATCO tasks make the mental workload rather high (monitoring and managing routine traffic, switching attention, solving conflicts, updating spatial mental picture, providing services). A high level of stress, including its physical component, might therefore be undesirable. Nevertheless, the tolerances to stress manifestation vary from one individual to another. It is thus not easy to say whether ATC is a stressing activity as such.'

The Royal Air Force, of course, employs its own controllers, known as Air Operations (Control) Officers, recruiting within the age group 17½ to 47. Required educational qualifications are: two A-levels or three Highers at Grade C or above. Five GCSEs at Grade C/4–5 or above, or SCE equivalent 5 or above, including English Language and Maths. At least two A2 Levels/3 Highers at Grade C or above (excluding General Studies or Critical Thinking), which must total a minimum of sixty-four UCAS points. Or hold a UK degree at Grade 2:2 or higher (or acceptable alternative). Training is undertaken at the Defence College of Air and Space Operations at RAF Shawbury in Shropshire.

The role of an Aerodrome Flight Information Service Officer (AFISO) is described in Chapter 9. Before a licence is issued by CAA, examinations in procedures, air law, navigation and meteorology have to be passed. After that a minimum of forty hours' practical experience has to be completed under the supervision of a qualified AFISO. A validation will then be granted for the particular airfield after a check-out by a CAA inspector. AFISO work is not well paid but it provides valuable experience for moving on to full ATC. Much of the study syllabus is almost identical for both disciplines.

Apart from being a controller, there are several other employment opportunities in ATC. Almost all ATC units employ Air Traffic Services Assistants (ATSAs). ATSAs provide support to controllers and perform administrative functions necessary for the air traffic service system to continue working (eg flight plan acceptance and pre-flight briefing for pilots). ATC units also require engineering support from Air Traffic Engineers (ATEs) to ensure that the equipment and navigation aids are maintained and operate correctly. You should contact your local airport directly to enquire about employment prospects as an ATSA or ATE. Some ATC units may sponsor suitable ATSAs for controller courses.

In addition to ATC services, NATS provides comprehensive engineering design and maintenance for all its systems including centres, radars, communications and navaids. It trains all its engineers in technical skills for a wide range of equipment installation and maintenance, safety management, and general skills.

So there you have it; a rewarding and interesting job with constant challenges. A real buzz when you get it right. I have been lucky enough to spend most of my time in ATC working in a tower environment. As one of my enthusiast colleagues observed, you get very well paid to watch aeroplanes all day. Simplistic, maybe, but not far from the truth!

Birmingham controller view at night. *RW*

Opposite: Coventry tower at sunset. *RW*

Section 2

Chapter 18

Airband Monitoring

Legalities

A reminder about the law relating to airband listening; it is illegal for the unlicensed. It is a myth that listening is permitted if one does not impart the information to anyone else. However, owning a scanner or any radio that can receive airband transmissions is not against the law. Judging by the number of radios apparent in public viewing areas at airports and at airshows, it would appear that officialdom tolerates what is essentially a harmless activity. Of serious concern is what the Civil Aviation Authority calls Malicious Interference to VHF Communications Services. There have been attempts by irresponsible, if not criminal, persons deliberately impersonating air traffic controllers and the types of messages they broadcast. The CAA says that problems caused by these incidents have so far been minimised owing to the experience of pilots and controllers receiving the transmissions.

All such incidents are investigated by the Office of Communications, commonly known as Ofcom, and evidence is gathered for prosecution. Listening to police messages is most definitely illegal, and there have been a number of cases involving heavy fines and confiscation of scanners. Merely having these frequencies in the receiver's memory is considered proof of guilt. You have been warned!

P-3 Orion of the German Navy displaying at a Cosford airshow.

Apart from airband listeners who use their radios as a means of logging aircraft registrations, there are others for whom this is of no more than academic interest. Their listening pleasure is derived from learning how aircraft are controlled and the way the ATC system operates. Those in the second category will soon begin to grasp the principles, and will want to find out more, whilst those in the first will recognise that a basic knowledge of them will assist in tracking the aircraft in which they are interested.

I should like first to cast some light on the jargon words that always puzzle the new airband listener. A comprehensive list can be found below, but the most frequently encountered are the terms QNH, QFE and flight level. The first two are codes rather than abbreviations and refer to the current atmospheric pressure at sea level and aerodrome level, respectively. When the value in hectopascals (this term has now replaced millibars but the measurements are identical) is set on the aircraft's altimeter, the instrument will indicate the distance above the appropriate datum. The term QFE Threshold refers, by the way, to the barometric pressure converted to that at the end of the runway.

Above a point known as the Transition Altitude, normally between 3,000ft and 6,000ft in the United Kingdom, a standard barometric setting of 1013.2 hectopascals is used, producing what is termed a flight level (abbreviated to FL). This ensures that all aircraft, particularly within controlled airspace, are flying on the same altimeter setting and can thus easily be separated vertically by the required amount. This removes the necessity of continually adjusting the altimeter to allow for local pressure variations over the route, any error being common to all aircraft in the system. FL70 is roughly equivalent to 7,000ft, FL230 to 23,000ft, and so on.

Times are given in the form of two figures; for example 14, pronounced one four, indicates fourteen minutes past the hour, while 42, four two, means forty-two minutes past the hour. The standard ATC time in the United Kingdom, and indeed in the entire aviation world, is Universal Time Constant (or Co-ordinated) known as UTC. In the winter it is the same as local or Alpha time in the United Kingdom, but British Summer Time is one hour ahead of it. This use of UTC ensures that there is no confusion with Flight Plans on aircraft flying through time zones.

The word squawk is often heard, particularly in route clearances, along with a four-figure code. This is set on the aircraft's transponder, a device that responds to automatic interrogations from a ground station by sending a return signal in coded form. The information appears on the radar display as a label, giving callsign, height and destination, adjacent to the appropriate aircraft position symbol. The word blip is obsolete, the image on the display (screen is obsolete too!) on modern radars being produced electronically via computer.

The term 'clearance' or 'cleared' is a legal one meaning that the aircraft may proceed under certain explicit conditions and that it will not be impeded by other traffic. It is confined mainly to route clearances and runway occupancy for take-off and landing, thus avoiding any possible confusion with the meaning.

Directions are given in degrees magnetic so that if an aircraft is heading 360 degrees it is flying due north, 090 degrees due east and so on. Note the difference between heading and actual path over the ground (track). If there is a strong crosswind, an aircraft may be pointing (heading) in a particular direction but travelling over the ground in a considerably different direction. There is an analogy here with rowing a small boat across a fast-flowing river; although you may be aiming for a point on the opposite bank, the current will also be deflecting you sideways. Simple right and left are used for direction changes, as in the instruction 'Turn right heading 340 degrees', port and starboard being long outmoded in aviation.

Speed is expressed in knots, one knot being equal to 1 nautical mile per hour. Four main speeds are used within the ATC environment:

1. Ground speed – the actual speed of the aircraft over the surface of the earth. With a true airspeed of 100kt and a tailwind of 20kt, the ground speed would be 120kt.
2. True airspeed (TAS) – the actual speed of the aircraft through the air and shown on the flight plan and controllers' flight progress strips.
3. Indicated airspeed (IAS) – read directly from the cockpit airspeed indicator and often used by ATC for speed control. It varies from the TAS dependent on altitude, air density and temperature.
4. Mach number – TAS expressed as a fraction of the local speed of sound. The speed of sound (Mach 1) is a function of temperature – colder (ie higher) equalling slower. In international standard atmosphere (ISA) conditions, at sea level Mach One is a little over 661kt TAS, but at FL360 it has decreased to 572kt and remains at that figure to around FL600–FL700.

Distances are measured in nautical miles (approximately 2,025yd). References to DME, as in 'Report 8 DME Wallasey', relate to the Distance Measuring Equipment carried aboard aircraft. This receives radio transmissions from ground beacons and enables the distance to or from the particular position to be presented automatically to the pilot as a continuous read-out in miles and tenths. The 'time to go' to the beacon can also be displayed to the pilot.

Runways are designated by two numbers derived from the heading in degrees. The runways at Manchester, for example, are 05/23 Left and Right. This is rounded down from the actual direction of 051/231° and the end zero omitted. Similarly a heading of 064/244° would be presented as 06/24. Other familiar examples are 09 Right/27 Left and 09 Left/27 Right at Heathrow and 08 Right/26 Left at Gatwick. Note that small annual changes in the bearing of the Magnetic Pole can affect the designation of runways. For example, Heathrow's directions were 10/28 until 1987 when the exact alignment became nearer to 090/270 degrees than 100/280 degrees.

Airband Reception

Good reception of airband transmissions obviously depends on your location relative to airports and air lanes. Since VHF radio waves follow approximate lines of sight, the higher the aircraft, the further away you can hear messages from it. Transmitter power is also a factor, but, generally speaking, high-flying aircraft can be received up to 200 miles away.

Ground stations may be screened by hills, buildings and other obstructions, so you may not be able to pick up the replies from the tower or approach even if you live quite close to the airport. The coverage for the Area Control Centres (ACCs) at London and Prestwick is very much better, however, there being few places in the flatter parts of the British Isles out of range of one or more of their powerful transmitters. This is because they are sited at some distance from their associated ground stations, usually on high ground. There may, however, be some 'blind spots' in reception for no apparent reason.

Prolonged periods of high pressure over and around the UK can cause some strange effects with VHF frequencies. For example, during July 2013 there was much breakthrough from European ATC frequencies at low level all over the UK. This was usually on approach frequencies, Amsterdam being one of the unintended culprits. This is known as ducting or anomalous propagation and, apart from high pressure, needs several other factors such as certain temperature and humidity values for it to occur. As noted above, VHF radio waves roughly follow lines of sight but tropospheric refraction can cause them to 'bend' over the horizon and retain a significant level of power. These ducting conditions are well known at radar frequencies since they happen quite frequently. In VHF band, although meteorological statistics show that they should be less frequent, their probability of occurrence is still important enough to have an operational effect on current VHF analogue communications.

The first thing to do after acquiring a new scanner is to establish which ground stations are within range and which can help you to identify aircraft flying in your local area. You can set up the appropriate frequencies on the scanner and monitor them when required. With experience you will soon know which station an aircraft is likely to be 'working', its height being a good clue as to whether the pilot is talking to the local airfield, ACC, radar unit etc. Unfortunately, in parts of Britain there are so many ATC units capable of providing a radar service that it may be difficult to discover to which a transit aircraft is talking. A flight below airways in the north Midlands, for example, might be in contact with Birmingham, East Midlands or Shawbury Radar, or simply the London Flight Information Region frequency. Of course, the pilot may not be talking to anyone, nor does he need to if he remains clear of aerodrome traffic zones and other restricted airspace.

Aircraft do not always use their registrations or military serial numbers as callsigns, and most commercial flights use a callsign totally unrelated to the aircraft registration. The answers to many of the questions that arise from airband monitoring are to be found in the network of Facebook pages, websites and commercial magazines, especially *RadioUser* and *Aviation News*. Almost every airfield in Britain features its own Facebook page run by local enthusiasts.

Since most transatlantic flights from north-west Europe have to cross Britain at some point, even those anonymous airliners with contrails can be identified. There are several privately produced publications available that match the callsign and registration of most of them. Identifying military aircraft can be very difficult as few, apart from some USAF transports, use the actual serial number. Military airfields generally use UHF frequencies to communicate with their own aircraft. The callsigns of first-line combat aircraft are changed frequently for security reasons.

Very useful for supporting airband listening are the various virtual radar websites, such as Flightradar24, PlanePlotter and ADS-B Exchange. See pages 142-143 for more details.

Chapter 19

Airband Scanners

Scanning receivers, better known simply as scanners, are available as hand-held portables and desktop sets, the latter often referred to as base stations. A hand-held is very useful in that it can double for use at home or outdoors and will usually cost less than a base station while having similar frequency coverage. Desktops are, however, usually easier to operate, as there is more room available on the front panel for additional buttons and controls, together with larger frequency and channel display. Often – but not always – in the case of budget models, base receivers give better technical performance than a hand-held in terms of their ability to receive weaker signals. A word of caution: most hand-held scanners have no keypad for entering frequencies. This is done via multi-function buttons. Younger enthusiasts, having grown up with technology, will have no difficulty coping with this, but their elders may find it unnecessarily complicated and definitely not user-friendly. It is possible, with some sets, to download frequencies from a PC.

The good news is that you can buy a fully operational hand-held airband scanner for under £100. These reasonably inexpensive sets only include the civil VHF airband, but for £140 upwards most scanners cover the full VHF/UHF bands, for those wishing to monitor the military, In fact, most stretch from at least 25MHz to 1300MHz.

Shawbury-based Griffon at Sleap.

These scanners can be divided into two types – the keypad-operated ones, and the 'menu'-driven ones. Most are now 'computer friendly', and with the right cable connection and PC programme acquired separately can be used in conjunction with a computer database, which can be downloaded to the set.

One should be aware that most manufacturers no longer supply rechargeable batteries or power supply charge as standard, although there are some exceptions. When we move to the more sophisticated sets, batteries/battery packs are usually, though not always, included in the box. Top of the market sets in the price band from about £200 upwards have moved away from the familiar 'banks and channels', to 'dynamic programming', which is more complicated to use when manually entering frequencies, but a lot easier when programming from a computer.

It is obvious that these sets are really for the experienced scanner user, and should be avoided by a beginner who has never used one before.

Scanner Basics

The following notes are presented as a guide to what the beginner should be looking for in a scanner for airband listening. There is also an explanation of some innovative features.

Frequency Coverage and Tuning Step Size

Ensure that the bands you want to listen to are present as, in general, only the so-called continuous coverage scanners will include the UHF aircraft band. The coverage you should be looking for is 108.00 to 137.00MHz with 8.33kHz spacing and 225 to 400MHz with 25kHz spacing, the civil and military airbands respectively. Both ranges are AM (Audio Modulation). Depending on the filter fitted to the receiver, the recovered audio can, in some cases sound very distorted, as the receiver cannot tune exactly to the wanted signal. The better receivers let you select from several tuning steps, typically. Many budget scanners offer airband coverage but don't include the UHF military airband range.

Scan

Scan is the term used to describe the type of operation where the receiver runs through frequencies that have been pre-programmed into the equipment memory channels by the user. For example, local airport and Area Control frequencies. The receiver scans through these memory channels and stops when a signal is detected. The number of memories that can be scanned depends on the make of the receiver, but most offer a minimum of twenty, with the facility to 'Lockout' or temporarily remove from the scanning cycle those memories that are not of interest at the moment.

Search

Search is a term often confused with Scan and this is the other main feature on most receivers. If you don't know the exact frequency that a particular service operates on, but you have a rough idea, or want to monitor activity on the civil or military airbands in general, then use can be made of the search facility. The user programs into the receiver the upper and lower frequency limits of the band to be searched and also the frequency step size that the receiver is to search with. The receiver then automatically searches over the set range and stops when a signal is detected.

Some of the more sophisticated sets offer a whole range of different signal detection systems for use in the search and scan modes. These are designed to prevent the receiver from staying on one frequency for too long if a continuous signal is present. You should decide whether you are going to make the most use of either the Scan or Search function and choose the receiver with the facilities to suit. The Priority Channel function, sometimes called the AUX or auxiliary facility, allows any one preset channel to be interrogated automatically every two seconds so that you won't miss anything on, say, the local tower frequency.

Close Call

Certain receivers incorporate a function that revolutionises scanner performance. Known as Close Call, it looks for active frequencies within range of the unit and automatically tunes them in. It is no longer necessary to have huge memory banks full of frequencies or to search frantically through the bands looking for a certain transmission. A specific waveband can be targeted, such as VHF airband when listening at an airport, so as to avoid picking up unwanted transmissions from other services. An amazing technical leap. Alinco has since introduced a similar feature called Flashtune that automatically tunes the receiver to a nearby transmitter.

Alpha Tagging

Names can be added to identify memory channels, although sometimes restricted to as few as six characters.

Antennas (Aerials)

Radio waves are attenuated (weakened) by a lot of things, including buildings. If you can get the antenna that is connected to your scanner outdoors and as high as possible, you will hear very much more. A further method of improving reception is a pre-amplifier (usually abbreviated to pre-amp), which fits between the antenna and the receiver on a hand-held model or inside the case of a base station. The device boosts the received signals and feeds them into the receiver. Results can vary but it may be possible to receive, for example, the ground transmissions from a distant airport that were previously audible only as 'noise'. Better-quality pre-amps have filters that can be switched in to suit the frequency range in which you are interested.

Batteries

Hand-held radio tend to eat batteries so investment in rechargeables and a transformer for home use is obviously desirable. The former are usually supplied with the set as standard, along with a mains transformer. It is a good idea to obtain a second rechargeable battery pack so that the two can be alternated; life between charges is only a few hours.

Birdies

All radios rely on internal oscillators, crystals etc. in order to operate. With the extremely wide coverage offered by most modern scanners, it is inevitable that the receiver will sweep across some of its own, internally generated frequencies (and often their harmonics and mixing products). These are sometimes sufficient to stop a search when there is nothing really there! They can also block a frequency you want to listen to. Manufacturers try their best to avoid the worst by careful design, but is impossible to eliminate them all. A good way to deal with them, once identified, is to use the Lockout facility. Some manufacturers list the offending frequencies in the handbook. The good news is that on some new designs it is possible to move the birdies if they are blocking a useful frequency.

Specifications

These can be very misleading! One of the best ways to see if a receiver is up to the mark is to read the reviews, particularly where measurements have been made. This is because the manufacturer's figures are usually a minimum standard and many models are much better than the published figures.

Sensitivity

This is the ability to hear signals and should be lower than 1milliV for 12dB S/N on AM and 0.5milliV for 12dB S/N on NBFM.

Selectivity

This is the ability to reject unwanted signals on adjacent frequencies. The best choice seems to be around +- 7.5kHz at –6dB for most services in Britain, but up to +- 12kHz at –6dB is useable.

Spurious Response/Image Rejection

This is the ability to reject unwanted signals. The image rejection is usually a problem with older designs of receiver and can result in other transmissions interfering with the wanted signal, as is possible with the lower frequency ranges. A minimum of 50dB rejection should be expected for both image and other spurious responses. However, a lower figure is to be expected on hand-held models as a result of design economies in order to get the circuitry to fit inside the outer case.

There are a great number of features on today's scanners and it is important to find out exactly what is or is not included in the purchase price. Some require separate aerials, others power supplies and battery chargers. All the specialised dealers hold stocks of accessories, such as aerials, headphones, earpieces, and assorted plugs, leads and adaptors.

As has been stated before, VHF reception is 'quasi line-of-sight', so the higher the aerial the better the result. If the usual telescopic aerial or rubber antenna supplied with the set proves inadequate, a remote airband antenna can be purchased. A wide variety of these are available for outside or loft mounting. They can in turn be improved by attention to the coaxial cable used to connect aerial to receiver. If by re-routeing it you can shorten it, great, but if you can't get it any shorter than about 40ft (13m), consider using UR67 coaxial cable –expensive but offering much lower reception losses than cheaper cable.

For VHF airband the ground plane type of aerial can be recommended. One designed for airband use will give better performance than almost any other aerial, including wide band types intended for general use with scanners. Ideally, it should be mounted as high as possible in the clear, but is still capable of good results if left swinging from a rafter in your loft!

However, if you want to listen to military UHF as well as civil VHF, an aerial is needed that will cover the whole range from 100 to 500MHz. The professionals use a discone aerial for this purpose. Although looking like a demented hedgehog, they are the only simple aerial to work over a wide frequency range and the performance is first class. For those who want to fit an airband aerial to a vehicle, a vertical whip aerial is easy to fix and use, especially with a magnetic mount. As all signals in the VHF airband are vertically polarised, it is likely to be quite efficient.

Newcomers to airband listening may want to buy one of the more inexpensive sets first to familiarise themselves with what is being said and its meaning and perhaps move up to a more ambitious receiver later on. Second-hand models are often advertised in radio magazines and many dealers offer a good selection of trade-ins. It can also be argued that right from the start investment in a proper airband scanner is desirable. As ever, it all depends on money!

Software-Defined Radio and Computer Interface

If you are interested in finding new frequencies, logging channel usage and many more functions, then this is the option to look for. Many receivers now boast computer ports and an increasing amount of software is available, making it very easy to get a sophisticated system running. The advantage of this type of programming is that no group/system/bank/channel is wasted. The user can have a memory as flexible as they want it, without wasting the storage capability of the set. Systems, groups, and even individual channels, can be specifically named using the set's built-in menu. Programs to help with this can be downloaded from the Internet, or in many cases from the manufacturer's website.

An 'activity count' mode is available where you can set the scanner searching a given bank of memory channels, with the program performing a percentage count of the activity on each. This can be for virtually any period you like and a printed report is supplied at the end. This is very useful for assessing the listening possibilities of particular airband frequencies. An almost infinite range of aviation information can be found on the web, including new frequencies and procedures discovered by enthusiasts and unusual visiting aircraft, often with advance warning of their arrival.

A Selection of Popular Hand-held Scanners Plus Two Desktops

Albrecht AE-125H

Frequency range: 25–88MHz, 108–174MHz, 225–400MHz, 400–512MHz, which includes civil and military airbands.

Price: £130

Seven pre-programmed memory banks. Close Call feature. Hyper Search up to 300 steps per second.

Supplied accessories include two AA NIMH rechargeable batteries, mains charger.

Alinco DJ-X11E

Frequency range: 0.05–1300MHz, which includes HF, civil and military airbands.

Price: £300

Power: lithium battery pack, mains adapter.

1,200 channel memory with alpha numerical tagging up to sixteen characters. The dual receive facility allows you to listen to two frequencies at the same time and there are three selectable scan speeds. The manufacturer claims that this scanner has more features than many desktop receivers. Battery life is up to fifteen hours.

Supplied accessories include battery pack, charger with mains adapter, rubber duck-style antenna, belt clip and carry strap.

Uniden Bearcat UBX-75XLT

Frequency range: 87–107.9MHz, 108–174MHz, which includes civil airband only.

Price: £110

Power: Three × NiMh batteries (not supplied)

300-channel memory. Twenty-five channels per second scan rate, Close Call.

Supplied accessories: none.

Uniden Bearcat BCT-15X (desktop)

Frequency range: 25–512MHz, 758–823.9, 849–868.9, 894–960, 1240–1300MHz, which includes civil and military airbands.

Price: £250

Power: mains power adapter and car power plug supplied.

9,000-channel memory with alpha numerical tagging of up to 999 of them. Close Call feature. Alphanumeric tagging.

Supplied accessories: Telescopic antenna, serial PC interface cable, mounting bracket and hardware.

Uniden Bearcat UBC-125XLT

Frequency range: 25–88,108–174, 225–512, 860–960MHz, which includes civil and military airbands.

Price: £140

Power: Two × NiMH batteries.

500-channel memory with alphanumerical tagging, ten banks of fifty channels. Close Call feature.

Supplied accessories include batteries, mains charger, belt clip, wrist strap.

Left to right: Albrecht AE125H. Alinco DJ-X30E.

Uniden Bearcat 75XLT.

Uniden Bearcat 125XLT.

AOR AR 8600.

Uniden Bearcat UBC-3600XLT-NXDN

Frequency range: 25–1300MHz, which includes civil and military airband.

Price: £480

Power: Three × AA NiMh batteries with built-in charger.

2,500-channel memory with alphanumerical tagging, ten search banks. Auto store function whereby the scanner can be set to scan and store any active frequencies into memory. Close Call feature.

Supplied accessories include batteries, mains adapter, belt clip, wrist strap.

Icom R6.

ICOM IC-R6E

Frequency range: 0.1–1310MHz, which includes civil and military airbands.

Price: £200

Power: Two × NiMh batteries, mains adapter.

1,300-channel memory, twenty-two memory banks. High-speed scanning – 100 channels per second. Drip-resistant outer casing for use in harsh weather.

Supplied accessories include NiMh batteries, AC adapter, flexible antenna.

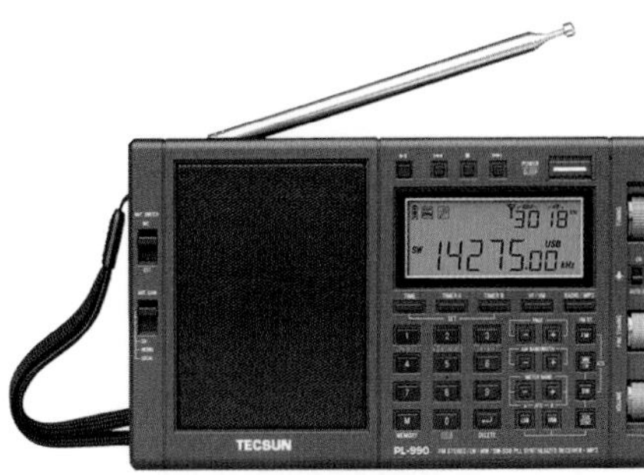

Tecsun PL-990.

Whistler TRX-2 (desktop)

Frequency Range: 25–1300 with some gaps, but includes civil and military airbands.

Price: £480

Power: Mains

Supplied accessories include antenna and power cable.

Principal airband and hobby suppliers

The Aviation Shop, Runway Visitor Park, Manchester Airport WA15 8XQ.
Tel: 0161 489 8324.

Haydon Communications, Haydon House, 1 Glencrofts, Hockley, Essex, SS5 4GN.
Tel: 01708 862524.

ML&S Martin Lynch, Wessex House, Drake Avenue, Staines, Middlesex TW18 2AP.
Tel: 0345 2300 599.

Moonraker (UK) Ltd, Cranfield Road, Woburn Sands, Bucks MK17 8UR.
Tel: 01908 281705.

Nevada Radio, Waters and Stanton & InnovAntennas, have combined to form the International Ham Stores Group, operating from a combined showroom and distribution centre at Unit 1, Fitzherbert Spur, Portsmouth, Hants, PO6 1TT.
Tel: 023 9231 3090.

Transair Pilot Shop, Brighton City Airport, Shoreham-by-Sea, West Sussex, BN43 5FF.
Tel: 01273 466000.

Gloucester Airport Shop, Terminal Building, Gloucestershire Airport, Cheltenham, GL51 6SR.
Tel: 01452 857700.

Solent Airport Distribution Centre, Hangar 9, Faraday Business Park, Solent Airport, Spitfire Way, Lee-on-the-Solent, PO13 9GA.

Left: Airbus Beluga airborne from Hawarden.

Below: Lufthansa Airbus A320 at Manchester.

Chapter 20

Virtual Radar for the Enthusiast

Virtual radar enables aircraft to be monitored on a computer display in real time, looking much like the ones that real controllers use. It utilises the Mode-S and ADS-B signals from aircraft. Mode-S is a Secondary Surveillance Radar (SSR) technique providing great integrity of data by practically eliminating false responses and garbling of data labels, particularly in busy airspace such as holding stacks. Mode-S provides the capability to down-link extra data automatically from the aircraft flight deck. ADS-B is the acronym for Automatic Dependent Surveillance – Broadcast. ADS-B equipped aircraft broadcast their precise position in space via a digital datalink along with other data, including airspeed, altitude, and whether the aircraft is turning, climbing, or descending. ADS-B receivers that are integrated into the air traffic control system or installed aboard other aircraft provide users with an accurate depiction of real-time aviation traffic, both in the air and on the ground.

The system relies on the satellite-based global positioning system to determine an aircraft's precise location in space. It then converts the position into a digital code, which is combined with the flight details. The digital code containing all of this information is updated several times a second and broadcast from the aircraft on a discrete frequency, called a datalink. Other aircraft and ground stations within about 150 miles receive the datalink broadcasts and display the information in user-friendly format on a computer screen. Pilots in the cockpit see the traffic on a Cockpit Display of Traffic Information (CDTI). Controllers on the ground can see the ADS-B targets on their regular traffic display, along with other radar targets. ADS-B has been in use over the Pacific and other areas outside conventional radar range for many years and has now become operational for North Atlantic traffic.

The elusive Lockheed U-2 can be tracked using PlanePlotter's unique Mode A/C function. *Stephen Walker*

With the right equipment, there is nothing to stop the amateur enthusiast from sharing all this data at an affordable price. The virtual radar boxes, such as the Kinetic SBS-3 described in the previous edition of this book, are no longer marketed, having been superseded by other electronic devices as described below.

Popular is the Mode-S Beast, a Mode-S and Mode-A/C receiver and decoder sold in kit form, which requires some soldering of components to the circuit board and screwing the case together. This takes anything up to an hour depending upon one's skill level, I am told. Alternatively, for an extra 24 Euros it can be supplied ready-assembled. To make it work, the Beast requires an external antenna and a USB connection to a PC enabled for PlanePlotter. Despite its relatively low cost of around 260 Euros, the Beast is a high-performance receiver. Also popular is the Radarcape, with similar capability to the Beast.

The GNS 5890 is a USB ADS-B receiver and fits directly into your PC. Being only slightly bigger than a standard USB stick, the GNS5890 is claimed to be the world's smallest ADS-B receiver. It tracks aircraft, allowing you to receive the data from ADS-B equipped aircraft within a 300km radius and have the information displayed on your PC or other USB-compatible device. The GNS 5890 does this with a highly sensitive 1090MHz ADS-B circuit and a bespoke antenna supplied with the purchase. The cost is around £120.

There are dozens of 'dongle' types of varying quality, although none are as good as the professional devices owing to their much lower sample rates. The only plus as far as the 'dongles' are concerned is that they are a lot cheaper. Deciding which of all these options is the best for you is difficult. I would strongly advise that you talk to a few radar receiver users if you can and view different receivers in operation. Radarspotting Forum (radarspotting.com) is a useful source of advice and information, and a careful read through the many threads will answer some of your questions.

If you don't want the bother and expense of a radar receiver, there are a number of free sites gathering their data from a vast network of enthusiasts. The best ones, in my opinion, are flightradar24.com, planefinder.net, RadarBox24.com and Radarvirtuel.com, as they are all in real time. Flightradar24 and Plane Finder are also available as phone apps for both iPhone and Android.

As these sites also operate a commercial service, they bow to operator pressure for confidentiality by rendering certain aircraft anonymous. They also filter out a lot of the military traffic. However ADS-B Exchange (www.adsbexchange.com) does not participate in what it calls the 'security theatre' performed by most other flight tracking websites that do not share data on military or certain private aircraft. It says that it exists to serve the aviation hobbyist/enthusiast first and foremost.

Similarly, the OpenSky Network is a non-profit, community-based receiver network that has been continuously collecting air traffic surveillance data since 2013. Unlike other networks, OpenSky keeps the complete unfiltered raw data and makes it accessible to academic and institutional researchers. With over 25 trillion ADS-B, Mode S, TCAS and FLARM messages collected from more than 3,500 sensors around the world, the OpenSky Network claims that it exhibits the largest air traffic surveillance dataset of its kind.

It remains to give a brief description of the formidable capabilities of PlanePlotter. PP relies on a global network of radar receiver users combining the signals they receive and making the results available via the internet. PlanePlotter can be downloaded free for a twenty-one-day trial, after which a 25 Euro (plus VAT for EU residents) one-off charge is payable online for continued use. You do not have to own a radar receiver, just a PC. PP is an amazing resource with continuous free upgrades to improve its capabilities. The website (www.planeplotter.com) details all these features, including Mlat (multi-lateration), which can locate aircraft not transmitting position, by measuring the pulse arrival times at several PP users. With that method, it can even locate aircraft that are operating basic Mode A only, and not Mode S at all.

Another unique feature in PlanePlotter is Beamfinder, which uses the 'ping' radar returns from an aircraft illuminated by several radar sites to determine its position, without requiring any other PlanePlotter stations in the area. If you own a radar receiver (some cost less than £30), you may choose to contribute your raw reception data to the network and thus enjoy the Mlat feature for no further charge. Otherwise the annual fee for these features is 12 Euros plus VAT.

PP users are warned that some of its advanced features are relatively complex and may involve unfamiliar concepts. There is an implicit requirement that users can cope with routine Windows operations, file manipulation etc. Also that they understand something about firewalls, routers and networks, can find their home position's latitude and longitude and that they are prepared to spend time studying the Help file so as to understand how to get the best out of these advanced features.

24-bit Aircraft Addresses

The CAA allocates a unique number for every UK-registered aircraft, known as the International Civil Aviation Organisation (ICAO) 24-bit aircraft address. One of the primary uses of the address is the unique identification of an aircraft via its Mode S transponder. An ICAO 24-bit aircraft address is allocated to every UK-registered aircraft regardless of whether it is ever likely to be fitted with a Mode S transponder. The address stays with a particular airframe for the period that the aircraft remains UK-registered. Blocks of numbers are allocated to each member state. Details of the allocated addresses are available via the online G-INFO UK Register database.

Typhoon with USAF KC-135 tanker as seen on ADS-B Exchange.

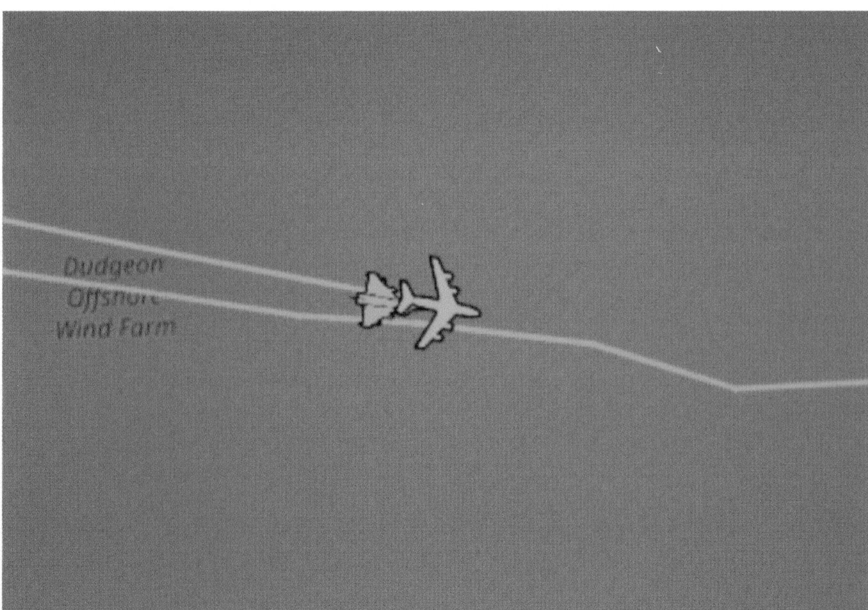

A theoretical total of 16,777,214 addresses is available and this worldwide system has been designed so that, at any one time, no address is assigned to more than one aircraft. Only one address can be assigned to an aircraft and it cannot be changed except under exceptional circumstances authorised by the state regulatory authority concerned. When an aircraft changes its state of registry, the previously assigned address is to be relinquished and a new address assigned by the new registering authority. It is essential that the aircraft address is periodically verified using ground tests.

Such checks must also be conducted when a major maintenance check has taken place and when the aircraft has changed registration, to ensure that a newly assigned address has been properly set. Inaccurate data can have a serious effect on flight safety. Notwithstanding, it is not uncommon for aircraft to broadcast an incorrect code and thus a wrong registration appears on virtual radar. In Europe (including the UK), ATC radar takes the registration from the flight plan via an interface with the Eurocontrol network, and not from a database of Mode S to registration tie-ups.

In particular, the airborne collision avoidance system, ACAS II, performs on the assumption that only a single, unique 24-bit aircraft address per airframe exists. The performance of ACAS II can be seriously degraded and in some instances disabled if an incorrect or duplicate address is installed on an aircraft. If an aircraft is fitted with Mode S, then the address has a number of uses for ATC and other services. If an aircraft is fitted with an emergency locator transmitter then this can also use the same address to identify the aircraft to search and rescue services.

Chapter 21

Charts and Official Documents

Almost as important as an airband radio itself is the acquisition of a set of radio navigation charts. They are essential to build up an overall picture of the UK airways system and the positions of beacons and reporting points.

En route charts are published by three organisations for the United Kingdom; the Royal Air Force, Aerad and Jeppesen. The US Air Force produces its own charts but these are more difficult to obtain. Obviously the information on the different charts is fundamentally the same, but the presentation differs quite considerably. There is also some variation in the areas covered. The RAF covers the UK with two charts; UK(H)2 for high altitudes and UK(L)2 for low altitudes.

The NavTech (formerly Aerad) chart for the UK is EU(H/L)2. NavTech also produce a wide range of other related documentation, including Standard Instrument Departure charts, Standard Arrival charts and airport and apron layouts. Navtech's other important publication, much prized by enthusiasts, is the Europe and Middle East Supplement, one of a set of four that cover the entire world. It is a soft-backed book packed with information on airports, including their aids, runway lengths and radio frequencies.

The other chart publisher is Jeppesen Inc, an American firm whose main distributor in the UK is Pooley's Flight Equipment at London Elstree Airport (www.pooleys.com). Four sheets cover the UK, two for high level (Ref E(HI)1 and 2) and three for low altitudes (Ref E(LO)1, and 3). The company also produces a wide variety of associated data, the most important of which are airport approach charts. Full details can be found at www.jeppesen.com.

Pitts Special at Sleap.

Eurocontrol do not actually publish their own charts, but make them downloadable as pdf files free of charge from their website www.eurocontrol.int. The relevant charts for the UK and Ireland are ERC-10/H for high-level and 10/L for low-level airspace.

The AIM Aeronautical Charting Department of NATS (AIM standing for Aeronautical Information Management) produces a wide range of charts including SIDs, STARs and let down plates. It is also responsible for the UK Aeronautical Information Publication, once known as the Air Pilot. The AIP itself is freely viewable online. It is divided into general information such as ATC rules and procedures, details of each aerodrome and an en route section listing all air routes and sub-divisions of airspace.

At first sight, radio navigation charts are a perplexing welter of intersecting lines, symbols and figures, but, like any other maps, there is a key and with a few minutes' study they become logical. The radio beacons are identified by name and a three or two-letter abbreviation. The Wallasey DVOR, for example, may be referred to by ATC and aircraft as Wallasey or Whiskey Alpha Lima. The frequency of 114.1MHz on which the beacon radiates will be adjacent to its name on the chart. Also shown on the chart are the designations of airways, their bearings in both directions, the distances in nautical miles between reporting points, the heights of their bases and upper limits and the lowest available cruising levels.

Many of the charts are stocked by airband radio suppliers but they can also be purchased direct from the publishers or their agents at the addresses listed below. Out-of-date charts are sometimes advertised in the aviation press at reasonably low prices and can also be found on eBay and airshow stalls. Provided that they are not too old, say more than twelve months, they can still be very useful.

Other Information Sources

AM 3000 Manual of Military Air Traffic Management. Available online.

CAP 168 Licensing of Aerodromes.

CAP 393 Air Navigation: the Order and Regulations. As with all the other Civil Aviation Authority publications listed here, it is available for free download on the CAA website.

CAP 413 Radio Telephony Manual. The Bible for correct UK phraseology.

CAP 413 Supplement 2. A Reference Guide to UK Phraseology for Aerodrome Drivers.

CAP 452 Aeronautical Radio Station Operator's Guide. Phraseology for Air/Ground operators.

CAP 493 Manual of Air Traffic Services Part 1. All you ever wanted to know about UK ATC and a lot you didn't! Student controllers will have to learn most of this in detail. Note that MATS Part 2 is not publically available. This is the section unique to each ATC unit, covering all local procedures, whether it be airport or Area Control centre.

CAP 584 Air Traffic Controllers – Training.

CAP 637 Visual Aids Handbook: A compendium of visual aids intended for the guidance of pilots and personnel engaged in the handling of aircraft.

CAP 670 Air Traffic Services Safety Requirements.

CAP 694 The UK Flight Planning Guide.

CAP 722 Unmanned Aircraft System Operations in UK Airspace.

CAP 744 Air Traffic Controllers – Licensing.

CAP 745 Aircraft Emergencies: Considerations for Air Traffic Controllers.

CAP 774 UK Flight Information Services.

CAP797 Flight Information Service Officer Manual.

CAP1430 UK Air Traffic Management Vocabulary (includes Abbreviations)

CAP1711 Airspace Modernisation Strategy

NAT Doc 007 North Atlantic Operations and Airspace Manual (ICAO European and North Atlantic Office) Available online.

SKYbrary

SKYbrary, Eurocontrol's Wikipedia-style website, can be found at www.skybrary.aero. It is a remarkable repository of safety knowledge related to flight operations, air traffic management and aviation safety in general. Recently added to the site are SKYclips, a growing collection of short animations of around two minutes' duration that focus on a single safety topic in aviation. Typical titles are Stopbars at Runway Entrances, Callsign Confusion, Conditional Clearances, Sensory Illusions, and Traffic Collision Avoidance System (TCAS) – Always Follow the Resolution.

YouTube

There is a lot of ATC-related content on this site, most of it American, but there are some very informative videos on the NATS and Eurocontrol channels.

Suppliers of Airways Charts, Flight Guides and related material

Royal Air Force, No. 1 Aeronautical Documents Unit, RAF Northolt, West End Road, Ruislip, Middlesex, HA4 6NG.

See also the list on page 140

Ottringham Doppler VOR beacon in East Yorkshire.

Chapter 22

ATC Terminology and Aviation Jargon

Phonetic Alphabet

The use of phonetics on radio to overcome the problems of confusing similar sounding letters like 'B' and 'P' or 'M' and 'N' dates back to the First World War when it was essential that such information as map references were passed accurately by aircraft spotting for the artillery. The phonetic alphabet of the time began A-Ack, B-Beer and gave rise to the phrase 'Ack-Ack' for anti-aircraft fire. By the time of the Second World War it had been replaced by an alphabet beginning A-Able, B-Baker and C-Charlie. In the 1950s, by international agreement, the British wartime code was superseded by a new alphabet designed to be more easily pronounced by aircrew whose native language is other than English.

Some of the original phonetics were retained but a number of words known throughout the world were now employed. The resulting alphabet was almost identical to that in use today, the exceptions being M-Metro, N-Nectar and X-Extra. The new offering sparked off some ribald comment that its originators seemed to have spent a lot of time hanging around in bars and dance halls, such was the emphasis on these admirable pursuits! The alphabet was overhauled once more in 1956 and remains in use to this day.

Certain universally accepted codes and abbreviations, such as QNH, QFE, ILS, SRA, QDM are not put into phonetics but said as written. There is also a standard way of pronouncing numbers and the word decimal, as used in radio frequencies, is supposed to be said as 'dayseemal', although this rarely happens in practice.

Current phonetic alphabet

A – Alpha
B – Bravo
C – Charlie
D – Delta
E – Echo
F – Foxtrot
G – Golf
H – Hotel
I – India
J – Juliet
K – Kilo
L – Lima
M – Mike
N – November
O – Oscar
P – Papa
Q – Quebec
R – Romeo
S – Sierra
T – Tango
U – Uniform
V – Victor
W – Whiskey
X – X-Ray
Y – Yankee
Z – Zulu

Transmission of numbers

0 – Zero
1 – Wun
2 – Too
3 – Tree
4 – Fower
5 – Fife
6 – Six
7 – Seven
8 – Ait
9 – Niner
Thousand – Tousand

Examples of number transmissions are: 10 – Wun Zero; 583 – Fife Ait Tree; 2,500 – Too Tousand Fife Hundred; 3,000 – Tree Tousand. Exceptions are Flight Level Wun Hundred, Too Hundred, Tree Hundred etc, said in this way to avoid the confusion that has sometimes occurred in the past with FL100/110 and FL200/210. All six figures are spoken when identifying radio frequencies spaced at 25kHz. Exceptionally, when the two final digits of the frequency are both zero, only the first four digits need be given. 119.000 – Wun Wun Niner dayseemal Zero; 122.500 – Wun Too Too dayseemal Fife. An 8.33kHz spaced frequency is quoted to four places of decimals, which is very inconvenient to say over the air. Therefore, it has been deemed that the channels are referred to in a simpler but consistent manner. For example, you might set 120.0416 on a scanner but the pilot will refer to it as 120.040.

Q-Code

A further note concerns the Q-Code, long obsolete in aviation, apart from certain enduring terms like QDM, QNH and QFE. It was an expansion of the Q-Code already in use by the merchant marine and it became possible to exchange information on practically all subjects that might be needed in aviation communications. These three-letter groups could be sent by wireless telegraphy (W/T) in Morse with great speed and overcame any inherent language difficulties. For example, an operator would send the code 'QDM' to a ground station, which meant 'What is my magnetic course to steer with zero wind to reach you?' The ground operator would transmit 'QDM' and the appropriate figure.

Standard words and phrases used in R/T communications

Word/Phrase	Meaning
Acknowledge	Let me know that you have received and understood this message
Affirm	Yes
Approved	Permission for proposed action granted
Break	Indicates the separation between messages
Break break	As above but in a busy environment
Cancel	Annul the previously transmitted clearance
Changing to	I intend to call __ (unit) on __ (frequency)
Check	Examine a system or procedure (no answer is normally expected)
Cleared	Authorised to proceed under the conditions specified
Climb	Climb and maintain
Confirm	I request verification of clearance, instruction, action or information
Contact	Establish radio communications with __ (unit) your details have been passed (The obsolete code 'QSY', which meant the same thing, is often still used by pilots)
Correct	True or accurate
Correction	An error has been made in this transmission (or message indicated). The correct version is ...
Descend	Descend and maintain
Disregard	Ignore

Fanstop	I am initiating a practice engine failure after take-off. (Used only by pilots of single-engine aircraft.) The response should be 'Report climbing away'.
Freecall (unit)	Your details have not been passed. Mainly used by military ATC
Hold short	Stop before reaching the specified location
How do you read	What is the readability of my transmission?
I say again	I repeat for clarity or emphasis
Maintain	Continue in accordance with the condition(s) specified in or in its literal sense. eg 'Maintain VFR'
Monitor	Listen out on (frequency)
Negative	No or permission not granted or that is not correct or not capable
Over	My transmission is ended and I expect a response from you
Out	My transmission is ended and no response is expected
Pass your message	Proceed with your message
Read back	Repeat all, or the specified part, of this message back to me exactly as received
Recleared	To be used only in relation to routeings and NOT for instructions to climb or descend
Report	Pass requested information
Request	I should like to know, or I wish to obtain
Roger	I have received all your last transmission (Note: under no circumstances to be used as an affirmative or negative
Say again	Repeat all, or the following part of your last transmission
Standby	Wait and I will call you. (Note: No onward clearance to be assumed. The caller would normally re-establish contact if the delay is lengthy. Standby is not an approval or denial
Unable	I cannot comply with your request, instruction or clearance
Wait	RAF equivalent of Standby
Wilco	I understand your message and will comply with it

If a pilot wants a check on the quality of his radio transmissions he will say: 'Tower, GCD radio check.' The tower may reply: 'GCD, readability 5.' The clarity of radio transmissions is expressed by the following scale:

Readability 1 – Unreadable

Readability 2 – Readable now and then

Readability 3 – Readable but with difficulty

Readability 4 – Readable

Readability 5 – Perfectly readable

Note that controllers in exasperation sometimes use non-standard phrases such as 'Strength a half' for really awful radios! Another phrase in common usage is 'Carrier wave only', indicating that an unmodulated transmission is being received by the ground station, ie it is just noise without the accompanying speech.

Aeronautical ground stations are identified by the name of the location, followed by a suffix that indicates the type of service being given.

Suffix	**Service**
Control	Area Control Service
Radar	Radar (in general)
Director Approach Control Radar	Approach Radar Controller dealing with either arriving or departing traffic
Zone	Military Aerodrome Traffic Zone crossing
Approach	Approach Control
Tower	Aerodrome Control
Ground	Ground Movement Control
Delivery	Clearance Delivery
Talkdown	Precision Approach Radar (Military)
Information	Flight Information Service
Radio	Aerodrome Air/Ground Communication Service

When satisfactory two-way communication has been established, and provided that it will not be confusing, the name of the location or the callsign suffix may be omitted. The basic rule is that the full callsigns of both stations must be used on the first transmission. For example:

Aircraft: 'Southend Tower GABCD.'

ATC: 'GABCD Southend Tower pass your message.'

Aircraft callsigns may take various forms but they must remain the same throughout the flight. However, if aircraft on the same frequency have similar callsigns ATC may instruct them to alter the format temporarily to avoid confusion. Aircraft in the heavy wake turbulence category must include the word 'Heavy' immediately after the callsign in the initial call. For the Airbus A380, 'Super' is used as a suffix. In both cases, this is to remind the controller that increased separation may be necessary for following aircraft.

To alert controllers to the fact that a student pilot is flying solo, the callsign prefix 'Student' is used in the initial call and then usually dropped until contact is made with another ATC unit. The controller can then make due allowance for the limited experience of student pilots and keep instructions as simple and straightforward as possible. 'Helicopter' is another possible callsign prefix. All Unmanned Air Systems (UAS) callsigns must include the word 'Umanned' on first contact with a controller, to ensure that he/she is fully aware that they are dealing with a UAS flight.

When receiving a radar service, certain ex-military aircraft types have been granted an exemption from the Air Navigation Order requirement to fly at an indicated airspeed less than 250kt below Flight Level 100. In order to alert the controller to this higher speed profile, pilots of exempted aircraft will, on initial contact, prefix the aircraft callsign with 'Fastjet' or 'Fastprop' depending on the type of propulsion. Use of the prefix is confined to initial contact with ATC agencies for periods of flight during which speeds in excess of 250kt are intended.

Aircraft are identified by one of the following types of callsigns:

(a) The registration of the aircraft, eg GBFRM, N753DA

(b) The registration of the aircraft preceded by the approved telephony designator of the operating company, eg Speedbird GBGDC

(c) The flight identification or trip number, eg Speedbird 501

Once satisfactory two-way communication with an aircraft has been established, controllers are permitted to abbreviate the callsign but only to the extent shown in the table below.

Full callsign	Abbreviation
GBFRM	GRM
Speedbird GBGDC	Speedbird DC
N31029	N029
Cherokee GBGTR	Cherokee TR
Speedbird 501	No abbreviation
Helicopter	GABCD Helicopter CD

In practice other variations are to be heard, some pilots using their company three-letter designator and flight number rather than the normal company name and flight number, eg ANE 232 or Air Nostrum 232. Either is correct and it is quite common for controllers, faced with an unfamiliar company designator on a flight progress strip, or simply forgetting what it stands for, to revert to the three-letter prefix.

The aim is to prevent incidents and potential accidents caused by callsign ambiguities but they still occur in sufficient numbers to cause concern. Regular bulletins of Mandatory Occurrence Reports (MORs) are circulated among pilots and controllers and they often contain reports of aircraft with similar callsigns taking instructions meant for each other by mistake.

Private aircraft normally use the aircraft registration letters or numbers as a callsign, as do some taxi and executive aircraft and sometimes airliners on training or empty positioning flights. Otherwise, commercial operators use their company designator and flight number as in (c) above. Intensive use of flight numbers often leads to callsign confusion when two aircraft with the same flight number are on frequency together, for example Air France 532 and Air Malta 532. The problem is under constant scrutiny and a partial solution is the use of alphanumerics, but poorly chosen ones can be awkward to say. Further confusion has been caused by callsigns resembling flight levels or headings, so operators have agreed, as far as possible, not to allocate flight numbers that end in zero or five. In practice, this means figures below 500.

Glossary of Aviation Terms Heard on Radio

See also Abbreviations and lists on pages 9-12 and 149-151.

Abeam	Passing a specified point at 90 degrees to the left or right
Abort	Abandon take-off or return prematurely
Active	The runway-in-use
Actual	The current weather conditions
Airprox	Official term for a near miss
Alternate	Alternate airfield if unable to land at destination
Approach plate	Another term for approach chart
Approach sequence	Position in traffic onto final approach
Approved Departure Time	See page 53
Autorotation	Helicopter practice forced-landing
ATIS (Ay-Tiss)	Automatic Terminal Information Service
Avgas	Aviation gasoline
Backtrack	Taxi back along the runway
Bandboxed	Two or more frequencies monitored by one controller during quiet periods
Base check	Periodic training flight to check the competency of commercial flight crew
Base turn	Turn on to final from an instrument approach when it is not a reciprocal of the outbound track
Basic Service	See page 77
The Bell	Colloquial term for the Belfast VOR
Blind transmission	A transmission from one station to another when two-way communication cannot be established but where it is believed that the called station is able to receive the transmission
Booking Out	See pages 52 and 105
The Boundary	Boundary between Flight Information Regions or alternatively the edge of a Control Zone
Box	Radio, Box One being the main set and Box Two the standby
Breakthrough	Transmissions on one frequency breaking through on to another
Build-ups	Cumulo-nimbus clouds
CAVOK	See page 79
CB	Also referred to as Charlie Bravo. Cumulo-nimbus clouds
Charlie	That is correct (common HF usage)
Chopping to	Military term for changing frequency to, for example, approach
Clearance limit	A specified point to which an ATC clearance remains effective
Closing heading	Heading to intercept the ILS
Coasting in/out	Crossing the coast inbound/outbound
The company	As in 'Follow the company', ie an aircraft belonging to the same operator as the subject

Conflict Alert	See page 31
Conflicting traffic	Other aircraft in the vicinity that may prove a hazard
Crosswind	Strength of wind from the side on final approach component
CTOT	See-Tot, Calculated Take-Off Time (Slot)
The Data	Temperature, QNH, runway-in-use etc
Deconfliction Service	See page 77
Detail	Intentions during a particular training flight
Direct	Flying from one beacon or waypoint straight to another
Discrete	Separate frequency usually devoted to one aircraft for PAR talk-down etc
Div Arrival	Arrival message sent to destination and other agencies when an aircraft diverts en route
Dogleg	Flying a zig-zag to lose height, etc
Drift	The effect of wind on an aircraft
En route	As in 'Report going en route', ie changing to another frequency
Established	Aligned or 'locked on' with the ILS
Expected Approach Time	See page 43
Fanstop	Practice engine failure
Fod	Jargon word for airfield debris, derived from the abbreviation of 'foreign object damage' but now deemed to be 'foreign object debris'
Four Dee	4 miles DME
Free call	A call to a ground station without prior co-ordination by landline between this and the previous ATC unit with which the aircraft was in contact. Mainly used by military ATC
Glide path	The final descent path to the runway on an ILS approach
Go around	Overshoot runway and rejoin circuit or carry out missed approach procedure
Going en route	Changing to another frequency
Good rate	Unofficial abbreviation for a good rate of climb or descent
The GOW	Colloquial term for Glasgow VOR
GPU	Ground Power Unit
Guard frequency	International Distress Frequency which is monitored continuously by aircraft flying long-distance routes
Guesstimate	Just what it implies!
Heading	Direction in which the aircraft is pointing. See also Track
Heavy	See page 90
Intentions	Course of action after a missed approach etc
IR Test	Instrument Rating Test
Jet A-1	Turbine fuel
Land after	See page 50
Localiser	See page 26
LVPs	Low-Visibility Procedures (spoken as in the abbreviation)

Mach	Speed expressed as a ratio of the speed of sound (Mach 1)
MOR	Mandatory Occurrence Report
Navex	Navigational Exercise
No ATC speed	Unofficial abbreviation for 'no ATC speed restriction'
Nosig	No significant change in weather
Notam	Notice to Airmen
Off blocks	The time the aircraft commenced taxiing or pushback
On task	Aircraft reporting on scene or job
Orbit	Circle, usually over a specified point
Pattern	American equivalent of circuit
Pax	Passengers
POB (Pee-o-Bee)	Total of persons on board
The Pole	Colloquial term for Pole Hill VOR
Popup traffic	Traffic that suddenly appears on radar perhaps because it has just climbed into coverage
Powerback	Reversing off an apron stand under an aircraft's own power
PPR	Prior permission by telephone required for landing
Practice asymmetric	Engine failure simulation on multi-engined aircraft
Procedural Service	See page 42
Procedure turn	Similar to base turn except that the aircraft retraces its steps on an exact reciprocal of the outbound leg
Pushback	Pushed out of an apron stand by a special tractor
QDM	Magnetic heading in zero wind
QFE	Altimeter setting to indicate height above aerodrome, runway threshold or helideck
QNH	Altimeter setting to indicate elevation above sea level when on the ground and altitude when in the air
QSY	Obsolete term for 'change frequency to' but still sometimes used
QTE	True bearing
Radar heading	Heading imposed by a radar controller
Radar overhead	Radar blind spot above aerial
Radar vectoring	Specified headings given by radar
Radial	Magnetic bearing line from or to a VOR
Ready message	Sent to NMOC in the hope of an earlier CTOT (slot)
Ready in sequence	Ready for departure on reaching head of queue at holding point
Recovery	Military term for land back at base
Release(d)	Control of a particular aircraft handed over from Area Controller to approach, or authorisation from area for an aircraft to take-off
Regional	The QNH for a defined area (see page 22)
Rejected take-off	Abandoned take-off procedure that is sometimes practised during pilot check-outs
Resume own	Revert to self-navigation after a period of radar vectoring

RVR	Runway Visual Range (see page 80)
Sector	Each leg of a series of (usually) scheduled flights. Also sub-divisions of an Area Control Service
Securité	Prefix to RAF flight safety message
Selcal	Selective Calling (see pages 71 and 173)
SID	Standard Instrument Departure
SIGMET	Significant met conditions (see page 81)
Slot time	See page 92
SNOCLO	Airfield closed during snow-clearing operations
SNOWTAM	See page 82
Special flight	A police, photographic survey or other flight for which special permission has been granted by the CAA
Speed Limit Point	Position before which an inbound aircraft entering a TMA must have slowed to the speed limit (normally 250kt). For departing traffic speed restriction is lifted here
Squawk	SSR code (see page 18)
Stand	Numbered parking position on apron
Standard Missed	Procedure to be followed if an aircraft is unable to land approach from an instrument approach
Stepdown Fix	A defined point on the final approach track indicating that a critical obstacle has been safely overflown and descent to the next specified level may be commenced
Stepped on	Someone else transmitted over you
Stratus	Low-lying cloud layer
Stud	Military pre-set frequency
TAD	Tactical Air Directive (frequency)
TAF	Terminal Aerodrome Forecast
Teardrop	A 180-degree turn to land back on the runway from which one has just departed. Often used by circuit training aircraft when runway-in-use is changed
Tech stop	En route diversion for technical reasons such as refuelling
Tempo	Forecast temporary weather change
Three greens	Indication of wheels down and locked
Toppo chart	Topographical chart
Track	The path of an aircraft over the ground
Traffic	Other aircraft known to be in the vicinity
U/s	Unserviceable
Volmet	See page 83
Wake turbulence	See page 89
Waypoint	A pre-selected geographical position used with a Flight Management System
Wind shear	See page 81

Chapter 23

Phraseology Used in ATC Communications

There are certain basic R/T rules with which pilots must comply. Aircraft flying in controlled airspace must obtain permission from the controlling authority before they can change frequency to another station. They should not, for example, call the tower until approach instructs them to do so. Pilots sometimes take instructions intended for other aircraft, particularly if the callsigns are similar. Controllers need to be constantly vigilant to the possibility of such errors.

When a ground station wishes to broadcast information to all aircraft likely to receive it, the message is prefixed by the callsign 'All stations'. No reply is expected to such general calls unless individual aircraft are subsequently called upon to acknowledge receipt. Direct communications between pilots and controllers can be adversely affected by simultaneous transmissions that, effectively, block all or part of intended messages. The controller is usually alerted to the fact that he has transmitted over another aircraft by a distinctive change in the sidetone in his headset. The word 'blocked' may be used when the controller hears simultaneous transmissions, also by a pilot hearing simultaneous transmissions and wanting to alert aircraft and ATC alike.

Another important point is that an ATC route clearance is not an instruction to take off or enter an active runway. The words 'take-off' are used only when an aircraft is cleared for take-off; at all other times the word 'departure' is used. The disastrous runway collision at Tenerife in 1977 was caused mainly by a flight crew apparently interpreting a route clearance as also implying a take-off clearance. They must have known better but there were pressing distractions and so the fatal error was made.

The much-missed Vulcan in formation with the Red Arrows.

There is also a stringent requirement to read back certain information because of the possible seriousness of a misunderstanding in the transmission and receipt of these messages. If the controller does not receive a read-back, the pilot will be asked to give one. Similarly, the pilot is expected to request that instructions be repeated or clarified if they are not fully understood. The following ATC instructions must be read back in full by the pilot: level, heading and speed instructions, airways or route clearances, runway-in-use, clearance to enter, land on, take off on, backtrack, hold short of, or cross an active runway, Secondary Surveillance Radar operating instructions, altimeter settings, VDF information, frequency changes, type of radar service and transition levels.

For example:

ATC: 'GBFVM cleared to cross Lima 975 at MALUD Flight Level 180.'
Aircraft: 'Cleared to cross Lima 975 MALUD Flight Level 180, GVM.'

ATC: 'GTE contact East Midlands Radar 120.025.'
Aircraft: 'East Midlands 120.025 GTE.'

Levels may be reported as altitude, height or flight level, according to the phase of flight and the altimeter setting, but a standard form of reporting is adhered to. An aircraft climbs, descends, maintains, passes, leaves or reaches a level.

For example:

'Shamrock 920 climb FL190.'
'Easy 58H maintain altitude 3,500ft.'
'Speedbird 58 report passing FL160.'
'Ryanair 842 report reaching FL190.'

Aircraft: 'Easy 581H request descent.'
ATC: 'Easy 581H descend FL60.'
Aircraft: 'Easy 581H leaving FL140 for FL60.'

Sometimes a changing traffic situation may necessitate an intermediate halt to a descent or climb. 'Shamrock 920 stop descent FL150.' Or perhaps for traffic reasons, a higher than normal rate of climb or descent may be requested to avoid eroding separation. 'Speedbird 58 climb to FL190, expedite passing FL150.'

Clearances to climb and descend must include the expression 'Flight Level', 'Altitude' or 'Height'. The word 'to' after the verb must be used when clearing an aircraft to an altitude or height. It must not be used when a flight level is involved. When pilots are instructed to report leaving a level, they should advise ATC that they have left an assigned level only when the aircraft's altimeter indicates that the aircraft has actually departed from that level and is maintaining a positive rate of climb or descent.

Where there is any doubt that an aircraft is approved for Reduced Vertical Separation Minima (RVSM).

ATC: '(callsign) Confirm RVSM approved.'
Aircraft: 'Negative (or affirm) RVSM.'
Aircraft: 'Unable RVSM due turbulence' or 'Unable RVSM due equipment' or 'Ready to resume RVSM'.

Conditional Clearances

These comprise the callsign of the aircraft being given the clearance, identification of the subject of the condition, eg aircraft, reporting point, level etc. and the clearance. Examples are:

'Speedbird 123, after passing Wallasey, fly heading 305.'

'Lufthansa 456, below FL150, reduce speed to 220 knots.'

'Scandinavian 721, behind the landing 757, line up Runway 27 behind.'

Speed Control

Speed control is used to facilitate a safe and orderly flow of traffic. This is achieved by instructions to adjust speed in a specified manner. Examples of phraseology relating to speed are: 'Report airspeed/Mach number.' 'Maintain present speed.' 'Maintain x knots.' 'Maintain x knots or greater.' 'Do not exceed x knots.' 'Increase/reduce speed to Mach x.' 'Increase/reduce speed to x knots'. 'Maintain x knots until 4-mile final.' 'Reduce to minimum approach speed.'

Background Noise

Airband listeners can often hear all kinds of background cockpit noises when a pilot transmits a message to ATC. The most common one is the buzzer that sounds when an aircraft is climbing or descending towards a cleared level. The level is pre-set on the Flight Management Computer (FMC) and the warning sounds a thousand feet below when climbing, and a thousand feet above when descending. It alerts the pilots so that they can request a higher or lower level and, if so cleared, avoid having to level off. Automatic radio altimeter callouts are a customer option on the Boeing 737 series and other types, using a synthetic voice. Cockpit aural warnings include fire bell, take-off configuration, cabin altitude, and landing gear configuration. Take-off configuration warnings are one cause of aborted take-offs. Maybe the flap setting is not quite right for the conditions or it can just be a spurious warning. Only certain warnings can be silenced while the condition exists.

There are a number of sites on the web that incorporate sound files of cockpit warnings. You can listen to such sharp annunciations as 'Terrain, Terrain'; 'Glideslope, Glideslope'; 'Wind Shear, Wind Shear'; 'Sink Rate, Sink Rate', all accompanied by a 'whoop, whoop' sound and guaranteed to grab the pilots' attention! TCAS (Traffic Collision Avoidance System – see page 31) has its own menu of warnings designed to resolve conflictions. TCAS generates a Traffic Advisory (TA) when another aircraft becomes a potential threat and is approximately forty seconds from the closest point of approach. No manoeuvres are required for a TA. If the intruder continues to close and becomes an imminent threat, a Resolution Advisory (RA) is generated when the other aircraft is approximately twenty-five seconds from the closest point of approach. The RA provides a vertical restriction or manoeuvre to maintain or increase separation from the traffic.

A TA is indicated by the aural annunciation 'Traffic, Traffic', which sounds once, and is then reset until the next TA occurs. If the other aircraft's transponder is operating in Mode C or S, altitude information and vertical motion, if applicable, are also displayed. RAs are indicated by one or more aural phrases, ranging from 'Monitor Vertical Speed', meaning avoid deviations from the current vertical speed, to the self-evident 'Climb, Climb, Climb', 'Descend, Descend, Descend', 'Reduce Climb, Reduce Climb', and 'Reduce Descent, Reduce Descent'. 'Clear of Conflict' is announced once the RA encounter is resolved. TCAS alerts are inhibited by the Ground Proximity Warning System and wind shear warnings, and at low altitudes where the Traffic Avoidance Manoeuvre could be dangerous.

ATC transmissions are sometimes accompanied by background noise as well. Visitors unused to control rooms always behave as though they are in church, but the working environment is not always quiet. In a typical tower, the controller's assistant calls out bits of information about last-minute parking stand changes and the like, ground vehicles blare on UHF loudspeakers, telephones buzz or ring and so on.

LiveATC Network

American-based Live ATC Network (www.liveatc.net) is the world's largest network of streaming audio feeds focused solely on aviation, currently covering nearly 1,000 airports around the world with around 3,000 different audio feeds, and growing daily. A LiveATC app for Android and iPhones is also available, which provides a quick and easy way to listen in on live exchanges between pilots and controllers near many airports worldwide. LiveATC lets you browse by US state or by country to find an airport and listen in to ATC. Before purchasing, phone owners are urged to check the website to make sure that their country, city and/or airports of interest are covered by LiveATC.

It is emphasised that no UK ATC channels are currently available and that situation is unlikely to change any time soon. Available airports are subject to change at any time, sometimes due to reasons beyond LiveATC's control. LiveATC owns and operates many of the receivers used in the network but most are provided by volunteers working in co-operation with LiveATC. Also, there is no guarantee that all feeds will be up 24/7, though they make their best effort to do so and have a good track record of uptime.

Area Control Phraseology

The phraseology used in Area Control is mainly self-evident. Common phrases to be heard are as follows:

Aircraft:	'Speedbird 345 request descent.'
ATC:	'Speedbird 345 maintain FL110 expect descent after Wallasey.'
ATC:	'Air France 045 descend to cross Honiley FL170 or above. After Honiley descend FL130.'

Unless otherwise instructed, subsequent frequency changes to new sector controllers include aircraft identification and level only:

'London Control, Shamrock 347, Flight Level 350.'
'Shamrock 347, London, Roger.'

If the aircraft is in level flight but cleared to another level, the call must include the aircraft identification followed by the current level and the cleared level.

Each major airport has one or more terminal fixes or beacons. Well known are the LBA at Leeds, the BEL at Belfast and the GOW at Glasgow. Even if the destination is not mentioned in transmissions while on airways, such routeings as Pole Hill–LBA will immediately give a clue. Similarly, knowledge of the runway designators at various airports will be useful. Since the trend is to a single main runway with an instrument approach at both ends, with perhaps one subsidiary for light aircraft, you can soon become familiar with those in your home area. Examples are Birmingham 15/33, Heathrow 09 Left and 09 Right/27 Left and 27 Right, Glasgow 05/23, and Manchester 05 Left and 05 Right, and 23 Left and 23 Right.

Secondary Surveillance Radar (SSR)

Nowadays, with comprehensive radar coverage of UK airspace, an aircraft's progress is monitored by the SSR read-out. This reduces the R/T loading considerably. Unless instructed otherwise or certain conditions apply, the initial call on a new frequency will be a simple 'London Control, Speedbird 501, Flight Level 350', to which the reply will be 'Speedbird 501, London, roger'.

Certain phrases concerning the operation of transponders are listed below. SSR in the United Kingdom was once confined almost exclusively to the ACCs, but most Approach Control units now have the capability. The use of the word 'squawk', by the way, seems to have been inspired by the wartime instruction to operate IFF (Identification, Friend or Foe, an early form of transponder), 'Make your cockerel crow' and the pilot's confirmation that the IFF equipment was switched off after landing, 'Cockerel strangled'.

SSR Phraseology

Phrase	Meaning
Squawk (code)	Set the code as instructed
Confirm Squawk	Confirm the code set on the transponder
Reset Squawk	Reselect assigned code
Squawk Ident	Operate the special position identification feature
Squawk Mayday	Select Emergency code
Squawk Stand-by	Select the standby feature
Squawk Altitude	Select altitude reporting feature
Stop Squawk Altitude	Deselect altitude feature
Confirm Level	Check and confirm your level. (Used to verify the accuracy of the Mode C-derived level information displayed to the controller.)

General Approach Control Phraseology

Since all major airports now use radar to direct their traffic, I shall deal with this aspect first. An aircraft must be identified before it can receive a radar control or advisory service; in other words, the controller must be sure that one particular blip on his display is the aircraft he is directing. This is simple with a radar handover from another ATC unit or by means of SSR, but in the event of a rare transponder failure the following procedure is employed:

ATC: 'GVM report heading and level.'
Aircraft: 'GVM heading 140 at 2,500ft.'
ATC: 'GVM for identification turn left heading 110 degrees.'

The identification turn must be at least 30 degrees different from the original heading. When the pilot reports steady on the new heading, and the controller is sure that he has related a specific blip on his display with the aircraft, he transmits: 'GVM identified 12 miles south of (airfield).' The service to be given is then added.

ATC: 'Vectoring for an ILS approach runway (designation).'

If in the initial call the aircraft makes the turn requested and is still not observed on radar, perhaps because it is out of range, in weather clutter, or below cover, the controller will say 'GVM not identified.

Resume own navigation'. D/F will then be used to home the aircraft towards the airfield for eventual radar pick-up. When identified, the aircraft will be vectored, that is given headings to steer, to fit it into the approach sequence or, if traffic is light, direct to final approach. Outside controlled airspace the aircraft may be vectored around unidentified traffic. Information will be given by use of the twelve-hour clock, twelve o'clock being straight ahead, three o'clock over the pilot's right shoulder and so on. The distance and relative direction of movement is also given, together with any information on speed, type of aircraft if known, etc. Typical traffic information is passed in this form: 'ABC123 unknown traffic ten o'clock, 5 miles crossing left to right, fast moving.'

If the pilot does not have the traffic in sight he may request avoiding action. This may, in any case, be initiated by the controller if he considers it necessary. Sometimes rapid action is required to avert the risk of collision: 'ABC123 avoiding action turn left immediately heading 110 degrees.' A few incidents have occurred where, by using a too relaxed tone of voice, the controller failed to convey to the pilot the urgency of the required action and the pilot's more leisurely response led to an awkward situation that might have been averted. The CAA eventually instructed all controllers to ensure that their tone of voice does not lull pilots into a false sense of security on these occasions!

At locations with no radar, procedural methods are used. The same applies when radar is normally available but unserviceable or seriously affected by weather clutter, or if the pilot wishes to carry out a procedural approach for training purposes. On transfer from the ACC, the first call will go something like this:

Aircraft: 'Inverness Approach GBC descending FL60, estimating INS at 42.'

ATC: 'GBC cleared for VOR/DME approach Runway 05, descend to altitude 3,500ft QNH 1021. Report beacon outbound.'

Subsequent reports will be made when 'base turn complete' and, if the beacon is several miles out on final approach, a 'beacon inbound' call will be made as well. These standard calls help the Tower Controller to plan his traffic, if there is no radar to give him ranges from touchdown.

Where the airport is equipped with ILS, permission to make a procedural approach is given thus: 'GMB cleared for ILS approach Runway 27, report beacon outbound QNH 1008.' Subsequent exchanges would be:

Aircraft: 'GMB beacon outbound.'

ATC: 'GMB report established inbound.' (The phrase 'report procedure turn complete' may be substituted.)

Aircraft: 'GMB established ILS inbound.'

ATC: 'GMB report 4 DME.'

Aircraft: 'GMB 4 DME.'

ATC: 'GMB contact Tower 118.1.'

Phraseology for Surveillance Radar Approaches includes the following:

During the Intermediate Procedure
'This will be a Surveillance Radar Approach, terminating at x miles from touchdown. Check your minima, stepdown fixes and missed approach point.'

Azimuth information
'Turn left/right x degrees, heading XXX. Closing (final approach) track (rate of closure eg

slowly, quickly) from the left/right. Heading of XXX is good. On track. Slightly left/right of track.'

Descent information
'Approaching x miles from touchdown, commence descent now to maintain an x degree glide path. x miles from touchdown – height should be x feet. Do not acknowledge further instructions. Check minimum descent height. Check gear.'

Completion
On track, half a mile from touchdown. Approach completed. Out.'

Aerodrome Control Phraseology

Aircraft: 'Liverpool Tower, Easy 163D Airbus 319, request start. Information Bravo QNH 1008.'

ATC: 'Easy 163D start approved. Information Bravo is current.'

The phrase 'Start-up at your discretion', together with an expected departure time, may be used so that the onus is on the crew to start engines at a convenient time. Note that the words 'at your discretion' are used by controllers to imply that any traffic delays, getting stuck in soft ground and other misfortunes will henceforth be the pilot's fault! Controllers have very definite responsibilities and they are understandably reluctant to take on any extra ones.

Aircraft: 'Heathrow Ground Alitalia 235 Stand E3 request pushback and start.'

ATC: 'Alitalia 235 pushback and start approved.'

Most airports now have nose-in parking at the terminal to save apron space and to facilitate passenger handling. Aircraft have to be pushed backwards by a tractor into a position from which they can taxi for departure. A variation is the 'powerback' in which a turboprop aircraft reverses under its own power. If there is no delay, 'Push and start-up approved' is passed, together with the outside air temperature in degrees Celsius. Most airfields will have an information broadcast referred to as an ATIS ('Ay-Tiss' Aerodrome Terminal Information Service (see page 80).

Aircraft: 'Liverpool Tower GLFSA at Kilo request taxi for local.'

ATC: 'GSA taxi Charlie hold Runway 09 via Alpha, Information Bravo is current, QNH 1001.'

Training flights are often referred to by the word 'detail', as in 'Coventry Tower GAXVW request taxi clearance, two on board circuit detail.' This is a throwback to military jargon, as is the term 'fanstop' for a practice engine failure after take-off. Taxi instructions must always specify a clearance limit, which is the point at which an aircraft must halt and ask for further permission to proceed. The limit is normally the holding point of the runway-in-use but it may also be an intermediate position, perhaps short of another runway that is in intermittent use. To maintain a smooth operation, controllers try to anticipate calls from taxiing aircraft so that they do not actually have to stop at intermediate points. Some UK airports have complex taxiway systems and each significant section is given an identifying letter (two in some cases). Holding points are allocated a number as a suffix to the taxiway designation, eg Alpha One.

The ideal is to establish a circular flow of taxiing aircraft so that the ones just landed do not get in the way of those moving towards the holding point. Alas, some airports have inadequate taxiway systems with two-way flows and bottlenecks. A refusal to give crossing clearance of an active runway is passed in the form: 'GVW hold short Runway 23.' Permission to continue is:

'GVW cross Runway 23, report vacated.' At some point before departure, the aircraft will be given a clearance to exit the control zone. A typical clearance at Liverpool, for example, is 'GYE is cleared to the zone boundary via Chester, Special VFR not above altitude 1,500ft Liverpool QNH 1002.'

Some types of aircraft, mainly piston engined, carry out engine run-up checks prior to departure and are not always ready for take-off when they reach the holding point, so the controller may say 'GVW report ready for departure.' When ready for take-off, permission is sought from the tower. If the runway is occupied by traffic that has just landed, the aircraft will be told to 'line-up and wait'. The American phrase 'taxi into position' is sometimes tried when a foreign pilot seems to have difficulty in understanding what is meant. (Controllers always have something up their sleeves to break the language barrier and we have all had to resort to plain speech to convey our meaning to some uncomprehending student pilot.)

If there is traffic on final, the aircraft at the holding point may be told: 'Behind the Cherokee on short final, line up Runway 27, behind.' Care must be taken that there is no possibility of confusion with another aircraft that may have just landed. Where a preceding aircraft is beginning its take-off roll, the second aircraft may be told: 'After the departing Cessna, line up and wait.' The use of the words 'cleared immediate take-off' means that the aircraft must go without delay in order to leave the runway free for landing traffic. It is only to be used where there is actual urgency so that its specific meaning is not debased.

For reasons of expedition, a controller may wish to line up an aircraft on the runway for departure before conditions allow take-off. 'Easy 34DC via holding point Alpha One line up and wait Runway 27, one aircraft to depart before you from Delta.' The aircraft should reply: 'Via holding point Alpha One line up and wait 27 number two for departure, Easy 34DC.'

When line-up will take place at a position other than for a full-length runway departure, the intermediate holding point designator will be included in the line-up instruction. Controllers may include the designator in any other line-up instruction when considered appropriate. 'GCD ready for departure.' ATC: 'GCD via Charlie Two line up Runway 28.' The detailed rules for runway occupancy can be found on page 50.

For inbound VFR aircraft, examples of circuit joining procedure phraseology are as follows:

Aircraft:	'Coventry Tower GAYMN at Ansty for landing.'
ATC:	'GMN join right-hand downwind Runway 05, QFE 1004,' or 'GMN join straight-in approach Runway 23, QFE 1004.'
Aircraft:	'GMN downwind.'
ATC:	'GMN Number 2, follow the Cessna 150 on base.'
Aircraft:	'GMN Number 2, traffic in sight.'
ATC:	'GMN extend downwind, number 2 to a Cessna 150 3 miles final on radar approach.'
Aircraft:	'GMN extending downwind.'

Aircraft on what used to be known as 'circuits and bumps' may wish to do a 'touch and go' landing; in other words, the aircraft lands, continues rolling and takes off again without a pause. The wording 'cleared touch and go' is the only one approved officially but pilots may ask for a 'roller', the military equivalent. (Somebody did once read back to me 'cleared for a hit and run' but such levity is not encouraged!) Instructions to carry out a missed approach may be given to avert an unsafe situation, such as when one aircraft is too close behind another on final. 'GTE go around, I say again, go around. Acknowledge.' Sometimes an aircraft on a practice instrument approach with an intended go-around will be instructed to do this not below 400ft because the runway is temporarily obstructed by an essential maintenance vehicle.

Depending on local procedures, a departing aircraft will be retained on the tower frequency until it is clear of the circuit, or changed to approach immediately. Airways flights will, of course, be transferred to Area Control just after take-off or as soon as they have been separated from any conflicting traffic. When the landing roll is complete, the arriving aircraft will be told to vacate the runway in the following manner:

ATC: 'GMN vacate left,' or 'GMN taxi to the end, report runway vacated,' or 'GMN take next right. When vacated contact Ground 121.750.' The appropriate taxiing instructions are then passed. Airborne and landing times may be passed by the tower, although there is no official requirement for this.

Strangely enough, controllers are not responsible for reminding pilots to put their wheels down on final, except when a radar approach is being provided. However, if an aircraft landed wheels-up in broad daylight, the controller would no doubt suffer some criticism, apart from the dent to his professional pride! Fortunately it is a rare occurrence these days but I once earned a pint from a Cessna 337 pilot whom I reminded just in time. (Cheap at the price – the saving in repairs would have paid my year's salary.)

One last point is defined as 'Essential Aerodrome Information'. It refers to any obstruction or unserviceability that is likely to affect operations. It is always prefixed 'caution', examples being 'Caution work in progress ahead just north of taxiway.' 'Caution PAPI Runway 27 unserviceable.' 'Caution large flock of birds north of Runway 27 threshold.'

As a footnote, I must emphasise that the above is merely an outline of common radio phraseology. Exhaustive coverage of the entire range can be found in CAP 413 Radio Telephony Manual, viewable online free of charge.

Airline Company Messages

Included in the VHF airband and listed in Appendix 3 are blocks of frequencies allocated for company operational communications. Within Europe, the designated bands are 131.400–132.000MHz and 136.800–136.875MHz inclusive. They are used for the exchange of information between commercial aircraft and their ground-based operations staff or handling agents. These behind-the-scenes messages are entirely separate from air traffic control but are essential for the safe and efficient running of an airline or cargo service. Further down the scale, but no less important to their users, many flying schools have a company frequency to pass weather information to their offices and discuss flying bookings etc.

In contrast to ATC exchanges, messages on company frequencies are very informal and often resemble a telephone conversation. An exception is where one frequency is shared by several operators or by one handling agent at a number of different airports. In this case the talking is kept to a minimum. Some larger operators have their own ops channels, Other airlines, especially foreign ones, find it uneconomical to maintain their own ops office at each airport and instead use the services of a handling agent. The best known is Servisair, a Stockport, Cheshire-based firm with offices at all the main and many regional airports. A comprehensive service is provided, including passenger and cargo handling, organising refuelling, catering requirements, aircraft cleaning, the filing of flight plans, arranging slot times, crew meals and hotel bookings.

There is no standard phraseology for company messages but the information is usually passed in a particular manner. In the initial call, the last two letters of the aircraft registration are often added as a suffix to the callsign. Sometimes the flight number is deleted altogether. Time 'off blocks' or 'off chocks', ie time taxiing commenced, is passed first, followed by airborne time and ETA at destination. Fuelling requirements for the next sector (next leg of a series of flights or the return trip) are given in the following manner: In tanks ... x tonnes or kilos. Burn off (or burn) ... x tonnes or kilos. Taxi ... x tonnes or kilos. Burn off is the amount of fuel estimated to be used. The term RTOW is sometimes heard. It stands for Regulated Take-Off Weight, the pre-computed weight for the aircraft plus passengers, fuel and cargo for a particular set of conditions. The latter include runway length, whether its surface is wet or dry, temperature and certain other factors.

Passenger information is usually included in various forms. The total number of fare-paying passengers is passed, followed by the number of non-fare paying infants, for example, 253 plus 2. The infants are sometimes referred to as tenths eg 2/10ths or as decimals (252.2 pax). 'No specials' indicates no special requirements. Disabled passengers may require a wheelchair for disembarkation; 'lift-off' if unable to walk, 'walk off' if able to get down the steps to the wheelchair.

Aircraft Communications and Reporting System (ACARS)

ACARS is also used for ops messages and is a digital datalink system for the transmission of messages between aircraft and ground stations. It once relied exclusively on VHF channels but more recently alternative means of data transmission have been added, with satellite communication providing worldwide coverage. Depending on the satellite system in use, coverage may be limited or absent at high latitudes where it is needed for flights over the poles. To remedy this, HF ACARS datalink has been introduced and increasingly replaced by satellite communication datalinks. Aircraft can now fly polar routes and maintain communication with ground-based systems such as ATC centres and airline ops. There has also been a rapid trend towards the integration of aircraft systems with the ACARS link for its use as an operational communications tool. Modern ACARS equipment now includes the facility for automatic as well as manual initiation of messaging.

Airshows

Airshow frequencies are generally the same as those normally used by the airfield concerned. Some may be allocated by CAA on a temporary basis for venues that are not airfields. If there is any doubt, the scanner search facility will soon locate the appropriate channels. Some receivers will search for active frequencies between preset upper and lower limits and automatically dump them into the memory banks. The receiver does all the work for you and at airshows the external aerial can be shortened or removed altogether so that only local frequencies will be found.

For those who prefer to plan ahead, airfield frequencies can be programmed in advance, and the search mode used to detect any non-standard ones that may be in use. If the location is a civilian airfield, the number of channels in use will be small. Military airfields normally have a much greater number of frequencies, some being secondary backup channels. On VHF, 122.1MHz is used as a standard frequency for Aerodrome Traffic Zone penetration by civil aircraft. This or another assigned frequency is almost always used for the control of military airshows so as to cater for civil participants.

Many small airfields do not have a full ATC service. A simple Air/Ground radio channel or a rather more formal Flight Information Service may be provided to pass basic data to pilots. When hosting an airshow, a few volunteer controllers may be on duty with a CAA temporary local validation of their ATC licences. The Royal International Air Tattoo, for example, relies on the same team of experienced controllers working in their spare time to handle Britain's biggest airshow.

Radio calls are kept to a minimum during airshows to avoid breaking a pilot's concentration during a complex sequence of manoeuvres. As his 'slot' nears its end, he will be given a check on minutes to go. Military display teams such as the Red Arrows have their own UHF frequency for interplane transmissions. The leader or his No. 2 monitors the VHF channel and relays any ATC messages. A few display teams simply use the airshow control frequency for their air-to-air communication, although this may be in a foreign language!

An expensive scanner is not essential at an airshow, as you are close to the transmitters and even the most basic set can perform well in those conditions. Your choice of antenna, usually so critical for quality reception, is also less restricted. Many listeners use a short length of flexible wire instead of the normal antenna, which means that the set can be stowed in a jacket pocket out of the way, with no loss of signal.

An important accessory is a pair of lightweight headphones or an earphone to overcome aircraft noise. Earphones offer another advantage: they increase your battery life and can make the difference between them lasting all day or dying in the middle of the show. The majority of modern receivers can use rechargeable cells, but these rarely last for more than four to six hours of continuous use, so a spare set of rechargeables is needed. Don't forget to top them up the day before – the charge can drain away if they are unused for a while.

Batteries are a very important consideration and many regular listeners use alkaline cells at an airshow. They are more expensive but will easily last ten to twelve hours. Some modern radios can run for twenty or more hours on a set and can thus last all weekend, which is very useful if the show is a two-day event like RIAT.

If your radio has memory banks, a good tip is to programme the basic ATC frequencies into one bank for rapid scanning and place display team channels into another for use during the individual routines. If you have a single-frequency set, the best plan is to locate the airshow controller (normally the Tower Controller) and stick to this all day. It will provide almost everything you need and some teams will also use it for their air-to-air communications.

There are several less obvious benefits to be derived from using an airband radio. Airshow photography has always relied upon split-second timing to get the best shots. Tuning in to the voices of the pilots as they synchronise manoeuvres can assist in getting that special picture. Display items sometimes catch the display commentator unawares – the fast, low arrival of a fighter, for example. The pilot has to inform ATC that he is running in and, if you are listening, you can be waiting, camera at the ready.

Extensive market areas are a feature of all major airshows and attract numerous aviation suppliers. Their wares range from books and magazines to airband radios and accessories and navigation charts.

Selected Display Team Frequencies

Aerostars Yak Display Team: 124.45

Asas de Portugal: 261.15

BBMF: 120.8 121.4 122.7 124.675

Black Cats: 266.725 232.55 254.4750 280.4750

Blue Angels: 237.8 250.975 255.2 275.35 284.25 302.1 305.5 346.5

Blue Eagles: 252.0 264.15 307.175 382.6

Breitling Jet Team: 136.95

The Blades: 121.05136.975

Frecce Tricolore: 123.475 362.625 263.25 307.8 351.825 381.0 387.525
Midnight Hawks (Finland): 122.55 140.625
Patrouille de France: 138.5 138.525 139.625 141.825 143.1 140.5 141.0 143.1
Patrouille Suisse: 142.30 141.725 266.175 312.35 359.45 388.75
Patrulla Águila (Spain): 130.05 130.3 337.975 264.725 241.95 252.5
RAF Falcons: 255.1 256.9 397.4
Red Arrows: 243.45 242.2 307.075
Turkish Stars: 225.75 264.4 279.6 141.475

A Duxford airshow general view.

Chapter 24

Military Airband Monitoring

Military ATC employs a block of frequencies between 225 and 400MHz, audio modulated (AM) as in the civil VHF airband. Although technically the Ultra High Frequency (UHF) band does not start until 300MHz, they are usually referred to as UHF and are normally spaced 25kHz apart. Theoretically, this produces 7,000 separate channels, and although many are in use for airfield and area ATC, it leaves a very large number available for a variety of uses. These include in-flight refuelling, bombing and gunnery range operations, air-to-air frequencies for formation flying, satellite links and, in the case of the USAF in Britain, numerous ops and Command Post channels. Blocks of frequencies, known as TADs from the acronym for Tactical Air Directive, are allocated mainly for air defence interception purposes by RAF radar units. Each channel has a code number such as TAD 122, to avoid saying the actual frequency over the air.

An anomaly is the use of a range of frequencies between 137 and 159MHz (AM) by various NATO air forces including the RAF and USAF. To save time-consuming manual tuning, many military aircraft have pre-set radio frequencies, referred to as Studs (Button or Push to the Americans). For example, a typical allocation might be:

Stud 1: Ground Movements Control; Stud 2: Tower; Stud 3: Departures; Stud 4: Approach; Stud 5: Radar/Director; Stud 6: Radar/PAR; Stud 7: London Mil; Stud 8: London Mil West ICF; Stud 9: London Mil SouthWest ICF.

It is possible that the military could adopt 12.5kHz spacing in the UHF airband or even 8.33, as in civil aviation. This would free up a large number of frequencies but it would have to spread throughout NATO, at great cost in radio equipment modification and reorganisation. Likely channel interference would be another problem.

R/T exchanges are often clipped and difficult for the layman to understand; for example, two clicks on the mike button on the mike button often serve as an acknowledgment. The use of oxygen mask microphones tends to depersonalise voices but it does, however, make many RAF transmissions instantly identifiable as such! Ground operations frequencies at RAF and USAF bases can be found in the 30–39, 68–69, 72–80 and 406–414MHz ranges, all NFM mode.

Military aviation thrives on initials and code words. Among the many to be heard on UHF are PD (practice diversion), RTB (return to base), Homeplate (base), Chicks (friendly fighter aircraft), Playmate (aircraft being worked with) and Pogo (switch to channel ...). Embellish is a code word signifying that an aircraft is prepared to act as a target for practice fighter interception. The USAF has its own jargon, such as Code One (a fully serviceable aircraft), RON (remain overnight), TOT (time on target), Lima Charlie (loud and clear), Victor freek (VHF frequency), and Uniform (UHF frequency).

The Initial Contact Frequencies (ICF) for each sector at London Mil, callsign 'Swanick Mil', are monitored permanently using dedicated UHF and VHF frequencies. Note that Swanwick is pronounced with a silent 'w', hence the callsign spelling to avoid confusion. The Central (Mil) Sector is the busiest of the sectors and includes the Lichfield Corridor. The others are East, Northeast, North, West, and Southwest. These areas include Scotland as far north as Shetland.

To preserve security, some military transmissions may employ DVP (Digital Voice Protection) techniques. The speech is electronically digitised, mixed at random and then transmitted. A compatible receiver then unscrambles the sequence and restores its intelligibility. There are several code words for this secure mode; USAF AWACS aircraft, for example, refer to it as 'in the green'. Other terms are 'going tactical' and 'going crypto'. Some NATO strike aircraft are able to engage a frequency-hopping communications system 'Have Quick', which uses eight channels in sequence to foil the eavesdropper. However, a receiver with a very fast scan rate can still monitor the messages. Recently introduced and soon to be fitted to most US military aircraft is encrypted Software Defined Radio, known as the Joint Tactical Radio System (JTRS). It has been nicknamed Jitters and its main task is to render inter-service communications completely seamless. For example, it is ideal for providing secure voice, data and video during exercises.

RAF aircraft use callsigns derived from two systems. First-line aircraft may use operational callsigns consisting of a three-character prefix of numbers and letters (a trigraph) suffixed by a two number (dinome) mission identifier. They can also use a word followed by the pilot's individual number, for example 'Rampage 08, 'Chaos 012' both used by Typhoons in 2021. Other Typhoon callsigns include 'Cobra', 'Havoc' and 'Nightmare'. Army Apache helicopters also follow an aggressive theme – 'Machete', 'Viper' and 'Prowler', to name but a few.

Callsigns for Flying Training Units (FTUs) and Search and Rescue (SAR) aircraft use fixed ICAO-allocated three-letter designators with figure suffixes as individual pilot number callsigns. For example, VYT22, a Valley-based Hawk. Standard clipped R/T phrases used by controllers can create problems for inexperienced basic flying students under some circumstances. Consequently, student pilots are allocated a three-figure suffix to their tri-graph in order to draw the attention of the controller to the inexperience of the pilot. In addition it should be noted that the three-figure suffixes 101–109 are reserved for SAR helicopter missions.

If two or aircraft are flying as a formation, the formation may be allocated an approved word callsign, in addition to the normal mission/pilot numbers allocated to each aircraft. The mission/pilot numbers will only be used in the event of a split. For the duration of the formation flight aircraft should be identified by adding the words 'one', 'two' etc. to the formation callsign, eg Bear One, Bear Two etc. Where formations operate using the callsign of the lead aircraft, controllers are to add the word 'flight' or 'formation' to the callsign, when transmitting instructions relevant to the whole group, eg Eagle 51 Flight. RAF Air Support Command uses 'Ascot' as a prefix, together with a four-digit Task number. Sometimes, a tactical callsign prefix is allocated, such as 'Comet' for an A400 Atlas.

The USAF makes considerable use of so-called tactical callsigns such as 'Doom 20' (a B-52), the number being the pilot's personal designation. These prefixes are changed periodically but, having said that, there are many that have been retained for years, and some are included in Appendix 6. When a formation is involved, the leader will handle all voice communications with the ground. To find out how many aircraft are in the flight, listen for a frequency change and count each aircraft checking in on the new channel. 'Shark 21 Flight, check' '2!', '3!','4!' etc. The same procedure is used for all formations, whether they be military or civil. The nature of some military operations prohibits compliance with certain ATC regulations. For example, clearance may be granted for a formation to enter controlled airspace provided the individual aircraft can maintain separation from each other visually or by the use of airborne radar.

They must also be able to communicate with the formation leader, who is in contact with the controlling authority. A formation may therefore be considered as a single unit for separation purposes provided that the formation elements are contained within 1 mile laterally and longitudinally and are at the same level. Standard UK military callsign procedures apply to formations. In instances where there is any doubt, such as when working USAF or foreign aircraft whose callsign procedures may be different, the suffix 'Flight' is used to indicate on R/T and landline that the call refers to a formation.

Examples:

'Blackcat' – denotes a UK formation

'Blackcat 1'- denotes a UK single element

'Deadly 31 Flight' – denotes a USAF formation

'Deadly 31' – denotes a USAF singleton

USAF Air Mobility Command transports generally use the aircraft serial, referred to as the 'tail number'. Alphanumeric codes are employed as well, eg Reach 7M8RH. On occasion the suffix has represented a particular exercise, eg 'FL' for 'Flintlock' and 'RF' for 'Reforger'. The US Navy is another alphanumeric user, Navy 6 Golf 086 for instance, the first two characters often referring to the code painted on the aircraft. Other foreign air forces use self-evident prefixes such as Danish, Saudi etc. 'Aussie' identifies the Royal Australian Air Force and 'Kiwi' the Royal New Zealand AF; the Greeks use 'Hellenic Air Force' but the Norwegians hide behind 'Juliet Whiskey'. French Air Force transport aircraft often use 'Cotam', the initials of this arm of the Air Force, while the French Navy uses 'FMN' or sometimes 'France Marine'. 'Mission' and up to four figures is frequently heard in use by German military aircraft and also by aircraft of other countries, including the RAF.

Air-to-Air Refuelling

Most air-to-air refuelling in UK airspace takes place under service from ATCRUs (Air Traffic Control Radar Unit), ISTAR (Intelligence, Surveillance, Target Acquisition and Reconnaissance) or ASACS (Air Surveillance and Control System) units. Most training refuelling is conducted on designated 'towlines', which are racetrack patterns some 60 to 100nm long, usually between FL100 and FL290. Tanking exercises are normally advised in advance and the relevant airspace notified as active to other interested agencies. As an example of refuelling over the North Sea, Flamborough West flights will initially be working London Mil, perhaps on the same frequency if tanker and receiver are making their way north around the same time. London Mil may play a part in setting up and arranging the join-up, as the AR/IP (Air Refuelling Initial Point) is in their airspace. Both aircraft will normally use the same frequency, with the receiver then only using the AR Primary (maybe after asking to switch to the tanker frequency). The tanker then identifies both as a 'Flight' in comms with ATC. Sometimes the receiver may stay in contact with ATC throughout. It is around this time that the join-up will be in progress with 'MARSA' being declared/accepted by the tanker, who will then be controlled by the receiver (squawking Standby) until they split. Military Accepts Responsibility for Separation of Aircraft (MARSA) applies to aircraft above FL245 that are under constant radar control. However, when aircraft join up with less than the 1,000ft minimum vertical separation, then the radar unit is no longer responsible for separation and aircraft 'accept MARSA'.

Airborne Warning and Control System (AWACS)

There are twelve AWACS Orbit areas around the UK, mainly off the coast but there are four over land spaced from Scotland to East Anglia. NATO documentation requires unidentified traffic not participating with the action in progress to be known as 'strangers'. This is important when providing tactical, picture building information because of the need to classify individual contacts as targets, friendly or stranger. This allows the military aircraft under control to take appropriate action against the correct aircraft while maintaining situational awareness on all non-participating aircraft. Use of the term 'traffic' would introduce another variable and add confusion. Therefore, AWACS controllers will use the word 'stranger' instead of the word 'traffic' when passing information on conflicting, non-participating aircraft.

Procedures and Phraseology at Military Aerodromes

It is Ministry of Defence (MoD) policy to encourage civil use of military aerodromes where this does not conflict with military flying operations. While the same general rules and procedures apply to aircraft at all aerodromes, the specific requirements of military operations mean that the way they are applied often makes them appear somewhat different from those to which civilian pilots have become accustomed.

Precision approach radar (PAR) may be provided, which can be likened to a ground-controlled ILS. The controller directs the pilot onto the final approach, and then gives heading directions to maintain his flight path on the runway centreline, telling him not to acknowledge such instructions unless requested. Once the aircraft reaches the glide path the controller will tell the pilot regularly whether he is above or below it, but will not give specific rate of descent directions. The pilot is expected to make his own adjustments to follow the glideslope down to his decision height. On any instrument approach, the controller will say 'carry out cockpit checks, advise complete' before the aircraft turns onto the base leg, and 'check gear, acknowledge' during the final approach.

Most military circuit patterns are oval. The downwind leg is flown closer than at most civilian aerodromes because the turn after take-off and the final turn both involve continuous 180-degree turns. The 'downwind' call is standard, but the call of 'final' is given as the aircraft starts its final turn at the end of the downwind leg. When practice forced landings are made, the terms High Key Point and Low Key Point may be heard. High Key varies in position and height according to the aircraft type but generally is the high dead side of the runway. Low Key is a point downwind opposite the runway threshold.

Civilian pilots must expect military traffic to be given priority as they tend to use a lot of fuel, and often do not carry much spare for diversion. Many military aerodromes require visitors to carry out a standard overhead join. However, depending on the direction of approach, ATC may give instructions to join downwind, or on base leg. Circuit patterns are usually flown at heights that depend on aircraft type. For example, a turboprop trainer may fly the pattern at 1,000ft on QFE, light piston aeroplanes at 800ft, and, if traffic is mixed, fast jet traffic at 1,200 or 1,500ft. The 'military standard join' involves approaching parallel with the runway-in-use from an 'initial point' outside the Aerodrome Traffic Zone on the dead side of the runway centreline, at circuit height or lower.

A call of 'initials' will be made at that 'initial point'. Some aircraft may approach at high speed for a 'run and break'. Approximately 1–1½ minutes after calling 'initials' the aircraft will turn steeply, level or climbing to the circuit height, from the dead side to downwind, calling 'on the break' instead of the normal 'downwind' call. If the aerodrome has 'no dead side' (often when helicopters operate together with aeroplanes) the run-in may take place over the runway itself. Any non-standard procedures would normally form part of the visiting aircraft brief.

Military controllers use 'two-in', 'three-in' etc. for the number of aircraft present in the circuit. As with civilian procedures, priority is normally given to instrument traffic. ATC will transmit the position of that instrument traffic along with the type of aircraft. It should be noted that USAF bases in Britain use their own style of American phraseology.

Chapter 25

HF Monitoring

In Britain there are a wide variety of listening possibilities, principally the civil stations (nets) controlling traffic over the Atlantic from Polar regions almost to the Equator, the US Air Force's extensive network and those of the RAF and airline operators. There are nearly 140 ATC centres operating on HF around the world and, depending on the performance of one's receiver and other factors, many of them can be monitored. During the transatlantic slack periods (i.e. between the late morning/early afternoon westbound flights and the eastbound flights in the early hours of the morning) one can listen in to other parts of the world. For example, aircraft in the Far East in the late afternoon, Africa in the evening, and then, for an hour or so either side of midnight, the Caribbean and the eastern seaboard of the USA are very busy.

HF stations use a block of radio frequencies to circumvent the effects of atmospheric conditions. HF transmissions 'bounce off' the ionising layers that lie above the earth but, since the layers are affected by day and night conditions, a suitable range of daytime frequencies might suffer severe interference at night and vice versa. Although having very long range, HF lacks the clarity of the VHF channels and the atmospheric noises and transmissions make it very tiring for crews to maintain a continuous listening watch.

The answer is SelCal, short for Selective Calling. By this method, crews need not monitor the frequency, but when the ground station wishes to communicate with them a tone is sent and decoded by the cockpit equipment. This unique code opens up the squelch on the HF radio when received by the unit, allowing pilots to hear only the radio calls for their aircraft. A 'bing-bong' sound can be heard on the radio and, on the flight deck, a chime or light signal also alerts the pilots to respond by R/T. Each aircraft with SelCal capability is allocated a four-letter code by Aviation Spectrum Resources Inc (ASRI), an American company that acts as registrar and agent to the ICAO to perform this function.

On the first contact with the controller, the SelCal will normally be checked and here is where the interest lies for anyone interested in aircraft registrations. The SelCal code remains with the aircraft as long as the 'box' does, despite changes of ownership. ASRI does not make public the registration /SelCal tie-ups but painstaking detective work by enthusiasts has tracked down most of them and lists can be found on the web by Googling 'Selcal'. Unfortunately, SelCal codes do not always stay with the aircraft for life and nor is it true that one particular SelCal code is only used by one aircraft. Just about every SelCal code is shared by at least one other aircraft, although they are likely to be flying in different hemispheres.

Outside VHF range, aircraft crossing the Atlantic communicate with ATC mainly by means of datalink, with HF as a backup. The same applies to any ocean or underdeveloped land mass where the short range of VHF radio waves would prove useless. However, datalink is rarely an option in many areas. Before the pandemic, an average of 1,300 commercial, military and general aviation flights crossed the North Atlantic each day, all being handled by Shanwick to the east of the halfway point. Aircraft requesting clearance to enter the Shanwick Oceanic Control Area from overhead the United Kingdom can be heard on certain VHF frequencies.

In addition, the track co-ordinates are broadcast on frequency 133.8MHz and this can be heard in many parts of the United Kingdom. Compared with the brief content of domestic airways clearances, these oceanic clearances are fairly long-winded because of the need to specify a number of latitude and longitude positions, although in certain circumstances they can be abbreviated.

Position reports are passed as the present position and a forward estimate for the next one. They are given in terms of latitude and longitude, 56 North 10 West being an example, or as a reporting point or beacon when nearing a land mass. Approximately one aircraft per hour is requested by the Oceanic Control Centre to 'Send Met' and will include weather information with each position report. This consists of outside air temperature, wind speed and direction derived from INS equipment, plus any other relevant observations. A typical position report is: 'Position Swiss 100 56 N 20 W 1235 Flight Level 330 estimate 56 N 30 W 1310, next 56 N 40 W.'

Virtually all shortwave aircraft communications use Single Side Band (SSB) signals. Without going into too many technicalities, the AM (Audio Modulation) method employed by HF transmissions is built up of three components; a lower side band, a carrier, and an upper side band. By removing the carrier and one of the side bands, the power of the signal is compressed into a smaller band width, which boosts reception at long range and reduces interference. However, an ordinary shortwave receiver that may have the necessary frequency bands (2–28MHz) will pick up SSB as something that has been described as 'sounding like Donald Duck'. To make the signal intelligible, the carrier has to be reintroduced and this can only be done if a Beat Frequency Oscillator (BFO) or crystal-controlled carrier oscillator is fitted. Beware of shortwave sets that receive only broadcast bands or else have no SSB capability. Advertisements are often misleading on these vital points, implying that the product will receive everything.

Unfortunately, a basic HF set with SSB costs considerably more than the equivalent simple VHF radio. However, for around £150 the Tecsun PL-660 will do the job admirably. It has digital tuning, which is highly desirable with HF as there are so many operational frequencies and it obviously helps to identify them precisely for future reference. The built-in aerial is only useful for strong local signals like Shanwick, and for wider coverage a long wire aerial is needed. The longer (10 to 30m) and higher the better, orientated as near horizontal as you can and if possible at right angles to the direction of the station you most want to listen to, eg N/S for Atlantic traffic. Beware of short circuits in the rain from whatever tree or pole you have attached it to, not to mention lightning strikes! An aerial tuning unit (ATU) is a good investment. It tunes the aerial length electronically and matches it to the receiver to produce a peak signal.

If you are able to move upmarket for higher performance, there are several choices, including the Icom and AOR ranges. Ideally, the enthusiast needs a scanner that can monitor VHF and UHF airband as well as HF air communications, but it is only recently that modern electronics have made this possible in a convenient package. Many scanners now feature HF SSB as well as VHF and UHF airband. Unfortunately, these so-called wide band scanners are inevitably a compromise between the demands of different sections of the frequency bands. A dedicated HF receiver will always outperform them. Of course, for this sort of equipment you are getting far more than the airbands.

These radios are communications receivers in the fullest sense of the word. For example, the AOR AR-8600 Mk II at around £650 spans virtually the entire radio spectrum, from long-wave broadcasts up to the limits of current usage.

Do not expect the quality of VHF airband reception on HF and be warned that you may have to work very hard and try a lot of frequencies before you intercept anything. HF propagation conditions can fluctuate enormously. Propagation forecasts available online are very useful in narrowing down the possibilities.

The North Atlantic HF network is divided into 'families' of frequencies to obtain a balanced loading of communications on the oceanic track system. They are designated NATA to F. Each family uses a primary frequency with a secondary one for use when reception is poor. The frequencies are shared by several Oceanic Control Centres, including Shanwick (Shannon/Prestwick), which serves aircraft between 45° North and 61° North and between 10 West and 30 West. The Iceland OCC at Reykjavik is responsible for traffic north of 61° North and Gander works aircraft to the west of 30° West.

Santa Maria in the Azores looks after traffic south of Shanwick's area and from 15° West to 40° West. New York OCC controls flights over a large proportion of the south-west of the North Atlantic, and with favourable reception conditions those from the Caribbean and South America can be heard as well. San Juan in Puerto Rico is responsible for aircraft south of New York's area, using the same frequencies.

Long Distance Operational Control Facilities (LDOCF) are operated by or on behalf of many airlines throughout the world for company messages similar to those heard on VHF airband. Some of these stations are equipped to provide direct voice communications between flight crews and their company operations using phone patch techniques. Alternatively, the ground radio operator will accept messages for relay over the normal telephone or telex circuits. Stockholm Radio and the American stations ARINC and PanAM radio provide similar facilities to many other airlines.

HF and Military Aviation

Military aircraft use HF frequencies within broadly the same range as do civil aircraft. Military radio traffic is, however, a lot more varied and much less predictable than civil. It is also difficult to find out enough background information to understand some of the things to be heard, which is perhaps just as well! Both the RAF and the USAF have their own networks, as do the Canadian Forces. Other foreign air forces are represented as well, but since the transmissions are made in the native language, they are of limited interest.

The RAF's Flight Watch HF network is known as the UK Defence Global HF System with the callsign 'Tascom', pronounced 'Tazcom'. Its task is to handle the military equivalent of company messages, arrange telephone patches to home stations and operations centres and provide met and other information on request. It utilises the Terrestrial Air Sea Communication (TASCOM) System. Allied military and other aircraft are provided support in accordance with agreements and international protocols. Stations operate from the UK, Cyprus, Ascension and Mount Pleasant in the Falklands.

The UK Air Defence System runs a separate HF net providing communications between Sector Operations Centres and interceptor aircraft on alert to cover the UK Air Defence Regions. Friendly, Unknown and Zombie (Russian) aircraft are investigated.

The USAF equivalent to TASCOM is the High Frequency Global Communications System (HF-GCS), which divides the world into fourteen Zones. The English base is at Croughton (first syllable pronounced as in 'crowd') in Northamptonshire, callsign Croughton Global. There are no operators here, the messages being relayed remotely from Andrews Air Force base in Maryland, USA. Its primary frequency is 11175kHz, sometimes referred to as 'Triple One Upper'. This is a common HF-GCS frequency used also by Incirlik in Turkey and Ascension Island, among others, and they too can be monitored under good reception conditions. Most frequent users are the transports of Air Mobility Command giving details of loads and unserviceabilities to their destinations or ops centres.

When an aircraft crew wish to call an Airlift Command Centre they often use the blanket callsign Mainsail to alert HF-GCS stations that a phone patch is required. The ground station will respond only if the aircraft signal is reasonably strong and clear. It is not uncommon for Croughton to have several aircraft 'queuing' for phone patches, so there are a number of backup frequencies available. Many of the calls involve met information known as Metro (pronounced 'Mee-tro'). Aircrew may offer PIREPS, pilot reports of weather conditions encountered en route. This can be useful because the aircraft serial number and type are usually quoted as well as its tactical callsign if one is in use. 'Capsule' messages can also be heard, periodically updating operation instructions to transport aircraft.

HF-GCS channels are interrupted frequently by Air Combat Command 'Foxtrot' routine mission status broadcasts, known as 'Skybird' after the blanket callsign for ACC ground stations. Part of the former Strategic Air Command (SAC) fail-safe system, now incorporated in ACC, they test communications between aircraft, ground stations and missile silos. Should the US have ever been involved in a nuclear exchange the 'go code' would have been transmitted via this network. Consisting of a string of alphanumerics, these coded messages have been going out on HF since at least the early 1960s. The ground stations' initial call to all SAC (Strategic Air Command) aircraft, 'Skyking, Skyking, do not answer, do not answer', will be familiar to regular HF listeners. The broadcasts on HF-GCS are repeats of those going out on the former SAC's own group of frequencies. A basic form of security is the use of a channel designator such as 'Sierra 391', rather than the actual frequency. As with many military HF frequencies, they can be 'dead' for long periods.

Ground stations employ imaginative callsigns that are changed daily, examples being Acidman, Chipmouse, Big Daddy and Red Cedar. The US Navy has its own HF net that often involves aircraft as well as ships. US Coast Guard aircraft can sometimes be heard over the Eastern Seaboard of the USA talking to their bases. Other miscellaneous users of the HF band include anti-drug-running aircraft and the so-called Hurricane Hunters tracking storms.

A Selection of HF Frequencies

Civil Air Route Regions (ICAO) frequencies and major ground stations are listed below. Do not expect to hear the very distant ones routinely. Virtually all frequencies listed are Upper Side Band (USB).

AFI = African; CAR = Caribbean; CEP = Central East Pacific; CWP = Central West Pacific; EUR = European; MID = Middle East; NP = North Pacific; SAM = South America; SAT = South Atlantic; SEA = South East Asia; SP = South Pacific.

NAT-A (southern tracks) 3.016 5.598 8.906 13.306 New York, Gander, Shanwick, Santa Maria

NAT-B 2.899 5.616 8.864 13.291 17.946 Shanwick, Gander

NAT-C 2.872 5.649 8.879 11.336 13.306 17.946 Gander, Shanwick, New York

NAT-D (polar routes) 2.971 4.675 8.891 11.279 13.291 17.946 Shanwick, Reykjavik

NAT-F (Assigned on a tactical basis) 3.476 6.622 8.831 13.291 17.946 Shanwick, Gander

NAT-H (Assigned on a tactical basis) 2.965 3.491 5.583 6.556 6.667 10.021 10.036 11.363

NAT-I (Assigned on a tactical basis) 2.869 2.944 2.992 3.446 3.4734.651 4.666 4.684 5.460 5.481 5.5595.577 6.547 8.843 8.954 11.276

CAR-A 2.887 5.550 6.577 8.918 11.396 13.297 17.907 New York, Paramaribo, San Juan

CAR-B 3.455 5.520 6.586 8.846 11.330 17.907 Barranquilla, Boyeros, Cayenne, Georgetown, Maiquetía, New York, Panama, Paramaribo, Piarco

MID-1 2.992 5.667 6.631 11.375 Ankara, Baghdad, Beirut, Damascus, Kuwait, Bahrain, Cairo, Jeddah

MID-2 3.467 5.658 10.018 13.288 17,961 Bahrain, Karachi, Bombay, Lahore, Delhi, Calcutta

SEA-1 3.470 6.556 10.066 13.318 17.907 Calcutta, Dhaka, Madras, Colombo, Malé, Cocos, Kuala Lumpur

SEA-2 3.485 5.655 8.942 11.396 13.309 Hong Kong, Manila, Kuala Lumpur

SEA-3 3.470 6.556 11.396 13.297 Manila, Singapore, Jakarta, Darwin, Sydney, Perth

AFI-1 3.452 6.535 8.861 13.357 17.955 Casablanca, Canaries, Dakar, Abidjan, Roberts

AFI-2 3.419 5.652 8.894 13.273 13.294 17.961 Algiers, Tripoli, Niamey, Kano

AFI-3 3.467 5.658 11.018 11.300 13.288 17.961 Lagos, Brazzaville, Luanda, Windhoek, Johannesburg, Lusaka

CEP-1/2 2.869 3.413 5.547 5.574 8.843 11.282 Honolulu, San Francisco

CWP-1/2 2.998 4.666 6.532 6.562 8.903 10.081 Hong Kong, Manila, Guam, Tokyo, 13.300 17.904 21.985 Honolulu, Port Moresby

SP-6/7 3.467 5.643 8.867 13.273 13.261 17.904 Sydney, Auckland, Nandi, Tahiti, Honolulu, Pascua

Base Stations

Stockholm 3.494 5.541 8.930 11.345 13.342 17.916 23.210; ARINC (New York) 6.640 8.933 11.348 13.297 13.306 13.348 PanAm Radio 2.890 5.511 9.210 10.033 17.901 21.955

VOLMET

RAF 5.450 11.253; Shannon: 3.413 5.505 8.957 13.264;
Gander/New York: 3.485 6.604 10.051 13.270; St John's: 6.754 15.034

Rescue

5.680 (primary) 3.023 3.085 5.695 8.364 (International Distress)

UK Defence Global HF System (TASCOMM)

3.146 4.742 6.733 9.031 11.205 13.257

US HF-GCS (callsign Croughton/Ascension/Incirlik/Lajes etc)

11.175 4.724 4.742 5.703 6.712 6.739 8.992 11.244 13.200 15.016 17.975

Note that the decimal point is normally omitted when frequencies are referred to during communications.

General rule: The higher the sun, the higher the frequency. The lower the sun, the lower the frequency. The longer the distance, the higher the frequency. The shorter the distance the lower the frequency.

Appendix 1

Beacons and Reporting Points

The centrelines of airways are marked by VOR/DME navigational beacons positioned at strategic intervals, such as where the airway changes direction or where one or more of them intersect. Many small airfields have an associated NDB used as a sole aid for instrument let-downs. Larger airports generally retain an NDB as a backup in the event of ILS unserviceability.

So-called Significant Points and Waypoints are hypothetical positions formed where certain radials from two VORs intersect, and are given a standard five-letter name. It may be related to a geographical feature such as the name of a nearby town, and is a distortion of the real name to arrive at five letters. Examples are EXMOR (Exmoor), ULLAP (Ullapool), LESTA (Leicester), NITON (Knighton), STAFA (Stafford), REXAM (Wrexham) and WOBUN (Woburn).

Others are purely artificial but often imaginative. KEGUN, used by Liverpool, refers to former footballer Kevin Keegan. GINIS is an appropriate name on the way to Dublin on Lima 975. Sadly, it seems that five-letter codes are now mostly computer-generated, producing a pronounceable but meaningless word such as IPNOX. There are now so many and they are replaced or discontinued so often that there is little point in listing them all.

Beacons and Selected Waypoints

VOR frequencies are in MHz and NDBs in kHz

Name	*Frequency*	*Code*	*Type*	*Approximate location*
ABBOT				Luton STARs
Aberdeen	114.3	ADN	VOR	Scottish East Coast
ALD	383.0		NDB	Alderney Airport
ASKEY				Stansted STARs
Barkway	116.25	BKY	VOR	Nuthampstead, Herts
Barra	316.0	BRR	NDB	Western Isles
Belfast	117.2	BEL	VOR	East of Belfast City
Benbecula	113.95	BEN	DME	Outer Hebrides
Berry Head	112.05	BHD	VOR	Near Torquay
BHX	406.0		NDB	Birmingham Airport
BIA	339.0		NDB	Bournemouth Airport
BLK	328.0		NDB	Blackbushe Airport
Biggin	115.1	BIG	DME	SE stack for Heathrow
Bovingdon	113.75	BNN	DME	NW stack for Heathrow
BPL	318.0		NDB	Blackpool Airport
Brecon	117.45	BCN	VOR	South Wales
BRI	414.0		NDB	Bristol Airport
Brookmans Park	117.5	BPK	VOR	North of London
Burnham	421.0	BUR	NDB	Berkshire
BZ	386.0		NDB	RAF Brize Norton
CAE	320.0		NDB	Caernarfon Airport

Name	***Frequency***	***Code***	***Type***	***Approximate location***
CAM	332.5			NDB Cambridge Airport
Carnane	366.5	CAR	NDB	Isle of Man
CBN	374.0		NDB	Cumbernauld airfield
CDF	388.5		NDB	Cardiff Airport
CHASE				Birmingham STARs
Chiltern	277.0	CHT	NDB	North of Heathrow
CL	328.0		NDB	Carlisle Airport
Clacton	114.55	CLN	VOR	Essex coast
Compton	114.35	CPT	VOR	Berkshire
Cork	114.6	CRK	VOR	Ireland
Costa	110.05	COA	VOR	Belgian coast
CWL	423.0		NDB	RAF Cranwell
Daventry	116.4	DTY	DME	South Midlands
DAYNE				Manchester STARs
Dean Cross	115.2	DCS	DME	West of Carlisle
Detling	117.3	DET	DME	Kent
Dieppe	115.8	DPE	VOR	French coast
DND	394.0		NDB	Dundee Airport
Dover	114.95	DVR	DME	Near town
Dublin	114.9	DUB	VOR	North of city
Dundonald	115.45	DUD	DME	Ayrshire
EAS	391.5		NDB	Southampton Airport
EDN	341.0		NDB	Edinburgh Airport
EGT	328.5		NDB	Londonderry/Eglinton
EKN	357.5		NDB	Enniskillen Airport
EME	353.5		NDB	East Midlands Airport
EMW	393.0		NDB	East Midlands Airport
Epsom	316.0	EPM	NDB	Heathrow stack when Ockham out of service
EX	337.0		NDB	Exeter Airport
FNY	338.0		NDB	Doncaster Sheffield Airport
Gamston	112.8	GAM	DME	South Yorkshire
Glasgow	115.4	GOW	DME	Glasgow Airport
GLW	331.0		NDB	Glasgow Airport
Goodwood	114.75		GWC	Chichester Goodwood Airport
Green Lowther	109.65	GLO	DME	Hilltop, Lanarkshire
GST	331.0		NDB	Gloucestershire Airport
Guernsey	109.4	GUR	VOR	Guernsey
HAV	328.0		NDB	Haverfordwest Airport
HAW	340.0		NDB	Hawarden Airport
HB	420.0		NDB	Belfast/City Airport
Henton	433.5	HEN	NDB	Bucks

Name	*Frequency*	*Code*	*Type*	*Approximate location*
Honiley	113.65	HON	VOR	S of Birmingham Airport
HRW	424.0		NDB	London Heathrow
Inverness	109.2	INS	VOR	Inverness Airport
Isle of Man	112.2	IOM	VOR	Southern tip of island
Jersey	112.2	JSY	VOR	Near airport
KEGUN				Liverpool STARs
Killiney	378.0	KLY	NDB	Near Dublin
KIM	365.0		NDB	Humberside Airport
Koksy	114.5	KOK	VOR	Belgian coast
KW	395.0		NDB	Kirkwall Airport
Lambourne	115.6	LAM	DME	NE stack for Heathrow
Land's End	114.2	LND	VOR	Land's End
Lashenden	340.0	LSH	NDB	Kent
LAY	395.0		NDB	Islay Airport
LBA	402.5		NDB	Leeds-Bradford Airport
LCY	322.0		NDB	London/City Airport
LE	383.5		NDB	Leicester Airport
London	113.6	LON	VOR	London Heathrow
LOREL				Stansted/Luton STARs
LPL	349.5		NDB	East of Liverpool Airport
LUT	345.0		NDB	Luton Airport
Lydd	114.05	LYD	DME	Lydd Airport
LZD	397.0		NDB	Lydd Airport
Machrihanish	116.0	MAC	VOR	Kintyre, Scotland
Manchester	113.55	MCT	VOR	Manchester Airport
Mayfield	117.9	MAY	DME	Sussex
Midhurst	114.0	MID	DME	Sussex
MIRSI				Manchester STARs
Newcastle	114.25	NEW	DME	Newcastle Airport
Nicky	117.4	NIK	VOR	Belgian coast
NOT	430.0		NDB	Nottingham Airport
NQY	347.0		NDB	Newquay Airport
NT	352.0		NDB	Newcastle Airport
NWI	342.5		NDB	Norwich Airport
OBN	404.0		NDB	Oban Airport
Ockham	115.3	OCK	DME	SW stack for Heathrow
Ottringham	113.9	OTR	VOR	Humberside
OX	367.5		NDB	Oxford Airport
OY	332.0		NDB	Belfast Aldergrove
Pampus	117.8	PAM	VOR	Holland
Perth	110.4	PTH	VOR	Central Scotland

Name	***Frequency***	***Code***	***Type***	***Approximate location***
PIK	355.0		NDB	Prestwick Airport
Pole Hill	112.1	POL	VOR	N of Manchester
REXAM				Liverpool SIDs Manchester STARs
ROKUP				East Midlands STARs
ROSUN				Manchester STARs
RWY	359.0		NDB	Isle of Man Airport
SBL	323.0		NDB	Sherburn-in-Elmet
St Abbs	112.5	SAB	VOR	Scottish east coast
St Inglevert	387.0	ING	NDB	French coast
Seaford	117.0	SFD	VOR	South coast
SH	426.0		NDB	Shobdon
Shannon	113.3	SHA	VOR	SW Ireland
SHM	332.0		NDB	Shoreham Airport
SND	362.5		NDB	Southend Airport
Southampton	113.35	SAM	DME	Southampton Airport
Spijkerboor	113.3	SPY	VOR	Holland
STM	321.0		NDB	St Mary's Scillies
Stornoway	115.1	STN	VOR	Outer Hebrides
Strumble	113.1	STU	VOR	Coast of SW Wales
Sumburgh	117.35	SUM	VOR	Shetland
SWN	321.0		NDB	Swansea Airport
Talla	113.8	TLA	VOR	South Scotland
TD	347.5		NDB	Teesside Airport
TIPOD				Liverpool STARs
Tiree	117.7	TIR	VOR	Hebrides
TNL	327.0		NDB	Tatenhill
Trent	115.7	TNT	VOR	North Midlands
Turnberry	117.5	TRN	DME	S of Prestwick Airport
Vesta	116.6	VES	VOR	Denmark
Wallasey	114.1	WAL	VOR	Wirral Peninsula
WBA	356.0		NDB	Wolverhampton Airport
Westcott	335.0	WCO	NDB	South Midlands checked
Whitegate	368.5	WHI	NDB	Manchester TMA, SW corner
Wick	113.6	WIK	VOR	Northern Scotland
WILLO				Gatwick STARs
WL	385.0		NDB	Barrow airfield
Woodley	352.0	WOD	NDB	Berkshire
WPL	323.0		NDB	Welshpool Airport
WTN	337.0		NDB	Warton airfield
YVL	343.0		NDB	Yeovil airfield

Appendix 2

Area Control Channel Allocation

London Area Control Centre (Swanwick) Sectors and Channels

Lakes Sector (NW England: 132.860, 133.705
Wirral Sector (Northern Irish Sea): 135.580
North Sea Sector (NE England): 126.780, 128.130
Daventry Sector (Midlands): 127.105, 127.880, 129.205, 131.130, 134.390
Clacton Sector (East Anglia): 118.480, 128.160, 133.940, 134.460
Bristol Sector (S Wales and W England): 129.380, 133.605, 134.755, 135.255
London Middle Sector: 132.165, 132.605
London Upper Sector: 127.430, 132.840, 134.460, 135.430
Dover Sector (SE England): 128.430, 133.485, 134.905
Berry Head Sector (SW England and W Channel): 126.080, 128.815, 132.955
Seaford Sector (South Coast): 135.330, 134.440
Hurn Sector (South Coast): 127.830, 129.430, 135.055

London Terminal Control (TC) Channels

118.830	Deps via Brookmans Park
119.780	Deps via Bovingdon
120.180	Inbounds from the south
120.530	Deps via Biggin
121.030	TC COWLY West
121.230	Inbounds via Lambourne
121.280	Inbounds via Bovingdon
124.930	TC East DAGGA Sector
127.955	TC Capital/VATON
128.480	TC WELIN East
129.280	TC North/LOREL
129.605	TC East/SABER
130.930	TC Midlands/WELIN
133.080	TC North/COWLY
133.180	TC South
134.130	TC South/Ockham
135.805	TC Capital/Compton

Scottish Area Control Centre Channels

Trent Sector: 118.780, 119.530
STAFA Sector: 134.430
Wallasey Sector: 128.055, 128.680
Isle of Man Sector: 133.055
Dean Cross Sector: 135.530, 135.855, 136.580
Humber Sector: 121.330, 133.805, 133.880
Antrim Sector: 123.780
Rathlin Sector: 129.105, 133.205
Talla Sector: 126.305, 130.980
Galloway Sector: 121.380, 124.830
Tyne Sector: 134.780
Tay Sector: 124.505
Montrose Sector: 126.930, 132.490
West Coast Sector: 127.280
Moray Sector: 129.230, 134.855
Central Sector: 132.730
Hebrides Sector: 133.680

Flight Information Region Channels

London Information: 124.75 (Wales and England west of a line roughly Manchester to Worthing) 124.6 (East of England from Manchester southwards) 125.475 (Northern England to Scottish Border)

Scottish Information: 119.875 (primary) 121.325 121.525 126.675 127.275 128.675 134.775 134.850 all shared with Control Sectors.

Note that you may be able to hear aircraft at far greater distances than normal VHF, as their messages on FIR may be cross-coupled and retransmitted. This is so that other pilots will be aware of them and thus not interrupt.

Dublin Area Control Centre Channels

Dublin Control: 129.180 133.655

London Control, Scottish Control and London Military Remote Transmitter Sites

Chedburgh, Suffolk; Clee Hill, Shropshire; Daventry, Northamptonshire; Davidstow Moor, Cornwall; Grantham, Lincolnshire; Great Dun Fell, Cumbria; Greenford, Middlesex; Preston, Lancashire; Reigate, Surrey; Snaefell, Isle of Man; Swingfield, Kent; Trimmingham, Lincolnshire; Ventnor, Isle of Wight; Warlingham, Surrey; Winstone, Gloucestershire.

Appendix 3

VHF Airband Channels

With the universal adoption of 8.33kHz frequency separation to overcome frequency congestion in the medium to long term, the resulting VHF frequencies are now referred to as channels. 25kHz channels ending in 00, 25, 50, 75 can easily be converted to 8.33kHz channels by adding 5 to the last digit, eg 05, 30, 55, 80. Full conversion charts for 8.33KHz frequency spacing and the associated channel numbers would take up too many pages to reproduce here, but can be found online.

For an 8.33kHz channel, the transmit frequencies will have at least four digits after the decimal. However, to reduce the potential for errors between the controller and pilot, the channel number has been allocated for each frequency that closely resembles the frequency. This is done in such a way that only three digits after the decimal are used. The purpose of this is to simplify the pronunciation of the frequency spoken over air and reduce the number of digits needed to be entered in the on-board radio.

As an example, to communicate on 118.0333MHz the pilot will need to dial in 118.035 as the channel number for an 8.33kHz-capable radio. This will be pronounced by the controller as 'One One Eight Decimal Zero Three Five'. On the other hand, if it was the old 25kHz radio then this would be pronounced 'One One Eight Decimal Zero Three Three' matching more closely the transmit frequency digits. The 8.33kHz equipment is designed in such a way that when the numbers are dialled in it will tune automatically tune into the actual transmit frequency 118.0333MHz.

Since VHF transmissions follow approximate lines of sight, those from high altitudes carry several hundred miles. This means that a larger number of separate frequencies have to be allocated or the protection range between a single frequency shared by two Area Control Centres greatly increased. The recommended limits for contacting the larger airports are 25 nautical miles at 4,000ft for tower and 25 miles from 10,000ft for approach. Mutual interference can also arise under conditions of enhanced radio propagation even while operating within protected limits. Such conditions normally exist very briefly and the planning of frequency allocation takes account of all but the worst of these situations. All pilot/controller conversations are recorded automatically for use in incident and accident investigations. Radar and computer exchange data is also recorded, although, since this is an ICAO recommendation only, the practice is not universal.

The ICAO designates 123.45MHz for use in VHF air-to-air communications to enable aircraft engaged in flights over remote and oceanic areas out of range of VHF ground stations to exchange necessary operational information and facilitate the resolution of operational problems. However, strangely enough, 123.45MHz is still used for air-ground communications in a number of neighbouring states and the CAA requires pilots to adhere to certain procedures. Pilots are only to use frequency 123.45MHz for the exchange of operational information. The recommended phraseology is as follows: As an aircraft may be maintaining watch on more than one frequency, the initial call should include the identification 'Interpilot'. For use when making a directed call to a specific aircraft: '(Callsign of aircraft being called) (Callsign of calling aircraft) interpilot, do you read.' For use when making a general call: 'Any aircraft vicinity of (specific position) (callsign of calling aircraft) interpilot (any additional appropriate information).' The condition about only using the frequency in remote and oceanic areas remains in force.

Channels for Airports and Airfields

Aberdeen: Tower: 118.105 GMC: 121.705 Approach/Radar:119.055/128.305 ATIS:121.855/114.3

Aberporth: See *West Wales (Aberporth)*

Aberporth Range: 119.655

Alderney Tower: 125.355 GMC: 130.505 Approach (Guernsey):128.655

Andrewsfield: A/G: 130.555

Anglia Radar (Aberdeen): 125.280 128.930

Arbroath: Gliders: 124.1

Ashcroft Farm: A/G: 122.520 (by arrangement)

Badminton: A/G: 123.180

Bagby: A/G: 123.255

Baldonnel/Casement: Tower: 123.505 GMC: 123.105 Approach/Radar: 122.005/123.005 ATIS: 122.805

Barkston Heath: Tower: 120.430 Departures: 124.455 ATIS: 132.130

Barra: AFIS: 118.080

Barrow (Walney): AFIS: 123.205

Beccles: A/G: 120.380

Bedford: A/G: 119.030

Belfast (Aldergrove): Tower: 118.3 GMC: 121.755 Approach/Radar: 128.5 120.905 ATIS: 126.130

Belfast City: Tower: 122.830 Approach/Radar: 130.85 134.8 ATIS: 124.580

Belle Vue (Microlights, Devon): A/G: 125.480

Bembridge, Isle of Wight: A/G: 123.255

Benbecula: Tower/AFIS/Approach: 119.205 ATIS: 113.95

Benson: Tower: 127.155 GMC: 121.805 Approach/Radar: 136.455/120.905

Biggin Hill: Tower: 134.805 Approach: 129.405 ATIS: 135.680

Birmingham: Tower: 118.305 GMP: 121.930 GMC: 121.805 Approach/Radar: 123.980 131.330 131.005 ATIS: 136.030

Blackbushe: AFIS/A/G: 122.305

Blackpool: Tower: 118.405 Approach/Radar: 119.955 ATIS: 127.205

Bodmin: A/G: 120.330

Boscombe Down: Tower: 130.755 Approach/Radar: 130.005/126.705

Bournemouth: Tower: 125.605 GMC: 121.705 Approach/Radar: 119.480 118.655 ATIS: 133.730

Breighton: A/G: 129.805

Brent Radar: 122.255 129.955

Brimpton/Walsing Lower Farm: A/G: 135.130

Bristol: Tower: 133.85 GMP: 121.930 Approach/Radar: 125.650 136.080

ATIS: 126.030

Brize Norton: Tower: 123.730 GMC: 121.730 Approach/Radar: 124.280/127.255/119.005/133.755 ATIS: 126.505 Ops: 130.080

Bruntingthorpe: A/G: 122.830

Caernarfon: A/G: 122.255

Cambridge: Tower: 125.905 Approach/Radar: 120.965/124.980 ATIS: 134.6

Campbeltown: AFIS: 125.905

Cardiff: Tower: 133.105 Approach/Radar: 119.155 125.855 ATIS: 132.480

Cark: A/G: 129.905

Carlisle: Tower/Approach: 123.605 ATIS: 118.430

Chalgrove: A/G: 125.410

Chatteris: A/G: 129.905

Chichester (Goodwood): AFIS: 122.455

Chivenor: A/G: 130.2

Clacton: A/G: 118.155

Clench Common Microlights (Devon): 119.305

Colerne: Approach: 120.080

Coll: A/G: 125.005

Colonsay: A/G: 123.805

Compton Abbas: A/G: 122.710

Coningsby: Tower: 124.680 GMC: 121.85 Approach/Radar: 119.205

Cosford: Tower: 128.655 Approach: 135.880

Coventry: AFIS: 123.830

Cranfield: Tower: 134.930 Approach: 122.855 ATIS: 121.880

Cranwell: Tower: 121.780 Approach/Radar: 124.455 ATIS: 126.330

Cromer: A/G: 118.265

Crowland/Spalding: A/G: 129.980

Culdrose: Approach: 134.055

Cumbernauld: A/G: 120.605

Damyns Hall (Hornchurch): A/G: 119.555

Deanland/Lewes: A/G: 129.730

Denham: A/G: 130.730

Derby: A/G: 118.355

Dishforth: Tower: 125.005

Doncaster Sheffield: Tower: 128.775 Approach/Radar: 126.225 129.055 ATIS: 134.955

Donna Nook Range: 122.755

Dublin: Tower: 118.605 GMP: 122.985 GMC: 121.805 Approach/Radar: 121.105 119.555 118.505 119.930 126.255 119.555 133.280 ATIS: 124.530

Dundee: Tower/Approach: 122.905 ATIS: 119.330

Dunkeswell: A/G: 123.480

Dunsfold: A/G: 119.1

Duxford: AFIS/A/G: 122.080

Eaglescott: A/G: 123.005

Earls Colne: A/G: 122.430

East Midlands: Tower: 124.005 GMC: 121.905 Approach/Radar: 134.180 120.130 126.180 ATIS: 122.680

Edinburgh: Tower: 118.705 GMP: 121.980 GMC: 121.755 Approach/Radar: 121.205 128.980 ATIS: 131.355

Eggesford: A/G: 123.5

Elmsett: A/G: 123.475

Elstree: AFIS/AG: 122.405

Elvington: A/G: 119.630

Enniskillen (St Angelo): A/G: 123.205

Enstone: A/G: 129.880

Eshott: A/G: 122.855

Eskmeals Range: 122.755

Essex Radar: See *London Stansted*

Exeter: Tower: 119.805 Approach/Radar: 130.055 125.250 133.440 ATIS: 119.330

Fairford: Tower: 124.805

Fair Isle: A/G: 118.030

Fairoaks: AFIS/AG: 123.430

Farnborough: Tower: 122.780 GMC: 121.815 Approach/Radar: 125.250 130.055 133.440 ATIS: 128.405

Fenland: AFIS/AG: 122.930

Fife/Glenrothes: A/G: 130.455

Fishburn Microlights (Co Durham): 118.280

Fowlmere: A/G: 135.705

Glasgow: Tower: 118.805 GMC: 121.705 Approach/Radar: 119.1 125.25 128.755 ATIS: 129.575

Gloucestershire (callsign Gloster): Tower: 122.905 Approach/Radar: 128.555 120.980 ATIS: 127.480

Gransden Lodge: A/G: 131.280

Guernsey: Tower: 119.955 GMC: 121.805 Approach/Radar: 128.655 118.9 124.505 ATIS: 109.4

Halfpenny Green: See *Wolverhampton-Halfpenny Green*

Halton: A/G: 130.430

Haverfordwest: A/G: 123.605

Hawarden: Tower: 124.955 Approach/Radar: 120.055 130.015 ATIS: 125.430

Henlow: A/G: 121.105

Henstridge: A/G: 130.255

Hinton in the Hedges: A/G: 119.455

Huddersfield (Crosland Moor): 128.380

Humberside: Tower: 124.905 Approach/Radar: 119.130 129.255 ATIS: 124.130

Husbands Bosworth: A/G: 127.580

Inverness: Tower: 118.405 Approach/Radar: 122.605 ATIS: 109.2

Islay: AFIS: 123.155

Isle of Man (Ronaldsway): Tower: 119.005 Approach/Radar: 135.905 120.855 125.305 ATIS: 123.880

Jersey Tower: 119.455 GMC: 121.905 Approach/Radar: 118.555 120.305 120.450 125.205 ATIS: 134.680

Kemble: AFIS: 118.430

Kinloss (monitored by Lossiemouth): Tower: 122.1

Kirkbride: A/G: 124.405

Kirknewton: Gliders: 124.1

Kirkwall: Tower/Approach/AFIS: 118.305 ATIS: 108.6

Lakenheath: Approach/Radar: 136.505 Civil transit: 128.905

Land's End (St Just): Tower/A/G: 120.255

Lasham: AFIS: 131.030

Lashenden (Headcorn): A/G: 122.210

Lee-on-Solent: AFIS: 118.925

Leeds-Bradford: Tower: 120.305 GMP: 121.805 Approach/Radar: 134.580 125.380 ATIS: 118.030

Leeds East (Church Fenton): A/G: 126.505

Leeming: Tower: 120.505 MATZ: 133.380

Leicester: A/G: 122.130

Lerwick (Tingwall): AFIS: 125.305

Leuchars: Tower: 119.230 Approach/Radar: 126.505

Linton-on-Ouse: Tower: 129.355 MATZ: 118.555

Little Gransden: A/G: 130.855

Little Rissington: A/G: 120.775

Little Snoring: A/G: 118.130

Liverpool: Tower: 126.355 GMC: 121.955 Approach/Radar: 119.855 118.455 ATIS: 124.330

London City: Tower: 118.080 129.455 GMC: 121.830 Approach/Radar: 125.030 132.705 133.455 ATIS: 136.355 Thames Director: 128.025 132.7

London Control: See Appendix 2

London/Gatwick: Tower: 124.230 134.230 GMP: 121.955 GMC: 121.805 Director: 118.95 126.825 129.025 ATIS: 136.525

London/Heathrow: Tower: 118.505 118.705 124.475 GMP: 121.980 GMC: 121.905 121.705 121.855 Director: 119.730 120.4 127.525 125.630 134.980 125.630 (Helis and SVFR) Arr ATIS: 128.080 113.75 117.0 Dep ATIS: 121.935

See Appendix 2 for detailed functions

London/Luton: Tower: 132.555 126.725 GMP: 121.885 GMC: 121.755

Approach/Radar: 129.55 128.75 Essex Radar: 129.55 ATIS: 120.580

London Stansted: Tower: 123.805 125.55 GMP: 121.955 GMC: 121.730 Director: 136.2 Essex Radar: 120.625 132.05 ATIS: 127.180 114.55

London (Battersea) Heliport: Tower: 134.280

Londonderry (Eglinton): Tower: 134.155 Approach: 123.625 ATIS: 119.380

Lossiemouth: Tower: 118.905 MATZ: 119.580

Lydd: Tower: 119.380 Approach: 120.705 ATIS: 129.230

Manchester: Tower: 118.630 119.405 GMP: 121.705 GMC: 121.855 Radar: 118.575 135.0 121.35 Arrival ATIS: 128.180 113.55 Dep ATIS: 121.980

Manchester/Barton: AFIS: 120.255

Manorbier Range: 122.755

Manston: Tower: 119.930

Marham: Tower: 118.330 MATZ: 124.155

Merryfield: Tower: 122.105

Middle Wallop: Tower: 118.605

Mildenhall: Tower: 122.555 GMC: 121.805 Ops: 131.980

Mona: Tower: 119.180 AFIS: 118.955

Netheravon: AFIS: 128.305 Salisbury Ops: 122.755 DZ: 128.305

Netherthorpe: A/G: 123.280

Newcastle: Tower: 119.705 GMC: 121.730 Approach/Radar: 124.380 125.830 ATIS: 118.380

Newquay: Tower: 134.380 GMC: 121.955 Approach/Radar: 133.405 127.930 ATIS: 127.405

Newtownards: A/G: 128.305
Northampton (Sywell): AFIS: 122.705
North Coates Microlights: 120.155
Northolt: Tower: 124.255 Approach/Radar: 119.335 128.330 ATIS: 128.630
North Weald: A/G: 123.530
Norwich: Tower: 124.255 Approach/Radar: 119.355 128.330 ATIS: 128.630
Nottingham: A/G: 134.880
Oaksey Park: A/G: 132.230
Oban: AFIS: 118.055
Odiham: Tower: 119.230 Approach/Radar: 131.305
Old Buckenham: A/G: 124.405
Old Sarum: A/G: 123.205
Old Warden (display days only): AFIS: 130.705
Oxford: Tower: 133.430 GMC: 121.955 Approach/Radar: 125.090 119.980 ATIS: 136.230
Pembrey: A/G: 124.405
Pembrey/Pendine Ranges: 122.755
Penzance Heliport: A/G: 120.060
Perranporth: A/G: 119.755
Perth/Scone: A/G: 121.080
Peterborough (Conington): A/G: 129.725
Peterborough (Sibson): A/G: 120.330
Plockton: A/G: 131.910
Plymouth Military Radar: 121.25/124.15
Pocklington: A/G: 118.685
Popham: A/G: 129.805
Prestwick: Tower: 118.155 127.155 Approach/Radar: 129.45 124.630 129.45 ATIS: 121.130
Redhill: Tower: 119.605 ATIS: 125.305
Retford/Gamston: A/G: 130.480
Rochester: AFIS: 122.255
Rufforth: A/G: 120.380
St Athan: Tower: 122.865 Approach (*Cardiff*): 119.150 125.855 ATIS: 130.560
Sandown: A/G: 119.280
Sandtoft: A/G: 130.415
Scilly Isles/St Mary's: Tower/Approach: 124.880
Scottish Control: See Appendix 2
Seething: A/G: 118.435
Shanwick Oceanic: 123.95 124.175 128.360 127.65 127.9 127.950
Shawbury: Tower: 122.105 MATZ: 133.155
Sherburn-in-Elmet: A/G: 122.610
Shipdham: A/G: 132.255
Shobdon: AFIS/AG: 118.155
Shoreham: Tower: 125.405 Approach: 123.155 ATIS: 130.980
Silverstone: A/G: 123.330
Skegness: A/G: 132.430
Sleap: A/G: 122.455
Southampton: Tower: 118.205 Approach/Radar: 122.730 Solent Radar: 120.230 ATIS: 130.880
Southend: Tower: 127.730 Approach/Radar: 130.780 128.955 ATIS: 136.055
Spadeadam Range: 128.725
Stapleford: A/G: 122.805
Stornoway: Tower/Approach/AFIS: 119.480 ATIS: 115.1
Stow Maries: A/G: 118.980
Strubby: A/G: 122.305
Sturgate: A/G: 130.305
Sumburgh: Tower: 118.255 Approach/Radar: 131.3 123.155 ATIS: 125.855
Swansea: A/G: 119.705
Swanwick Mil: 133.330 (East) 135.080 (North East) 134.305 (North West) 136.380 (North) 127.455 (West) 135.155 (South West)
Syerston: A/G: 128.530 123.380
Tain Range: 122.755
Tatenhill: A/G: 124.080
Teesside: Tower: 119.805 Approach/Radar: 118.855 128.855 ATIS: 132.380
Tern Hill: Tower: 122.105
Thames Radar: 132.7
Thruxton: A/G: 118.280

Tibenham: A/G: 129.975
Tilstock: A/G: 118.105
Tiree: AFIS: 22.705
Topcliffe: Tower: 21.455 Approach/Radar: 25.005
Tresco Heliport: A/G: 118.205
Truro: A/G: 129.805
Turweston: A/G: 122.175
Unst: AFIS/A/G: 130.355
Upavon: A/G: 124.105
Valley: Tower: 122.105 Approach/Radar: 122.230 ATIS: 120.730
Waddington: Tower: 122.305 Approach/Radar: 128.955 119.505
Wainfleet Range: 122.755
Walton Wood Heliport: A/G: 123.625
Warton: Tower: 130.805 Approach/Radar: 129.530 129.730 ATIS: 121.730
Wattisham: Tower: 122.105 Approach/Radar: 125.805
Wellesbourne Mountford: AFIS: 124.030
Welshpool: A/G: 128.005
Western Radar: 132.305 131.055
West Freugh/Kirkcudbright Range: 130.055
Weston on the Green: DZ: 133.655
West Wales (Aberporth): AFIS/AG: 122.155
White Waltham: AFIS/AG: 122.605
Wick: Tower/Approach/AFIS: 119.705 ATIS: 113.6
Wickenby: A/G: 122.455
Wittering: Tower: 127.930 Approach/Radar: 119.680 135.205 ATIS: 123.930
Wolverhampton Halfpenny Green: AFIS: 123.005
Woodvale: Tower: 119.755 Approach: 121.005
Wycombe Air Park: A/G: 126.555
Wyton: Tower: 126.855
Yeovil (Westland): Tower/AG: 125.405 Approach/Radar: 130.805
Yeovilton: Tower: 120.805 MATZ: 127.355

Airband Channels in Numerical Order

MHz	
118.030	Leeds ATIS/Fair Isle A/G
118.055	Oban AFIS
118.080	London City Tower/Barra AFIS
118.105	Aberdeen Tower/Tilstock A/G
118.105	Aberdeen Tower
118.130	Little Snoring A/G
118.155	Shobdon AFIS/A/G/Prestwick Tower/Clacton A/G
118.205	Southampton Tower/Tresco Heliport A/G
118.255	Sumburgh Tower
118.265	Cromer A/G
118.280	Thruxton A/G/Fishburn Microlights
118.305	Birmingham Tower/Belfast (Aldergrove) Tower/Kirkwall Tower/Approach/AFIS
118.330	Marham Tower
118.355	Derby A/G
118.380	Newcastle ATIS
118.405	London City Tower/Blackpool Tower/Inverness Tower
118.430	Kemble ATIS/Carlisle ATIS
118.435	Seething A/G
118.455	Liverpool Radar
118.505	Heathrow Tower/Dublin Radar
118.555	Jersey Radar/Linton-on-Ouse MATZ
118.575	Manchester Radar
118.605	Middle Wallop Tower/Dublin Tower
118.630	Manchester Tower
118.655	Bournemouth Radar
118.685	Paraglider Common Frequency
118.705	Heathrow Tower/Edinburgh Tower
118.75	East Fortune A/G
118.805	Glasgow Tower
118.855	Teesside Approach
118.90	Guernsey Radar
118.905	Lossie Tower
118.925	Lee-on-Solent AFIS
118.95	Gatwick Radar
118.955	Mona AFIS
118.980	Stowe Maries A/G

119.005	Isle of Man Tower/Brize Zone
119.030	Bedford A/G
119.055	Aberdeen Approach/Exeter Radar
119.10	Glasgow Radar/Dunsfold A/G
119.130	Humberside Approach
119.155	Cardiff Approach/Radar
119.180	Mona Tower
119.205	Coningsby Approach/Benbecula Tower/Approach/AFIS
119.230	Odiham Tower/Leuchars Tower
119.280	Sandown A/G
119.305	Clench Common Microlights
119.330	Dundee ATIS/ Exeter ATIS
119.335	Northolt Approach
119.355	Norwich Approach
119.380	Lydd Tower/Londonderry (Eglinton) ATIS
119.405	Manchester Tower
119.455	Jersey Tower/Hinton in the Hedges A/G
119.480	Bournemouth Radar/Stornoway Tower/Approach/AFIS
119.505	Waddington Radar
119.555	Dublin Approach/Damyns Hall (Hornchurch) A/G
119.580	Lossie MATZ
119.605	Redhill Tower
119.630	Elvington A/G
119.655	Aberporth Range
119.680	Wittering Approach
119.705	Newcastle Tower/Swansea A/G/Wick Tower/Approach/AFIS/Swansea A/G
119.730	Heathrow Director
119.755	Woodvale Tower/Perranporth A/G
119.805	Teesside Tower/Exeter Tower
119.855	Liverpool Approach
119.930	Dublin Approach/Manston Tower
119.955	Blackpool Radar/ Guernsey Tower
119.980	Oxford Radar
120.055	Hawarden Radar
120.060	Penzance Heliport
120.080	Colerne Approach
120.130	East Midlands Radar
120.155	North Coates Microlights
120.230	Solent Radar
120.255	Manchester Barton AFIS/Land's End Tower/A/G
120.305	Leeds Tower/Jersey Radar
120.330	Sibson A/G
120.330	Bodmin A/G
120.380	Rufforth A/G/Beccles A/G
120.40	Heathrow Director
120.430	Barkston Tower
120.45	Jersey Radar
120.505	Leeming Tower
120.580	Luton ATIS
120.605	Cumbernauld A/G
120.625	Essex Radar
120.705	Lydd Approach
120.730	Valley ATIS
120.775	Little Rissington A/G
120.805	Yeovilton Tower
120.855	Ronaldsway Radar
120.905	Belfast (Aldergrove) Radar/Benson Zone
120.965	Cambridge Radar
120.980	Gloster Radar
121.005	Woodvale Approach
121.075	Silverstone A/G
121.080	Perth A/G
121.105	Dublin Approach/Henlow A/G
121.130	Prestwick ATIS
121.205	Edinburgh Radar
121.25	Plymouth Military Radar
121.35	Manchester Radar
121.455	Topcliffe Tower
121.50	Emergency Frequency
121.60	Fire service/pilot direct comms
121.705	Heathrow GMC/Glasgow GMC/Manchester GMP/Bournemouth GMC/Aberdeen GMC
121.730	Stansted GMC/Brize GMC/Newcastle GMC/Warton ATIS
121.755	Belfast (Aldergrove) GMC/Edinburgh GMC/Luton GMC
121.780	Cranwell Tower

121.805 Leeds GMP/Dublin GMC/Guernsey GMC/Gatwick GMC/Mildenhall GMC/Birmingham GMC/Benson GMC
121.815 Farnborough GMC
121.830 London City GMC
121.855 Heathrow GMC/Aberdeen ATIS/Coningsby GMC/Manchester GMC
121.880 Cranfield ATIS
121.885 Luton GMP
121.905 Heathrow GMC/East Midlands GMC/Jersey GMC
121.930 Birmingham GMP/Bristol (Lulsgate) GMC
121.955 Oxford GMC/Newquay GMC
121.935 Heathrow Dep ATIS
121.955 Gatwick GMP/Liverpool GMC/Stansted GMP
121.980 Heathrow GMP/Edinburgh GMP/Manchester Dep ATIS
122.005 Baldonnel Approach
122.055 Company Ops
122.080 Duxford AFIS/A/G
122.105 RAF Common Tower Channel
122.130 Leicester A/G
122.155 West Wales AFIS/A/G
122.175 Turweston A/G
122.210 Lashenden (Headcorn) A/G
122.255 Caernarfon A/G/Rochester AFIS/Brent Radar
122.305 Blackbushe AFIS/Waddington Tower/A/G/Strubby A/G
122.355 Company Ops
122.405 Elstree AFIS/A/G
122.430 Earls Colne A/G
122.455 Sleap A/G/Chichester (Goodwood) AFIS/Wickenby A/G
122.480 Balloons Common Channel
122.520 Ashcroft Farm A/G
122.555 Mildenhall Tower
122.605 Inverness Approach/White Waltham AFIS/A/G
122.610 Sherburn A/G
122.680 East Midlands ATIS
122.705 Sywell AFIS/Tiree AFIS
122.710 Compton Abbas A/G
122.730 Southampton Tower
122.755 Donna Nook Range/Eskmeals Range/Manorbier Range/Salisbury Plain Range/Pembrey Range/Tain Range/Wainfleet Range
122.775 Crowfield A/G
122.780 Farnborough Tower
122.805 Stapleford A/G
122.830 Belfast City Tower/Bruntingthorpe A/G
122.855 Cranfield Approach/Eshott A/G
122.865 St Athan Tower
122.905 Gloster Tower/Dundee Tower/Approach
122.930 Fenland AFIS/A/G
122.985 Dublin GMP
123.005 Halfpenny Green AFIS/Eaglescott A/G
123.105 Baldonnel GMC
123.155 Shoreham Approach/Islay AFIS/Sumburgh Radar
123.180 Badminton A/G
123.205 Barrow (Walney) AFIS/At Angelo A/G/Old Sarum A/G
123.255 Bagby A/G/Bembridge A/G
123.280 Netherthorpe A/G
123.30 RAF Common PAR Talkdown Channel
123.330 Silverstone A/G
123.380 Syerston A/G
123.430 Fairoaks AFIS/A/G
123.45 Air-to-Air frequency for operational use only
123.475 Elmsett A/G
123.480 Dunkeswell A/G
123.50 Eggesford A/G
123.505 Baldonnel Tower
123.530 North Weald A/G
123.605 Carlisle Tower/Approach/Haverfordwest A/G
123.625 Eglinton Approach/Walton Wood HeliportA/G
123.730 Brize Tower
123.805 Stansted Tower/Colonsay A/G
123.830 Coventry AFIS

123.880	Ronaldsway ATIS
123.930	Wittering ATIS
123.95	Shanwick Oceanic
123.980	Birmingham Radar
124.005	East Midlands Tower
124.030	Wellesbourne AFIS
124.080	Tatenhill A/G
124.10	Arbroath gliders/Kirknewton gliders
124.105	Upavon A/G
124.130	Humberside ATIS
124.155	Marham LARS/Plymouth Military Radar
124.175	Shanwick Oceanic
124.230	Gatwick Tower
124.255	Norwich Tower/Northolt Tower
124.280	Brize Radar
124.330	Liverpool ATIS
124.380	Newcastle Approach
124.405	Kirkbride A/G/Old Buckenham A/G/Pembrey A/G
124.455	Cranwell Zone/Barkston Departures
124.475	Heathrow Tower
124.505	Guernsey Radar
124.530	Dublin ATIS
124.580	Belfast City ATIS
124.630	Prestwick Radar
124.655	Dublin Control
124.680	Coningsby Tower
124.805	Fairford Tower
124.880	St Mary's Tower/Approach
124.905	Humberside Tower
124.955	Hawarden Tower
124.980	Cambridge Radar
125.005	Topcliffe Approach
125.030	London City Radar
125.005	Dishforth Tower/Topcliffe Approach/Coll A/G
125.090	Oxford Approach
125.205	Jersey Radar
125.225	Valley Radar
125.25	Glasgow Radar/Exeter Radar/Farnborough Radar
125.280	Anglia Radar
125.305	Ronaldsway Radar/Redhill ATIS/Lerwick AFIS
125.355	Alderney Tower
125.380	Leeds Radar
125.410	Chalgrove A/G/Yeovil Tower/A/G
125.405	Shoreham Tower
125.430	Hawarden ATIS
125.480	Belle Vue Microlights (Devon) A/G
125.555	Stansted Tower
125.605	Bournemouth Tower
125.630	Heathrow Director
125.655	Bristol (Lulsgate) Radar
125.725	Scottish Volmet
125.805	Wattisham Approach
125.830	Newcastle Radar
125.855	Cardiff Radar/Sumburgh ATIS
125.905	Cambridge Tower/Campbeltown AFIS
126.030	Bristol (Lulsgate) ATIS
126.130	Belfast (Aldergrove) ATIS
126.180	East Midlands Radar
126.225	Doncaster Approach/Radar
126.255	Dublin Radar
126.330	Cranwell ATIS
126.355	Liverpool Tower/London City ATIS
126.505	Brize ATIS/Leeds East Approach/Leuchars Approach
126.555	Wycombe A/G
126.60	London Volmet North
126.705	Boscombe Zone
126.725	Luton Tower
126.825	Gatwick Radar
126.855	Wyton Tower
127.00	Dublin Volmet
127.155	Prestwick Tower/Benson Tower
127.180	Stansted ATIS
127.205	Blackpool ATIS
127.255	Brize Approach
127.355	Yeovilton Radar
127.405	Newquay ATIS
127.455	Swanwick Mil (West)
127.480	Gloster ATIS
127.525	Heathrow Director
127.580	Husbands Bosworth A/G

127.65	Shanwick Oceanic
127.730	Southend Tower
127.90	Shanwick Oceanic
127.930	Wittering Tower/Newquay Approach
127.95	Shanwick Oceanic
128.005	Welshpool A/G
128.025	Thames Director
128.080	Heathrow Arrival ATIS
128.180	Manchester Arrival ATIS
128.305	Aberdeen Radar/Netheravon AFIS/Newtownards A/G
128.330	Northolt Radar/Norwich Radar
128.360	Shanwick Oceanic
128.380	Huddersfield Crosland Moor A/G
128.405	Farnborough ATIS
128.50	Belfast (Aldergrove) Radar
128.530	Syerston A/G
128.555	Gloster Radar
128.60	London Volmet South
128.630	Northolt ATIS /Norwich ATIS
128.655	Guernsey Radar/Cosford Tower
128.725	Spadeadam Range
128.755	Glasgow Radar/Luton Radar
128.775	Doncaster Tower
119.80	Truro A/G
128.855	Teesside Radar
128.905	Lakenheath Ops (Civil transit)
128.930	Anglia Radar
128.955	Southend Radar/Waddington Radar
128.980	Edinburgh Radar
129.025	Gatwick Radar
129.055	Doncaster Radar
129.180	Dublin Control North
129.230	Lydd ATIS
129.255	Humberside Radar
129.355	Linton-on-Ouse Tower
129.405	Biggin Hill Approach
129.45	Prestwick Radar
129.530	Warton Radar
129.55	Essex Radar
129.575	Glasgow ATIS
129.725	Peterborough Conington A/G
129.730	Warton Radar/Deanland A/G
129.755	Company Ops
129.805	Breighton A/G/Popham A/G/Truro A/G
129.825	Common Microlight Channel
129.880	Enstone A/G
129.905	Cark A/G/Chatteris A/G/Langar A/G/Strathallan A/G
129.955	Brent Radar
129.980	Gliding sites Common Channel
130.005	Boscombe Radar
130.055	West Freugh Range
130.015	Hawarden Radar
130.055	Exeter Radar/Farnborough Radar
130.080	Brize Ops/
130.130	Glider Common Channel
130.175	Company Ops
130.20	Chivenor A/G
130.255	Henstridge A/G
130.305	Sturgate A/G
130.355	Unst AFIS/A/G
130.380	Company Ops
130.405	Glider Common Channel
130.415	Sandtoft A/G
130.430	Halton A/G
130.45	Fife/Glenrothes A/G
130.480	Gamston A/G
130.505	Alderney GMC
130.535	Parachute Drop Zone
130.555	Andrewsfield A/G
130.560	St Athan ATIS
130.605	Swissport Ops
130.630	Company Ops
130.655	Company Ops
130.705	Old Warden AFIS
130.730	Denham AFIS/A/G
130.755	Boscombe Down Tower
130.780	Southend Approach
130.805	Warton Tower/Yeovil Radar
130.85	Belfast City Approach/Little Gransden A/G
130.880	Southampton ATIS
130.980	Shoreham ATIS
131.005	Birmingham Radar
131.030	Lasham AFIS

131.055	Western Radar
131.280	Gransden Lodge A/G
131.30	Sumburgh Approach
131.305	Odiham Approach
131.330	Birmingham Radar
131.355	Edinburgh ATIS
131.405	Company Ops
131.430	Company Ops
131.455	Company Ops
131.485	Company Ops
131.505	Company Ops
131.705	Company Ops
131.805	Company Ops
131.905	Company Ops
131.910	Plockton A/G
131.930	Company Ops
131.980	Company Ops
131.980	Mildenhall Ops
132.05	Essex Radar
132.130	Barkston ATIS
132.230	Oaksey Park
132.255	Shipdham A/G
132.305	Western Radar
132.380	Teesside ATIS
132.430	Skegness A/G
132.480	Cardiff ATIS
132.555	Luton Tower
132.70	Thames Director
132.705	London City Radar
132.90	Temporary allocation for airshows etc
133.105	Cardiff Tower
133.155	Shawbury MATZ
133.280	Dublin Radar
133.330	Swanwick Mil (East)
133.380	Leeming MATZ
133.405	Newquay Approach
133.430	Oxford Tower
133.440	Exeter Radar
133.455	London City Radar
133.655	Weston on the Green DZ
133.730	Bournemouth ATIS
133.755	Brize Director
133.85	Bristol (Lulsgate) Tower
134.055	Culdrose Approach
134.155	Eglinton Tower
134.180	East Midlands Radar
134.230	Gatwick Tower
134.280	London (Battersea) Heliport Tower
134.305	Swanwick Mil (North West ICF)
134.380	Newquay Tower
134.580	Leeds Radar
134.60	Cambridge ATIS
134.680	Jersey ATIS
134.805	Biggin Hill Tower/Belfast City Radar
134.880	Nottingham A/G
134.930	Cranfield Tower
134.955	Doncaster ATIS
134.980	Heathrow Radar
135.00	Manchester Radar
135.080	Swanwick Mil (North East)
135.155	Swanwick Mil (South West)
135.130	Brimpton A/G
135.205	Wittering Approach
135.480	SAFETYCOM
135.680	Biggin Hill ATIS
135.705	Fowlmere A/G
135.880	Cosford Approach
135.905	Isle of Man Radar
136.030	Birmingham ATIS
136.055	Southend ATIS
135.080	Swanwick Mil (North East)
136.080	Bristol (Lulsgate) Radar
136.15	Dublin Control
136.20	Stansted Director
136.230	Oxford ATIS
136.355	London City ATIS
136.375	London Volmet Main
136.380	Swanwick Mil (North)
136.455	Benson Talkdown
136.505	Lakenheath Approach/Radar
136.525	Gatwick ATIS
136.75	ACARS Datalink
136.80	ACARS Datalink
136.85	ACARS Datalink
136.875	ACARS Datalink
136.90	ACARS Datalink

Appendix 4

UHF Airband Frequencies

As the RAF has yet to use 8.33 spaced allocations, the term 'frequencies' is used rather than 'channels'. This listing has been compiled from official sources available to the general public. There are, of course, many other allocations, including air-to-air, TADs, Ops and satellite communications. Note that some of the Swanwick Mil frequencies rebroadcast aircraft transmissions so that when a single controller is handling more than one frequency, aircraft on one frequency are able to hear those on another and thus not inadvertently interrupt. Swanwick Mil has a number of unpublished UHF frequencies that are allocated by the Initial Contact Frequency (ICF) controller as required.

Frequencies of Military Airfields and Radar Units

Aberporth Range: 338.925

Barkston Heath: Tower: 277.725 GMC: 389.625 Approach (*Cranwell*): 388.775 Radar: 278.775/232.35/264.9 ATIS: 290.65

Benson: Tower: 233.95 GMC: 343.575 Approach/Radar: 343.525/342.1 PAR: 246.65/277.675 ATIS: 397.575

Boscombe Down: Tower: 369.425 GMC: 374.45 Approach/Radar: 340.250 PAR: 373.15 ATIS: 232.85 Ops: 376.725

Boulmer: A/G: 249.625

Brize Norton: Tower: 269.175 GMC: 341.2 Approach/Radar: 278.35/231.95/339.025 PAR: 362.225 Ops: 369.9/373.1 ATIS: 284.975

Chetwynd: A/G: 307.3 Approach (*Shawbury*): 369.175

Colerne: Tower: 372.575 Approach: 374.825 ATIS: 277.85

Coningsby: Tower: 298.975 GMC: 357.125 Approach/Radar: 234.675/255.95/379.95 PAR: 234.575/276.775 ATIS: 278.80 Ops: 379.35

Cosford: Tower: 278.65 GMC: 278.675 Approach: 306.7

Cranwell: Tower: 370.55 GMC: 344.125 Approach/Radar: 338.775/355.575 240.95 PAR: 369.45/255.675/264.9 ATIS: 279.275

Culdrose: Tower: 370.65 GMC: 241.925 Approach/Radar: 279.9/231.775/313.6 PAR: 336.3/336.525 ATIS: 278.9

Dishforth: Tower: 371.975

Doncaster: Tower/Radar: 283.425

Donna Nook Range: 369.3 264.725

Eskmeals Range: 337.975

Fairford: Tower: 338.225 GMC: 234.25

Holbeach Range: 281.375 375.225

Kinloss: Tower: 277.225 Approach/Radar: (*Lossie*) 315.150/362.775/308.85 ATIS (*Lossie*): 369.15

Lakenheath: Tower: 373.775 GMC: 397.35 Approach/Radar: 275.825/264.575/275.825/315.7/242.05 ATIS: 341.05 Ops: 244.475/379.8/257.75/284.425

Leconfield: A/G: 369.175

Leeming: Tower: 376.85 GMC: 379.9 Approach/Radar: 278.225/372.3/233.9 PAR: 245.625/373.55 ATIS: 369.475 Ops: 377.75

Leuchars: Tower: 257.8 GMC: 275.375 Approach/Radar: 278.7/292.35/372.75 PAR: 309.6/299.75 ATIS: 368.85 Ops: 396.9

Linton-on-Ouse: Tower: 259.575 GMC: 278.125 Approach/Radar: 370.725/363.4 PAR: 340.775

Lossiemouth: Tower: 279.05 GMC: 268.625 Approach/Radar: 315.15/277.525/308.85 PAR: 378.775/255.925 ATIS: 369.150 Winter Ops: 291.15

Manorbier Range: 279.125 369.3

Marham: Tower: 278.175 GMC: 360.4 Approach/Radar: 343.975/378.7/357.0 PAR: 232.15/356.15 ATIS: 245.675 Ops: 284.0

Merryfield: Tower: 355.95

Middle Wallop: Tower: 345.175 A/G: 397.475 Approach/Radar: 233.375/233.575 PAR: 253.475 ATIS: 240.8

Mildenhall: Tower: 370.25 GMC: 337.975 Approach (*Lakenheath*): 309.2/250.3 ATIS: 375.5 Ops: 308.85/313.55 Metro: 284.425

Mona: Tower: 398.525 Approach/Radar (*Valley*): 266.125/269.1

Netheravon: AFIS: 398.2 A/G: 277.8 (Salisbury Ops)

Newcastle: Approach/Radar: 284.6

Northolt: Tower: 279.925 PAR: 343.75 ATIS: 299.8 Ops: 389.45

Odiham: Tower: 267.4 GMC: 339.825 Approach/Radar: 275.45/313.375 PAR: 245.625 ATIS: 370.75

Otterburn Range: 279.0

Pembrey Range: 264.725

Plymouth Military Radar: 281.475/370.85

Predannack: Tower: 285.1 Approach (*Culdrose*): 282.575

Prestwick: Ops: Navy Prestwick: 279.05

Scampton: Tower: 340.675 GMC: 336.525 Approach (*Waddington*): 345.075 PAR: 251.525

Shawbury: Tower: 362.0 Approach/Radar: 269.425/369.175/373.225 PAR: 377.775/360.45 ATIS: 341.65

Spadeadam Range: 308.775 ATIS: 341.975

Swanwick Mil: Initial Contact Frequency: East: 259.6 Northeast: 277.775 North: 282.625 Central: 252.875 West: 277.625 Southwest: 278.6 Southeast: 275.625 Lichfield Corridor: 292.525

Syerston: A/G: 292.45

Tain Range: 339.8/279.125

Ternhill: Tower: 386.675 GMC: 241.925 Approach (*Shawbury*): 369.175

Valley: Tower: 389.275 GMC: 369.5 Approach/Radar: 266.125/363.65/269.1 PAR: 313.55

Waddington: Tower: 241.325 GMC: 342.125 Approach/Radar: 345.075/232.7/280.175 PAR: 344.2/376.2 ATIS: 291.675 Vulcan Ops: 369.4

Warton: Tower: 369.275 Approach/Radar: 232.2/356.05

Wattisham: Tower: 388.35 Approach/Radar: 369.225/398.05 PAR: 386.275/265.675 ATIS: 277.925

West Freugh Range (Luce Bay): 368.975

Wittering: Tower: 379.1 GMC: 276.85 Approach/Radar: 234.075/344.6/276.65/372.125

Woodvale: Tower: 233.675 Approach: 280.65

Wyton: Tower: 372.2 GMC: 278.35 Approach: 369.525 ATIS: 279.15

Yeovilton: Tower: 376.3 GMC: 362.85 Approach/Radar: 234.3/240.575 PAR: 247.4/397.05 ATIS: 244.55

Miscellaneous Common Frequencies

Tower: 257.8 Approach: 362.3 Radar: 344.0 Approach: 362.3 PAR: 385.4 Distress: 243.0 Scene of Search: 282.8/156.0 (FM)/156.8 (FM)

UHF Airband Frequencies in Numerical Order

MHz

231.775 Culdrose Radar
231.95 Brize Radar
232.15 Marham PAR
232.20 Warton Radar
232.35 Barkston Heath Radar
232.70 Waddington Radar
232.85 Boscombe Down ATIS
233.375 Middle Wallop Radar
233.475 Fairford Ops
233.575 Middle Wallop Radar
233.675 Woodvale Tower
233.90 Leeming Radar
233.95 Benson Tower
234.075 Wittering Radar
234.25 Fairford Ground
234.30 Yeovilton Radar
234.575 Coningsby PAR
234.675 Coningsby Radar
240.575 Yeovilton Radar
240.80 Middle Wallop ATIS
240.95 Cranwell Radar
241.325 Waddington Tower
241.925 Ternhill GMC/Culdrose GMC
242.05 Lakenheath Radar
243.00 UHF Distress
244.475 Lakenheath Ops
244.55 Yeovilton ATIS
245.625 Leeming PAR/Odiham PAR
245.675 Marham ATIS
246.65 Benson PAR
247.40 Yeovilton PAR
249.625 Boulmer A/G
251.375 NATO Combined SAR Training
251.525 Scampton PAR
252.875 Swanwick Mil ICF Central
253.475 Middle Wallop PAR
255.675 Cranwell PAR
255.925 Lossiemouth PAR
255.95 Coningsby Radar
256.425 Lakenheath Radar
257.75 Lakenheath Ops
257.80 NATO Common Tower
259.575 Linton-on-Ouse Tower
264.575 Lakenheath Radar
259.60 Swanwick Mil ICF East
264.725 Donna Nook Range/Pembrey Range
264.90 Cranwell PAR
265.675 Wattisham PAR
266.125 Valley Radar
267.40 Odiham Tower
268.625 Lossiemouth GMC
269.10 Valley Radar
269.175 Brize Tower
269.425 Shawbury Radar
269.675 Lakenheath Radar
275.375 Leuchars GMC
275.45 Odiham Radar
275.625 Swanwick Mil ICF Southeast
275.825 Lakenheath Radar
276.65 Wittering Radar
276.775 Coningsby PAR
276.85 Wittering GMC
277.225 Kinloss Tower
277.525 Lossiemouth Radar
277.625 Swanwick Mil ICF Central
277.675 Swanwick Mil ICF West
277.725 Barkston Heath Tower
277.775 Swanwick Mil ICF Northeast
277.80 Salisbury Ops
277.85 Colerne ATIS
277.875 Lossie Approach
277.925 Wattisham ATIS
278.125 Linton-on-Ouse GMC
278.175 Marham Tower
278.225 Leeming Radar
278.35 Brize Radar/Wyton GMC
278.60 Swanwick Mil ICF Southwest
278.65 Cosford Tower
278.675 Cosford GMC
278.70 Leuchars Radar
278.775 Barkston Heath Radar
278.80 Coningsby ATIS
278.90 Culdrose ATIS

279.00	Otterburn Range
279.05	Lossiemouth Tower/Prestwick Navy Ops
279.125	Tain Range/Manorbier Range
279.15	Wyton ATIS
279.275	Cranwell ATIS
279.90	Culdrose Radar
279.925	Northolt Tower
280.175	Waddington Radar
280.65	Woodvale Approach
281.375	Holbeach Range
281.475	Plymouth Military Radar
282.575	Culdrose Approach for Predannack
282.625	Swanwick Mil ICF Northwest
282.80	Scene of Search NATO
283.425	Doncaster Tower
284.00	Marham Ops
284.425	Fairford Metro/Lakenheath Metro/Mildenhall Metro
284.60	Newcastle Radar
284.975	Brize ATIS
285.10	Predannack Tower
290.65	Barkston Heath ATIS
291.15	Lossiemouth Winter Ops
291.675	Waddington ATIS
292.35	Leuchars Radar
292.45	Syerston A/G
292.525	Swanwick Mil ICF Central
298.975	Coningsby Tower
299.75	Leuchars PAR
299.80	Northolt ATIS
300.80	NATO Low-flying
306.70	Cosford Approach
307.30	Chetwynd A/G
308.775	Spadeadam Range
308.85	Lossiemouth Radar/Mildenhall Ops
309.20	Lakenheath Approach
309.60	Leuchars PAR
313.375	Odiham Radar
313.55	Mildenhall Ops/Valley PAR
313.60	Culdrose Radar
315.15	Lossiemouth Radar
315.70	Lakenheath Radar
335.00	ILS Glide path Transmitters
336.30	Culdrose PAR
336.525	Culdrose PAR/Scampton GMC
337.975	Mildenhall GMC/Eskmeals Range
338.225	Fairford Tower
338.775	Cranwell Radar
338.925	Aberporth Range
339.025	Brize Radar
339.80	Tain Range
339.825	Odiham GMC
340.25	Boscombe Down Radar
340.675	Scampton Tower
340.775	Linton-on-Ouse PAR
341.05	Lakenheath ATIS
341.20	Brize GMC
341.65	Shawbury ATIS
341.975	Spadeadam Range ATIS
342.10	Benson Radar
342.125	Waddington GMC
343.525	Benson Radar
343.75	Northolt PAR
343.575	Benson GMC
343.975	Marham Radar
344.00	NATO Common Radar
344.125	Cranwell GMC
344.20	Waddington PAR
344.60	Wittering Radar
345.075	Waddington Radar
345.175	Middle Wallop Tower
355.575	Cranwell Radar
355.95	Merryfield Tower
356.05	Warton Radar
356.15	Marham PAR
356.725	Lakenheath ATIS
357.00	Marham Radar
357.125	Coningsby GMC
360.075	Lakenheath Radar
360.40	Marham GMC
360.45	Shawbury PAR
362.00	Shawbury Tower
362.225	Brize PAR
362.30	NATO Common Approach
362.85	Yeovilton GMC

363.40	Linton-on-Ouse Radar
363.65	Valley Radar
368.85	Leuchars ATIS
368.975	West Freugh (Luce Bay Range)
369.150	Lossiemouth ATIS
369.175	Leconfield A/G/Shawbury Radar
369.225	Wattisham Radar
369.275	Warton Tower
369.30	Donna Nook Range/Manorbier Range
369.40	Vulcan Ops (Waddington)
369.425	Boscombe Down Tower
369.45	Cranwell PAR
369.475	Leeming ATIS
369.50	Valley GMC
369.525	Wyton Approach
369.90	Brize Ops
370.25	Mildenhall Tower
370.55	Cranwell Tower
370.65	Culdrose Tower
370.725	Linton-on-Ouse Radar
370.75	Odiham ATIS
370.85	Plymouth Military Radar
371.975	Dishforth Tower
372.125	Wittering Radar
372.20	Wyton Tower
372.30	Leeming Radar
372.575	Colerne Tower
372.75	Leuchars Radar
373.10	Brize Ops
373.15	Boscombe Down PAR
373.225	Shawbury Radar
373.55	Leeming PAR
373.775	Lakenheath Tower
374.45	Boscombe Down GMC
374.825	Colerne Approach
375.225	Holbeach Range
375.50	Mildenhall ATIS
376.20	Waddington PAR
376.30	Yeovilton Tower
376.725	Boscombe Down Ops
376.85	Leeming Tower
377.75	Leeming Ops
377.775	Shawbury PAR
378.70	Marham Radar
378.775	Lossiemouth PAR
379.10	Wittering Tower
379.35	Coningsby Ops
379.80	Lakenheath Ops
379.90	Leeming GMC
379.95	Coningsby Radar
385.40	NATO Common PAR
386.275	Wattisham PAR
386.675	Ternhill Tower
386.75	Valley Tower
388.35	Wattisham Tower
389.485	Northolt Ops
389.625	Barkston Heath GMC
396.90	Leuchars Ops
397.05	Yeovilton PAR
397.35	Lakenheath GMC
397.475	Middle Wallop A/G
397.575	Benson ATIS
398.05	Wattisham Radar
398.20	Netheravon AFIS
398.525	Mona Tower

Appendix 5

ICAO Aircraft Type Designators

The three- or four-character designators below are used for flight planning purposes and also by ATC on flight progress strips. The aircraft name or designation in full is normally used on R/T, but many of the abbreviated versions may also be heard. This list is just a sample and gives an idea of how the system works. The full and very lengthy list can be found online in ICAO DOC 8643 – Aircraft Type Designators.

A109	Agusta 109
A310	Airbus A310
A318	Airbus A318
A319	Airbus A319
A320	Airbus A320
A321	Airbus A321
A333	Airbus A330-300
A337	Airbus Beluga XL
A345	Airbus A340-500
AC12	Commander 112
AC14	Commander 114
AN26	Antonov AN-26
AN72	Antonov AN-72
A124	Antonov AN-124
AS65	Dauphin
AJET	Alphajet
B733	Boeing 737-300
B734	Boeing 737-400
B738	Boeing 737-800
B74F	Boeing 747F
B74S	Boeing 747SP
B753	Boeing 757-300
B762	Boeing 767-200
B773	Boeing 777-300
B77L	Boeing 777-200LR
BDOG	Bulldog
BE9L	Beech King Air 90
BE20	Super King Air 200
BE40	Beechjet 400
BE55	Beech Baron
BE60	Beech Duke
BE76	Beech Duchess
BN2P	Islander
BN2T	Turbine Islander
C130	C-130 Hercules
C152	Cessna 152
C172	Cessna 172
C208	Cessna Caravan
C310	Cessna 310
C401	Cessna 401
C421	Cessna 421
C550	Citation II
C56X	Citation Excel
CL60	Challenger
D228	Dornier 228
D328	Dornier 328
DA40	Diamond DA-40 Star
DA42	Diamond DA-42 Twin Star
DH8D	Dash 8 400
E121	Xingu
EC55	Eurocopter 155
EUFI	Eurofighter Typhoon
FA50	Falcon 50
F900	Falcon 900
FK10	Fokker 100
FK50	Fokker 50
FK70	Fokker 70
GLF4	Gulfstream IV
GLF6	Gulfstream 650
GA7	Cougar
GLEX	Global Express
H25B	HS125 800
H47	Chinook
HR20	Robin HR20
IL62	Ilyushin IL-62
IL76	Ilyushin IL-76
JS31	Jetstream 31
JS41	Jetstream 41
LJ35	LearJet 35
LJ60	LearJet 60
P180	Piaggio Avanti
PA27	Piper Aztec
PA28	Piper Cherokee
PA34	Piper Seneca
PA38	Piper Tomahawk
PA30	Piper Twin Comanche
PA31	Piper Navajo
PAYE	Piper Cheyenne I/II
PN68	Partenavia P68
PREM	Premier 1
SF34	Saab 340
SR22	Cirrus SR-22
SW4	Merlin IV/Metro
T204	Tupolev TU-204
TAMP	Tampico
TEX	Texan
TOBA	Tobago

Appendix 6

Aircraft Radio Callsigns

Callsign prefixes and three-letter codes are allocated by the ICAO on a worldwide basis. The use of either is permitted but most operators tend to use the spoken prefix rather than the three-letter code. Sometimes you will hear both in succession, especially when the controller is unable to understand an unfamiliar prefix in a foreign accent and uses the code noted on his flight progress strip instead. On HF frequencies, the three-letter code is often used in preference to the spoken prefix because it is easier to hear over the usual atmospherics and interference. As an example, I have heard a BA aircraft over Africa using BAW rather than the usual Speedbird.

ICAO three-letter designators will normally only be assigned to: (a) aircraft operating agencies engaged in air transport operations in accordance with a full Aircraft Operators Certificate (AOC) that are considered to have a need for an exclusive designator; (b) Aircraft operating agencies engaged in aerial work operations that can demonstrate a need for an exclusive designator; (c) Government aircraft operating agencies; (d) Government authorities and services providing air navigation, communication and other services for international aviation; (e) Organisations, other than government organisations, providing services for international civil aviation.

For individual flights, the general advice from CAA to airline operators is: 'Many airlines continue to utilise their IATA commercial flight numbers as a callsign suffix. However, because they tend to be allocated in batches of sequential and very similar numbers, callsign confusion can occur. Several airlines have switched to alphanumeric systems with some success over recent years. However, if every operator adopts alphanumerics, the limited choices available within the maximum of four elements allowed in the callsign suffix means that similar confusion to the numeric system is likely to result.

'Before changing to an effective numeric system, which involves a significant amount of work, especially for a large airline, it is recommended that operators review their existing numeric system to deconflict similar callsigns. Where there is no effective solution to those callsigns that have a potential for numeric confusion, alphanumerics can be adopted.'

The following is a summary of the guidelines for operators when allocating callsigns. Avoid use of similar flight numbers within the same company; co-ordinate advance planning, whenever possible, with other operators to avoid using similar numbers; after implementation, ensure that there is a tactical response to review and amend callsigns where necessary; consider starting flight number elements sequences with a higher number, eg six and above; try to minimise use of callsigns involving four digits and, whenever possible, use no more than three; try to avoid using alphanumeric callsigns that correspond to the last two letters of the destination's ICAO location indicator, eg ABC 96LL for a flight inbound to Heathrow where the location indicator is EGLL; if similar-numbered callsigns are inevitable, allow a significant time and/or geographical split between aircraft using similar callsigns; when useful capacity in the allocation of flight numbers and alphanumerics has been reached, consider applying for and using a second company designator such as 'Shuttle'; avoid, whenever practicable, flight numbers ending in a zero or five, eg five may be confused visually with S, and zero when combined with two digits, ie 150, may be confused with a heading or level; avoid use of similar/reversed digits/letters in alphanumerics, eg ABC 87MB and ABC 78BM. Finally, avoid phonetic letters that can be confused with another airline designator prefix, eg D – the airline Delta.'

Requests for the registration of or change in a designator will only be recognised by the ICAO when received from the state having jurisdiction over the aircraft operating agency. Conversely, when a designator is no longer required, the ICAO should be informed immediately but undertake not to reassign it until a period of at least sixty days has elapsed. Some years ago, the ICAO issued a safety bulletin highlighting the fact that the word 'Air' was used either as prefix or suffix in more than one in five radiotelephony designators in use worldwide. Furthermore, one of its derived translations, 'Aero' in the Spanish language, represented 270 cases worldwide. 'Avia' used by many Russian operators occurred 174 times, 'Jet' 155, 'Trans' 134, 'Express' and 'Cargo' 83 times each. Less numerous examples included 'Flight', 'Star', 'Service', 'Charter', and 'Wings'. The situation is little changed today and the potential for callsign confusion leading to dangerous situations is obvious.

In the case of individual flight numbers, a Callsign Similarity Service (CSS) has been set up by Eurocontrol to tackle the ongoing problem of callsign confusion that can lead to crews taking instructions meant for other aircraft, with obvious safety implications. Some years ago, Eurocontrol declared that research had shown that over 80 per cent of callsign similarities could be resolved by a central management service. This would deconflict callsign similarities during the flight planning phases with the aid of a dedicated software application. This pan-European CSS solution has since taken the form of a co-ordinated service operated by Eurocontrol's Network Manager Operations Centre (NMOC).

Military callsigns are further explained in Chapter 170, many being changed frequently for security reasons. This is not a problem for training aircraft, and many three-letter codes reflect their bases, examples being 'VYT' and 'WIT' for the Valley and Wittering Flying Training Units respectively. Many have been assimilated into the ICAO system. I have endeavoured to include as many as possible of the civil prefixes heard over Britain and further afield on HF, but the list is far from exhaustive. I have added the state of origin where it is not obvious from the operator's name.

R/T callsign	**Operator**
Abex	ABX Air (USA)
ABG	Luxaviation Belgium
Aceforce	Allied Command Europe
Acropolis	Acropolis Aviation (UK)
Advanced	Advanced Flight Training Ltd
Aegean	Aegean Airlines
Aeroflot	Aeroflot Russian Airlines
Aeromexico	Aeromexico
Aeronaut	Cranfield University
Aeros	Flight Training (UK)
African West	African West (Senegal)
Aigle Azur	Aigle Azur
Aim Air	Aim Air (Moldova)
Air Albania	Air Albania
Air Alpha	Air Alpha Greenland
Air Baltic	Air Baltic
Airbridge Cargo	Airbridge Cargo Airlines
Air China Freight	Air China Cargo
Airbus Industrie	Airbus Industrie
Air Cadet	RAF Air Cadet Schools
Air Canada	Air Canada
Airest Cargo	Airest Cargo (Estonia)
Airevac	USAF Ambulance
Air Force One	US President
Air Force Two	US Vice-President
Air France	Air France
Air Ghana	Air Ghana
Air Hamburg	Air Hamburg
Air Hong Kong	Air Hong Kong
Air India	Air India
Air Malta	Air Malta
Air Mauritius	Air Mauritius
Air Nav	Air Navigation & Trading
Air Portugal	Air Portugal
Air Serbia	Air Serbia
Air Silesia	Air Silesia (Czech Republic)
Air Sweden	West Air Sweden
Air Tahiti	Air Tahiti
Air Tony	Spectrum Aviation

Air Ukraine	Air Ukraine
Air Zimbabwe	Air Zimbabwe
Albastar	AlbaStar (Spain)
Alitalia	Alitalia
All Weather	UK Civil Aviation Authority
AME	Spanish Air Force
American	American Airlines
Amerijet	International
Arabia Maroc	Air Arabia Maroc
Aravco	Aravco
Arcus Air	Arcus Air (Germany)
Arena	Arena Aviation (UK)
Argentina	Aerolineas Argentinas
Armyair	Army Air Corps
Ascot	RAF Transport
Asiana	Asiana Airlines
Astanaline	Air Astana (Kazakhstan)
Astonjet	Astonjet (France)
Atlanta	Air Atlanta (Iceland)
Atran	Aviatrans Cargo (Russian Fed)
Audeli	Audeli Air Express (Spain)
Austrian	Austrian Airlines
Avcon	Execujet Europe (Switz)
Aviabreeze	Breeze (Ukraine)
Avianca	Avianca (Columbia)
Azal	Azerbaijan Airlines
Ayline	Aurigny Air Services
Balado	Kapital Aviation (UK)
Balkan Holidays	BH Air (Bulgaria)
Bangladesh	Bangladesh Biman
Barkston	Barkston Heath FTU
Base	Budapest Air Service
Bavarian	ACM Air Charter
Beauty	TUI Fly (Belgium)
Beeline	Brussels Airlines
Belavia	Belavia (Belarus)
Beluga	Airbus Transport International
Binair	Bin Air (Germany)
Bioflight	Bioflight (Denmark)
Bizjet	Hamlin Jet
Black Sea	MNG Airlines (Turkey)
Bluescan	TUIfly Nordic (Sweden)
Blackadder	Bournemouth Commercial Flight Training
Blackbox	Boscombe Down DERA
Blue Air	Blue Air (Romania)
Blue Cargo	Bluebird Nordic (Iceland)
Bluefin	Blue 1 Finland
Blue Island	Blue Islands
Bluelift	Airlift (Norway)
Bond	Bond Helicopters
Bonus	Bonus Aviation (UK)
Border	Border Air Training
Brabazon	CAA Airworthiness Division
Bristow	Bristow Helicopters
British	British Intl Helicopters
Broadsword	2 Excel Aviation Ltd
Broadway	Fleet Requirements Unit
Brunei	Royal Brunei Airlines
Brunel	Bristol Flight Training Centre
Buzzard	Butane Buzzard Aviation
Caddy	Heliaviation Ltd
Calibrator	Cobham Flight Inspection
Camber	US Transportation Command
Camairco	Camair-Co (Cameroons)
Cambrian	Dragonfly Air Charter
Cameo	Cam Air Management
Cana	Sky Cana (Dominican Republic)
Canforce	Canadian Armed Forces
Cargo	FlySafair (South Africa)
Cargoblue	ASL Airlines (UK)
Cargojet	Cargojet Airways (Canada)
Cargo Line	Cavok Air (Ukraine)
Cargolux	Cargolux Airlines
Carpatair	Carpatair (Romania)
Catex	Catex (France)
Cathay	Cathay Pacific
Causeway	Woodgate Aviation
Cedar Jet	Middle East Airlines
Cega	Cega Aviation (UK)
Challenge	Challenge Airlines (Belgium)
Channex	Jet2.com
China Eastern	China Eastern Airlines

China Southern	China Southern Airlines
Chukka	Polo Aviation Ltd
City	KLM Cityhopper
Cityliner	Alitalia Cityliner
Cityhun	Cityline Hungary
Clever	Cargoair (Bulgaria)
Clifton	Centreline (UK)
Cloud Runner	247 Jet Ltd
Clue	HQ Euscom (USAF)
Coastguard	HM Coastguard
Commodore	Commair Aviation Ltd
Comex	Comed Group
Compass	Compass International (USA)
Condor	Condor Flugdienst
Connie	Kalitta Air (USA)
Contract	ASL Airlines Ireland
Corsair	Corse Air International (France)
Corsica	Air Corsica
Costock	East Midlands Helicopters
Cotam	French AF Transport
Coyne Air	Coyne Aviation
Cranwell	Cranwell FTU
Croatia	Croatia Airlines
CSA Lines	Czech Airlines
Cubana	Cubana
Cyprus	Cyprus Airways
Dagobert	Quick Air Jet Charter (Germany)
Danish	Danish Air Transport
Dark Blue	Aeropartner (Czech Republic)
Dark Knight	Excellent Air (Germany)
Dartmoor	Airways Flight Training
Delta	Delta Airlines
Diamond Air	Diamond Aircraft UK Ltd
Donair	Donair Flying Club
Duke	Jubilee Airways
Dynasty	China Airlines (Taiwan)
Eastflight	Eastern Airways
Easy	easyJet
Edelweiss	Edelweiss Air (Switzerland)
Edge	Leading Edge Aviation (UK)
Egyptair	Egyptair
El Al	El Al
Emerald	Westair Aviation (Ireland)
Emirates	Emirates
Endeavour	Victoria Aviation (UK)
Endurance	RVL Aviation (UK)
Enterair	Enter Air (Poland)
Eole	Airailes (France)
Etihad	Etihad Airways
Ethiopian	Ethiopian Airlines
Eurocat	Cat Aviation (Switzerland)
Eurofly	Eurofly (Italy)
Europa	Air Europa (Spain)
Eurotrans	European Air Transport
Eurovan	Van Air Europe (Czech Republic)
Euroviking	Air Atlanta Europe
Eurowings	Eurowings (Germany)
Eva	Eva Air (Taiwan)
Ever Flight	Eisele Flugdienst
Exam	CAA Flight Examiners
Exclusive Jet	XJC Ltd
Exxon	43rd Air Refuelling Wing
Fairfleet	Fleet Air International (Hungary)
Fairoaks	Fairoaks Flight Centre
Falconjet	Falcon Jet Centre (UK)
Fastlink	Linksair Ltd
Fedex	Federal Express
Finesse	Finesse Executive
Finforce	Finnish Air Force
Finnair	Finnair
Firebird	CargoLogicair (UK)
First City	First City Air (UK)
Flairjet	Flairjet Ltd
Flexair	Flexjet (UK)
Flexjet	Flexjet (USA)
Flight Cal	Flight Calibration Services (UK)
Flightvue	AD Aviation (UK)
Flying Bulgaria	Bulgaria Air
Flyinglux	Flying Group Luxembourg
Flying Group	Flying Service Belgium
Formula	Formula One Management

Fraction	Netjets Europe
France Soleil	Transavia France
Freebird	Freebird Airlines (Turkey)
Gama	Gama Aviation
Gauntlet	Boscombe Down DERA
Gemini	Global Crossings Airlines (USA)
German Air Force	German Air Force
German Wings	German Wings
German Cargo	Aerologic (Germany)
Gestair	Gestair (Spain)
Giant	Atlas Air (USA)
Gold	NHV Helicopters (UK)
Grand Prix	Williams Grand Prix Engineering
Grid	National Grid Co
Griffon	The 955 Preservation Group
Gulf Air	Gulf Air
Gypsy	Eagle Aviation (UK) Ltd
Hainan	Hainan Airlines (China)
Hansaline	Lufthansa CityLine
Helibus	CHC Helikopter Service (Norway)
Helimed	UK Helicopter Med Emergency
Helvetic	Helvetic Airways
Herky	37th Airlift Sqn
Highfield	BCA Charters (UK)
Highflyer	Private Sky (Ireland)
Hyperion	Hyperion Aviation (Malta)
Iberia	Iberia
Iceair	Icelandair
Images	Air Images
Indonesia	Garuda Indonesia
Iranair	Iran Air
Iraqi	Iraqi Airways
Irish	Irish Air Corps
Island Flyer	Island Aviation Ltd
Isle Avia	Island Aviation
Jaymax	J-Max Air Services
Janes	Janes Aviation (UK)
Japanair	Japan Airlines
Javelin	Leeming FTU
Jester	Executive Aviation Services
Jet Airways	Jet Airways
Jet Executive	Jet Executive (Germany)
Jetflite	Jetflite (Finland)
Jetnetherlands	JetNetherlands
Jet Nova	Jet Nova (Spain)
Jet Test	Jet Test and Transport (USA)
Jordanian	Royal Jordanian
Jumprun	Business Wings (Germany)
Kalitta	Kalitta Charters (USA)
Kemblejet	Delta Engineering Aviation
Kenya	Kenya Airways
Key Air	Key Air (USA)
Kingdom	GB Helicopters Ltd
Kitty	Royal positioning flights
Kittyhawk	32 (The Royal) Sqn
Kiwi	Royal New Zealand Air Force
KLM	KLM
Koreanair	Korean Airlines
Kuwaiti	Kuwait Airways
LAN	LATAM Airlines (Chile)
Landmark	Grantex Aviation
Legend	Air X (Malta)
Libair	Libyan Airlines
Lizard	Plymouth School of Flying
Logan	Loganair
Lomas	Lomas Helicopters 235
London City	London City Airport Jet Centre
Lonex	London Executive Aviation
Longtail	Longtail Aviation (Bermuda)
Lot	LOT (Poland)
Lotus Flower	Lotus Airline (Egypt)
Lufthansa	Lufthansa
Lufthansa Cargo	Lufthansa Cargo
Luxair	Luxair
Lyddair	Lyddair (UK)
Lynden	Lynden Air Cargo (USA)
Mahan Air	Mahan Air (Iran)
Mailman	Zimex Aviation Austria
Majan	Royal Omani Air Force
Malaysian	Malaysian Airline System
Maleth	Maleth-Aero (Malta)
Malta Star	DC Aviation

Manhattan	Manhattan Air (UK)
Marshall	Marshall Aerospace
Martin	Martin-Baker
Martinair	Martinair
MAS Cargo	MasAir (Mexico)
Mayoral	Dominguez Toledo (Spain)
Medops	IAS Medical (UK)
Meridian Cherry	Meridian (Ukraine)
Merlin	Rolls-Royce (Military Aviation)
Mermaid	Air Alsie (Denmark)
Metman	Met Research Flight
Midnight	Sundt Air (Norway)
Mitavia	RAF Avia (Latvia)
Moldcargo	Aerotranscargo (Moldova)
Moonflower	Neos (Italy)
Mozambique	LAM-Mozambique
Mozart	Salzburg Jet Aviation
Multi	NATO Support Agency (Netherlands)
NASA	National Aeronautics and Space Administration
National Cargo	National Airlines (USA)
Navigator	Nova Airlines (Sweden)
Navy	Royal or US Navy
Neptune	West Atlantic UK
Nericair	Neric (UK)
Netherlands Air Force	Royal Netherlands AF
Netherlands Navy	Netherlands Navy
Newpin	Hawker Beechcraft Hawarden
New Zealand	Air New Zealand
Nippon Cargo	Nippon Cargo Airlines
NOAA	National Oceanographic and Atmospheric Administration
Norbrook	Haughey Air (UK)
Nordvind	Avion Express (Lithuania)
Nor Shuttle	Norwegian Air Shuttle
Nor Star	Norwegian Air Long Haul
North Flying	North Flying (Denmark)
Northolt	32 (The Royal) Squadron
Northumbria	Northumbria Helicopters
Norwegian	Royal Norwegian Air Force

Nostru Air	Air Nostrum (Spain)
Nouvelair	Nouvel Air Tunisie
Obelix	Avcon Jet Malta
Olympic	Olympic Air
Oman	Oman Royal Flight
Omega	Aeromega (UK)
Omni	Omni Aviation (Portugal)
On Track	On Track Aviation Ltd
Open Skies	Open Skies Commission
Opera Jet	Opera Jet (Slovakia)
Orbest	Orbest Portugal
Orystar	Oryxjet Ltd
Osprey	PLM-Dollar Group
Oxford	Oxford Aviation Academy
Pad Aviation	Pad Aviation (Germany)
Pakistan	Pakistan International
Para	Army Parachute Centre
Pat	US Army Priority Air Transport
Pendley	Pen-Avia Ltd
Philippine	Philippine Airlines
Pilatus Wings	Pilatus Flugzeugwerke
Pipeline	Pipeline inspection flight
Player	Play (Iceland)
Podilia	Podilia-Avia (Ukraine)
Polar	Polar Air Cargo (USA)
Police	Police Aviation Services
Port	Skyworld Airlines (USA)
Powerline	UK Powerline Inspection
Poyston	Haverfordwest Air Charter
Prestige	Capital Air Ambulance
Proflight	Langtry Flying Group
Propstar	Propstar Aviation Ltd
Qantas	Qantas
Qatari	Qatar Airlines
Quadriga	Windrose Air (Germany)
Rabbit	Rabbit-Air Zurich
Rafair	Royal Air Force
Rainbow	32 (The Royal) Sqn
Rapex	HD Air (UK)
Raven	Ravenair
Reach	USAF Air Mobility Command

Redair	Redhill Aviation Ltd
Red Angel	FAI Rent-a-Jet (Germany)
Red Devils	Red Devils Parachute Team
Redhawk	Sovereign Business Jets (UK)
Red Head	Babcock Onshore Services (UK)
Rednose	Norwegian Air UK
Red Pelican	JDP France
Red Star	Goodridge (UK)
Relief	Relief Transport Services (UK)
Richair	Rich International Airways (USA)
Ripple	Skyblue Aviation (UK)
Rollright	Rollright Aviation Ltd
Rolls	Rolls-Royce (Bristol Engine Division)
Romaf	Romanian Air Force
Rooster	Hahn Airlines
Royal Air Maroc	Royal Air Maroc
Royal Nepal	Royal Nepal Airlines
Rubystar	Ruby Star Airlines (Belarus)
Rushton	FR Aviation
Rwandair	Rwandair
Ryanair	Ryanair
Safiran	Safiran Airlines (Iran)
Saint Athan	St Athan MU
Saints	Solent Flight Ltd
Saltire	Air Charter Scotland
Sam	Special Air Mission (USAF)
Samson	Samson Aviation Ltd
Santa	BA Santa Flights
Saudia	Saudi-Arabian Airlines
Saxonair	Saxon Air (UK)
Scandinavian	Scandinavian Airlines System
Science	Natural Environment Research Council
Scillonia	Isles of Scilly Sky Bus
Sentry	USAF AWACS
Seabird	FSB Flugservice (Germany)
Seychelles	Air Seychelles
Shamrock	Aer Lingus
Shawbury	Shawbury FTU
Shell	Shell Aircraft
Shepherd One	Papal flight (Alitalia)
Shuttle	British Airways Shuttle
Siberian	S7 Airlines
Silkair	Silkair (Singapore)
Silk West	Silk Way West Airlines (Azerbaijan)
Silver Arrow	Global Jet (Luxembourg)
Silver Cloud	Silver Cloud Air (Germany)
Singapore	Singapore Airlines
Sirio	Sirio (Italy)
Sky Camel	KS Avia (Latvia)
Skydrift	Skydrift (UK)
Sky Elite	European Business Jets (UK)
Sky Flyer	Hi Fly (Portugal)
Skyjet	ASA Airlines Spain
Skynews	British Sky Broadcasting
Skytravel	Smartwings (Czech Republic)
Sloane	Sloane Aviation
Snoopy	Air Traffic GmbH
Solway	Apollo Air Services (UK)
Sonas	Acass Ireland
Southcoast	South Coast Aviation Bournemouth
Southern Air	Southern Air (USA)
Sovereign	Tag Aviation UK
Spar	58th Airlift Sqn USAF
Special	Specialist Aviation Services (UK)
Speedbird	British Airways
Springbok	South African Airways
Striker	Wittering FTU
Sudanair	Sudanair
Sunnyheart	Thomas Cook Airlines (Spain)
Sunscan	Sun Air of Scandinavia
Sunturk	Pegasus Airlines
Support	Prescott Support Co (USA)
Surinam	Surinam Airways
Surveyor	Cooper Aerial Surveys (UK)
Swedeforce	Swedish Armed Forces
Swift	Swiftair (Spain)
Swiss	Swiss Airlines

Swiss Ambulance	Swiss-Air Ambulance
Synergy	Synergy Aviation (UK)
Syrianair	Syrian Arab Airlines 389
TAM	LATAM Airlines Brazil
Tampa	Avianca Cargo (Colombia)
Tarnish	Warton Military Flight Ops
Tarom	Tarom (Romania)
Tayflite	Tayflite Ltd
Tayside	Tayside Aviation
Teemol	Mann Air Charter
Tester	Empire Test Pilots School
Thai	Thai International
Thanet	TG Aviation Ltd
Thunder Cat	Catreus AOC (UK)
Tigris	Tiger Helicopters (UK)
Til	Tajikistan International
Tomjet	TUI Airways
Topcat	Helicopter Services (UK)
Topcliffe	Topcliffe FTU
Topswiss	easyJet Switzerland
Towline	AirTanker (UK)
Trafalgar	Bluestream Aviation (UK)
Trans Arabian	Trans Arabian Air Transport (Sudan)
Transat	Air Transat (Canada)
Transavia	Transavia (Netherlands)
Trans Europe	Air Transport (Slovakia)
Trident	Atlas Helicopters (UK)
Truman	Truman Aviation
Tuifly	Tuifly (Germany)
Tunair	Tunisair
Turkish	Turkish Airlines
Turkmenistan	Turkmenistan Airlines
Twin Goose	Air-Taxi Europe (Germany)
Twinjet	Twin Jet (France and UK)
Typhoon	Coningsby FTU
Tyrol Ambulance	Tyrol Air Ambulance
Tyroljet	Tyrolean Jet Service
Ukraine Alliance	Ukraine Air Alliance
Ukraine International	Ukraine International Airlines
United	United Airlines
UPS	United Parcel Service (USA)

Uzbek	Uzbekistan Airways
Valljet	Valljet (France)
Vampire	Execujet Scandinavia (Denmark)
Vectis	BN Group (UK)
Vickers	BAe Systems Marine
Victor Victor	US Navy
Viking	SunClass Airlines (Denmark)
Virgin	Virgin Atlantic
Vista Jet	Vista Jet (Malta)
Volante	Executive Jet Charter (UK)
Volga	Volga-Dnepr Airlines
Voluxis	Voluxis (UK)
Vortex	Support Helicopter Force RAF
Vueling	Vueling Airlines
Vulcan	Waddington FTU
Vulkan Air	Vulkan Air (Ukraine)
Watchdog	Ministry of Fisheries
Westland	Leonardo MW Ltd
White Knight	DEA Aviation (UK)
Whitestar	Star Air (Denmark)
Widerøe	Widerøe (Norway)
Wizz Air	Wizz Air
Wizz Go	Wizz UK
Wizard	Micromatter Technology (UK)
Wondair	Wondair on Demand Aviation (Spain)
Woodstock	Capital Air Services (UK)
World Express	DHL Air (UK)
Wycombe	Booker Aviation (UK)
Wyton	No. 1 Elementary Flying Training School
Xray	Xjet Ltd (UK)
Yemeni	Yemen Airways
Yorkair	Multiflight Ltd
Zap	Titan Airways
Zimex	Zimex Aviation (Switzerland)
Zitotrans	Aviacon Zitotrans (Russia)
Zorex	Zorex Air Transport (Spain)

Suffixes to the flight number can have various

meanings:

A	Extra flight on the same route. If more than one, B, C etc. may be used
F	Freight
P	Positioning flight
T	Training flight
Heavy	Reminder to ATC that aircraft is wide-bodied with a strong vortex wake
Super	Airbus A380 An-225

Be aware that there are exceptions to these, such as British Airways' Shuttle callsigns, eg 'Shuttle 6M'. The letter suffixes change alphabetically for each service throughout the day. And, of course, there are the alphanumerics as described above.

Royal Flights

Royal Flights by No. 32 (The Royal) Squadron (and whenever No. 10 Squadron or No. 216 Squadron aircraft are being utilised for Royal/VIP flights) are designated by the callsign 'Kittyhawk' (three-letter code TQF), followed by an identification number and the suffix 'R'. For helicopters it is 'Rainbow', an identification number and the suffix 'S'.

Civilian chartered helicopters use 'Sparrowhawk', three-letter KRH, followed by an identification number. Callsigns for positioning flights are as follows: No. 32 (The Royal) Squadron – the three-letter operator designator RRF and the radiotelephony callsign 'Kitty', followed by an identification number. Civilian chartered fixed-wing aircraft will use their normal company callsign.

ICAO Company Designators

Three-letter code	Operator
AAB	Luxaviation Belgium
AAC	Army Air Corps
AAE	Air Atlanta Europe
AAF	Aigle Azur
AAG	Atlantic Aviation
AAL	American Airlines
AAM	Aim Air (Moldova)
AAR	Asiana Airlines
ABD	Air Atlanta (Iceland)
ABN	Air Albania
ABR	ASL Airlines Ireland
ABV	ASL Airlines UK
ABW	Airbridge Cargo Airlines
ABX	ABX Air (USA)
ACW	RAF Air Cadet Schools
ADB	Antonov Airlines (Ukraine)
ADI	Audeli Air (Spain)
ADR	Adria Airways
AEA	Air Europa (Spain)
AEE	Aegean Airlines
AEG	Airest (Estonia)
AFB	Bulgarian Air Force
AFP	Portuguese Air Force
AHA	Air Alpha (Denmark)
AHK	Air Hong Kong
AHO	Air Hamburg
AHY	Azerbaijan Airlines
AJT	Amerijet International
ALI	Airlift (Norway)
ALK	Sri Lankan Airways
ALS	Air Alpe (France)
AMC	Air Malta
AME	Spanish Air Force
AMR	Air America
AMX	Aeromexico
ANA	All Nippon Airways
ANE	Air Nostrum (Spain)
ANZ	Air New Zealand
AOS	Aeros Flight Training (UK)
ARG	Aerolineas Argentinas
ASJ	Astonjet (France)
ASL	Air Serbia

ATG	Aerotranscargo (Moldova)
ATJ	Air Traffic GmbH (Germany)
AUA	Austrian Airlines
AUI	Ukraine International Airlines
AUR	Aurigny Air Services
AVA	Avianca (Columbia)
AVB	Aviation Beauport
AWC	Titan Airways
AXY	Air X Charter (Malta)
AYZ	Atlant Soyuz
AZD	Zimex Aviation Austria
AZE	Arcus Air (Germany)
AZG	Silk Way West Airlines (Azerbaijan)
AZS	Aviacon Zitotrans (Russia)
AZW	Air Zimbabwe
BAE	BAe Systems
BAF	Belgian Air Force
BBB	Swedejet Airways
BBC	Bangladesh Biman
BBD	Bluebird Nordic (Iceland)
BCI	Blue Islands
BCS	European Air Transport
BCY	CityJet
BDN	Boscombe Down DERA
BEE	Jersey European
BEL	Brussels Airlines
BGA	Airbus Transport International
BGH	BH Air (Bulgaria)
BHL	Bristow Helicopters Group
BID	Bin Air (Germany)
BIO	Bioflight (Denmark)
BKH	Barkston Heath FTU
BLA	Blue Air (Romania)
BLF	Blue 1 Finland
BLX	TUIfly Nordic (Sweden)
BON	B & H Airlines
BOS	Openskies (France)
BOX	AeroLogic (Germany)
BPS	Budapest Aircraft Service
BRT	British International Helicopters
BTI	Air Baltic
BVA	Buffalo Airways
BVR	ACM Air Charter
BWA	Caribbean Airlines
BWY	Fleet Requirements Air Direction Unit
BZN	Brize Norton FTU
CAL	China Airlines (Taiwan)
CAO	Air China Cargo
CAT	Cat Aviation (Switzerland)
CCM	Air Corsica
CAZ	Cat Aviation (Switzerland)
CBY	Coningsby FTU
CCA	Air China
CEG	Cega Aviation (UK)
CES	China Eastern
CFC	Canadian Armed Forces
CFD	Cranfield University
CFG	Condor Flugdienst
CFU	CAA Flying Unit
CGD	HM Coastguard
CGF	Cargo Air (Bulgaria)
CHG	Challenge Airlines (Belgium)
CHH	Hainan Airlines (China)
CJT	Cargojet Airways (Canada)
CKS	Kalitta Air
CLG	Challair (France)
CLH	Lufthansa CityLine
CLU	CargoLogic Air (UK)
CLX	Cargolux Airlines
CMB	US Transportation Command
CMF	Compass International (USA)
CNB	Cityline Hungary
COA	Continental Airlines
CPA	Cathay Pacific
CRL	Corse Air International
CRN	Aero Caribbean
CRV	Acropolis Aviation (UK)
CSA	Czech Airlines
CSN	China Southern Airlines
CTB	Thomas Cook Airlines (Spain)
CTM	French Air Force Transport
CTN	Croatia Airlines
CUB	Cubana
CVK	Cavok Air (Ukraine)
CWL	Cranwell FTU
CWY	Woodgate Aviation

CYP	Cyprus Airways
CYL	Alitalia Cityliner
DAH	Air Algerie
DAL	Delta Airlines
DCN	German Federal Armed Forces
DCW	DC Aviation (Malta)
DEV	Red Devils Parachute Team
DFC	Aeropartner (Czech Republic)
DHK	DHL (UK)
DHL	DHL Air Ltd
DKE	Jubilee Airways
DTA	TAAG Angola
DTR	Danish Air Transport
DUK	Ducair (Luxembourg)
EAT	Air Transport (Slovakia)
EBJ	European Business Jets
ECA	Excellent Air (Germany)
EDC	Air Charter Scotland
EDY	Apollo Air Services (UK)
EEU	Eurofly (Italy)
EFD	EFD Eisele Flugdienst
EFF	Westair Aviation (Ireland)
EIN	Aer Lingus
ENT	Enter Air (Poland)
EOL	Airailes (France)
ETH	Ethiopian Airlines
ETP	Empire Test Pilots School
EVA	Eva Air (Taiwan)
EWG	Eurowings (Germany)
EXM	CAA Flight Examiners
EXN	Exin (Poland)
EXS	Jet2.com
EZS	easyJet Switzerland
EZY	easyJet
FAF	French Air Force
FBF	Fine Airlines (USA)
FCO	Aerofrisco (Mexico)
FDX	Federal Express
FGN	Gendarmerie Nationale
FHY	Freebird Airlines (Turkey)
FIN	Finnair
FJC	Falcon Jet Centre (UK)
FJI	Air Pacific (Fiji)
FNS	Finesse Executive (UK)
FNY	French Navy
FPY	Play (Iceland)
FRA	FR Aviation
FRF	Fleet Air International (Hungary)
FSB	Flight Service Berlin
FYG	Flying Service Belgium
FYL	Flying Group Luxembourg
GAF	German Air Force
GCO	Gemini Air Cargo
GEC	Lufthansa Cargo
GES	Gestair (Spain)
GFA	Gulf Air
GHN	Air Ghana
GIA	Garuda Indonesia
GLJ	Globaljet Austria
GMA	Gama Aviation
GRL	Air Greenland
GTI	Atlas Air (USA)
GWI	German Wings
GXA	Global Crossing Airlines (USA)
HAF	Greek Air Force
HFY	Hi Fly (Portugal)
HHN	Hahn Airlines
HLE	UK HEMS
HYP	Hyperion Aviation (Malta)
ICE	Icelandair
ICG	Icelandic Coastguard
ICL	CAL Cargo (Israel)
IFA	FAI Rent-a-Jet (Germany)
IMX	Zimex Aviation (Switzerland)
IOS	Isles of Scilly Sky Bus
IQQ	Caribbean Airways
IRA	Iran Air
IRM	Mahan Air (Iran)
IYE	Yemen Airways
JAF	TUI Fly (Belgium)
JAI	Jet Airways
JAL	Japan Airlines
JAT	Air Serbia
JDP	JDP France
JEF	Jetflite (Finland)
JEI	Jet Executive (Germany)

JME	EJME (Portugal) Aircraft Management
JMP	Business Wings (Germany)
JNL	JetNetherlands
JNV	Jetnova (Spain)
JTN	Jet Test and Transport (USA)
KAC	Kuwait Airways
KAL	Korean Airlines
KEY	Key Air (USA)
KFS	Kalitta Charters (USA)
KHA	Kitty Hawk Air Cargo
KIN	Kinloss FTU
KLC	KLM Cityhopper
KQA	Kenya Airways
KRP	Karpatair (Romania)
KSA	KS Avia (Latvia)
KZR	Air Astana
LAA	Libyan Airlines
LAM	Linhas Aereas Mocambique
LAN	LATAM Airlines Chile
LAP	Lineas Aereas Paraguayas
LAV	AlbaStar (Spain)
LBC	Albanian Airlines
LBT	Nouvel Air Tunisie
LCN	Lineas Aereas Canarias
LCO	LATAM Cargo Chile
LCS	RAF Leuchars
LDG	Leading Edge Aviation (UK)
LEE	Leeming FTU
LGL	Luxair
LGT	Longtail Aviation (Bermuda)
LNQ	Linksair
LOP	Linton-on-Ouse FTU
LOS	Lossiemouth FTU
LOT	Lot Poland
LSP	Spectrum Aviation
LTC	Latcharter (Latvia)
LTU	Small Planet Airlines (Lithuania)
LXJ	Flexjet (USA)
LYC	Lynden Air Cargo (USA)
LZB	Bulgaria Air
MAA	MasAir (Mexico)
MAC	Air Arabia Morocco
MAH	Malev
MAS	Malaysian Airline System
MAU	Air Mauritius
MBE	Martin-Baker
MBL	First City Air (UK)
MDI	IAS Medical (UK)
MDT	Sundt Air (Norway)
MEA	Middle East Airlines
MEM	Meridian (Ukraine)
MET	Meteorological Research Flight
MGR	Magna Air (Austria)
MLT	Maleth-Aero (Malta)
MMD	Air Alsie
MMF	NATO Support Agency (Netherlands)
MNB	MNG Airlines (Turkey)
MOZ	Salzburg Jet Aviation (Austria)
MPH	Martinair (Netherlands)
MRH	Marham FTU
MSR	Egyptair
MTL	RAF Avia (Latvia)
MYO	Dominguez Toledo
NAF	Royal Netherlands Air Force
NAX	Norwegian Air Shuttle
NCA	Nippon Cargo
NCR	National Airlines (USA)
NFA	North Flying (Denmark)
NGA	Nigeria Airways
NHZ	NHV Helicopters (UK)
NJE	Netjets Europe
NLH	Norwegian Air Long Haul
NMB	Air Namibia
NOH	32 (The Royal) Squadron
NOS	Neos (Italy)
NOW	Royal Norwegian Air Force
NPT	West Atlantic UK
NRN	Royal Netherlands Navy
NRS	Norwegian Air UK
NVD	Avion Express (Lithuania)
NVR	Nova Airlines (Sweden)
NVY	Royal Navy
OAV	Omni Aviation (Portugal)
OAW	Helvetic Airways
OBS	Orbest Portugal
OMB	Omni Air International

OMG	Aeromega (UK)
OPJ	Opera Jet (Slovakia)
ORF	Oman Royal Flight
ORZ	Zorex Air Transport (Spain)
OSY	Open Skies Commission
OVA	Aero Nova (Spain)
OXF	Oxford Aviation Academy
PAC	Polar Air Cargo
PAL	Philippine Airlines
PAT	US Army Priority Air Transport
PBU	Air Burundi
PCH	Pilatus
PDA	Podilia-Avia (Ukraine)
PEA	Pan Européenne (France)
PGT	Pegasus Airlines (Turkey)
PIA	Pakistan International
PJS	Jet Aviation (Switzerland)
PLC	Specialist Aviation Services
PNR	ASL Airlines Spain
PSK	Prescott Support Co (USA)
PSW	Pskovavia
PTG	Privat Air Dusseldorf
PVD	Pad Aviation (Germany)
QAJ	Quick Air Jet (Germany)
OAL	Olympic Air
QFA	Qantas
QGA	Windrose Air (Germany)
OHY	Onur Air (Turkey)
QTR	Qatar Airways
RAM	Royal Air Maroc
RAX	Royal Air Freight (USA)
RBA	Royal Brunei Airlines
RBB	Rabbit-Air (Switzerland)
RCH	USAF Air Mobility Command
RCJ	Hawker Beechcraft Hawarden
REN	Arena Aviation (UK)
RFR	Royal Air Force
RGL	Regional Airlines (France)
RHD	Babcock Onshore Services (UK)
RIA	Rich International (USA)
RJA	Royal Jordanian
RJZ	Royal Jordanian Air Force
RNA	Royal Nepal Airlines

ROT	Tarom (Romania)
RRL	Rolls-Royce (Military Aviation)
RRR	Royal Air Force (Air Transport)
RRS	Boscombe Down DERA
RSB	Ruby Star Airlines (Belarus)
RTS	Relief Transport Services
RUA	Rwanda Airlines
RVR	Ravenair
RWD	RwandAir
RYR	Ryanair
RYT	Raya Jet (Jordan)
SAA	South African Airways
SAZ	Swiss Air-Ambulance
SBI	S7 Airlines
SCR	Silver Cloud Air (Germany)
SEY	Air Seychelles
SFR	FlySafair (South Africa)
SHF	Support Helicopter Force
SHT	BA Shuttle
SIA	Singapore Airlines
SIO	Sirio (Italy)
SLK	Silkair (Singapore)
SLM	Surinam Airways
SMX	Alitalia Express
SNA	Sky Cana (Dominican Republic)
SON	Acass Ireland
SOO	Southern Air (USA)
SPC	Skyworld Airlines (USA)
SRD	SAR 22 Sqn
SRG	SAR 202 Sqn
SRR	Star Air (Denmark)
STN	St Athan Maintenance Unit
SUA	Silesia Air (Czech Republic)
SUD	Sudan Airways
SUS	Sun Air of Scandinavia
SVA	Saudi-Arabian Airlines
SVF	Swedish Armed Forces
SVW	Global Jet Luxembourg
SWI	Swiftair (Spain)
SWN	West Air Sweden
SWT	Swift Air (Spain)
SYG	Synergy Aviation
SYR	Syrian Arab Airlines

SYS	Shawbury FTU
TAM	LATAM Airlines Brazil
TAP	TAP (Portugal)
TAR	Tunisair
TAS	Lotus Airlines (Egypt)
TAY	TNT
TCP	Transcorp Airways
TEX	Catex (France)
TFL	Arke (Netherlands)
THA	Thai Airways
THY	Turk Hava Yollari
TIL	Tajikistan International
TJT	Twin Jet (France)
TJS	Tyrolean Jet Service
TJT	Twin Jet (France)
TOF	Topcliffe FTU
TOM	TUI Airways
TOW	AirTanker (UK)
TPA	Avianca Cargo (Colombia)
TRA	Transavia (Netherlands)
TRT	Trans Arabian Air Transport (Sudan)
TSC	Air Transat (Canada)
TUA	Turkmenistan Airlines
TUG	Government of Turkmenistan
TUI	Tuifly (Germany)
TVF	Transavia France
TVS	Smartwings (Czech Republic)
TWE	Transwede
TWF	247 Jet (UK)
TWG	Air-Taxi Europe (Germany)
TYW	Tyrol Air Ambulance
UAA	Leuchars UAS/AEF
UAD	Colerne UAS/AEF
UAE	Emirates
UAH	Cranwell AEF
UAJ	Glasgow UAS/AEF
UAL	United Airlines
UAM	Woodvale UAS/AEF
UAO	Benson UAS/AEF
UAQ	Leeming UAS/AEF
UAU	Boscombe Down UAS/AEF
UAV	Wyton UAS/AEF
UAW	St Athan UAS/AEF
UAX	Church Fenton UAS/AEF
UAY	Cosford UAS/AEF
UGA	Uganda Airlines
UKL	Ukraine Air Alliance
UPS	UPS
UTN	Air Ukraine
UZB	Uzbekistan Airways
VAA	Van Air Europe (Czech Republic)
VAS	Aviatrans Cargo (Russian Fed.)
VCG	Catreus (UK)
VCJ	Avcon Jet Malta
VCN	Execujet Europe (Switzerland)
VDA	Volga-Dnepr Airline
VIP	Tag Aviation UK
VIR	Virgin Atlantic
VJT	Vista Jet (Malta)
VKA	Vulkan Air (Ukraine)
VKG	SunClass Airlines (Denmark)
VLG	Vueling Airlines (Spain)
VLJ	Valljet (France)
VLL	Valley SAR Training Unit
VMP	Execujet Scandinavia (Denmark)
VOR	Flight Calibration Services (UK)
VSB	BAe Systems Marine
VTA	Air Tahiti
VYT	Valley FTU
VXS	Voluxis (UK)
WAD	Waddington FTU
WDG	Min of Ag & Fish
WHE	Leonardo MW Ltd
WIF	Widerøe (Norway)
WIT	Wittering FTU
WKT	DEA Aviation (UK)
WLC	Welcome Air (Austria)
WNR	Wondair (Spain)
WTN	Warton Military Flight Ops
WYT	No. 1 Elementary Flying Training School, RAF Wyton
WUK	Wizz Air UK
XJC	Exclusive Jet Ltd
XJT	Xjet (UK)

Appendix 7

UK SSR Code Assignment Plan

Aircraft are identified by Secondary Surveillance Radar (SSR) using transponder codes comprised of four digits (0–7). These codes are assigned following the International Civil Aviation Organisation's (ICAO) Originating Region Code Assignment Method (ORCAM). ORCAM is based on the strategic allocation of sets of codes to individual states and on the alternate use of transit and local definitions of codes per participating area (PA). This allows the same codes to be used for transit in one PA and for local purposes in adjacent PAs. Together they cover the entire ICAO EUR region.

However, this structure fails to provide sufficient SSR codes for today's demand due to increased levels of traffic and also changes in traffic flows. Eurocontrol, in its capacity as Network Manager (NM), has overcome the shortage of codes by developing a pan-European solution called Centralised Code Assignment and Management System (CCAMS). This provides efficient SSR code allocation to cope with increasing air traffic, mitigating the limitations of the existing ORCAM. It is a specific service carried out on behalf of the ICAO.

CCAMS consists of a central server located at Eurocontrol's premises. It provides a unique code for general air traffic operating in the region, which includes the UK. This server automatically selects and sends a code to all the units along the flight's route, based on the information available from other NM systems. It responds to code requests received from ATC units. It ensures a code conflict-free trajectory for the flight, allowing the code to be retained in the CCAMS area.

SSR codes can provide many clues to aircraft operations and are thus very useful to virtual radar enthusiasts. Most codes are assigned by ATC units but some can be selected by the pilot where the situation requires or allows it. An example is 7000, the Conspicuity Code that, as the name implies, makes an aircraft not in receipt of an ATC service more conspicuous on radar. This can be very useful to a controller providing radar service outside controlled airspace. For IFR flights, the squawk code is assigned as part of the airways clearance and remains the same throughout the flight. Airfield radar units are allocated a block of codes to assign at their discretion for local traffic. Some non-radar-equipped ATC units will allocate squawk codes, notably towers who assign 7010 to circuit training traffic. The main reason is that the aircraft will show up on flight deck TCAS displays. This will provide an alert in the event of an inexperienced pilot wandering too close to the final approach, despite being instructed to hold well clear.

Frequency Monitoring SSR codes (often referred to as 'listening out squawks') have been allocated for use in the vicinity of certain airports. These codes have played a vital role in reducing infringements of controlled airspace (CAS) by enabling controllers to alert pilots if their aircraft appears to be going to infringe CAS. Any aircraft fitted with a Mode A/C or Mode S SSR transponder can use these codes. By entering the relevant four-digit SSR code into the transponder and listening to the published radio frequency, a pilot signifies to ATC that they are actively monitoring radio transmissions on that frequency.

Codes/Series	Controlling Authority/Function
0000	SSR data unreliable
0001	Height Monitoring Unit
0002	Ground Transponder Testing
0003	Surrey/Sussex HEMS
0004–0005	Scottish Non-standard Flights
0006	British Transport Police ASU
0007	Off-shore Safety Area (OSA) Conspicuity
0010	Aircraft operating outside Birmingham Controlled Airspace Zone and monitoring Birmingham Radar frequency
0011	Aircraft operating outside Southampton/Bournemouth Control Zone and monitoring Bournemouth Radar West
0012	Aircraft operating outside Heathrow/London City/Gatwick CAS and monitoring Thames Radar frequency
0013	Aircraft operating outside Luton/Stansted CAS and monitoring Luton Radar frequency
0014	Kent Air Ambulance (HLE21)
0015	Essex Air Ambulance (HLE07)
0016	Thames Valley Air Ambulance (HLE24)
0017	London Air Ambulance (HLE27)
0020	Air Ambulance Helicopter Emergency Medevac
0021	Fixed-wing aircraft (receiving service from a ship)
0022	Helicopter(s) (Receiving service from a ship)
0023	Aircraft engaged in actual SAR Operations
0024	Radar Flight Evaluation/Calibration
0025	Scottish Non-standard Flights
0026	Special Tasks (Mil) – activated under Special Flight Notification
0027	London Control (Swanwick) Ops Crossing/Joining Controlled Airspace
0030	FIR Lost. An aircraft receiving a radar service from D & D
0031	Hertfordshire Air Ambulance (HLE55)
0032	Aircraft engaged in police air support operations
0033	Aircraft paradropping
0034	Antenna trailing/target towing/glider towing
0035	Selected Flights – Helicopters
0036	Helicopter Pipeline/Powerline Inspection Flights
0037	Royal Flights – Helicopters
0041–0061	Police Air Support
0062–0077	No. 1 Air Control Centre
0100	NATO Exercises
0101–0117	Transit (ORCAM) Brussels
0120–0137	Transit (ORCAM) Germany
0140–0177	Transit (ORCAM) Amsterdam
0200	NATO Exercises
0201–0277	Allocated to NATS as CCAMS redundancy
0300	NATO Exercises
0301–0377	Assigned by CCAMS
0400	NATO Exercises
0401	RAF Leeming Conspicuity
0401–0417	Birmingham Approach
0401–0437	Ireland Domestic
0401–0450	Exeter Approach
0401–0467	RAF Lakenheath
0402–0426	RAF Leeming
0420	Coventry Conspicuity
0421–0427	Farnborough Radar/LARS
0427	RAF Leeming (Topcliffe) Conspicuity
0430	Hawarden Conspicuity
0441–0443	Edinburgh Approach
0447	Farnborough LARS – Blackbushe Departures
0450–0456	Blackpool Conspicuity

0453	Liverpool Bay Helicopter Conspicuity
0455	Eskofix RMZ
0457	Farnborough Zone Conspicuity
0460–0466	Farnborough Zone VFR
0460–0466	Farnborough Radar/LARS
0467	Farnborough Zone Conspicuity
0470–0477	Allocated to NATS as CCAMS redundancy
0500	NATO Exercises
0501–0577	Assigned by CCAMS
0600	NATO Exercises
0601–0637	Transit (ORCAM) Germany
0640–0677	Transit (ORCAM) Paris
0700	NATO Exercises
0701–0727	Transit (ORCAM) Maastricht
0730–0767	Assigned by CCAMS
0770–0777	Transit (ORCAM) Maastricht
1000	IFR GAT flights operating in designated Mode S Airspace
1001–1067	Transit (ORCAM) Spain
1070–1077	Assigned by CCAMS
1100	NATO Exercises
1101–1137	Transit (ORCAM) Germany
1140–1176	Assigned by CCAMS
1177	London Control FIS
1200	NATO Exercises
1201–1277	Channel Islands Domestic
1300	NATO Exercises
1301–1327	NATO – Air Policing (Air Defence Priority Flights)
1330–1357	Transit (ORCAM) Bremen
1360–1377	Transit (ORCAM) Munich
1400	NATO Exercises
1401–1407	Irish CCAMS Contingency Codes
1410–1477	Assigned by CCAMS
1500–1577	NATO Exercises
1600–1677	NATO Exercises
1700–1727	NATO Exercises
1730–1744	Newquay Approach
1730–1746	Farnborough LARS East
1730–1767	RAF Spadeadam
1730–1776	RAF Coningsby
1745	Newquay Fixed-wing
1746	Newquay Helicopters
1747	Newquay Conspicuity
1750–1757	Newquay Approach
1750–1757	Farnborough Zone
1760–1777	RNAS Yeovilton Fighter Control
1777	RAF Coningsby Conspicuity
2000	Aircraft entering UK airspace from a non SSR environment, or on the aerodrome surface in accordance with certain conditions
2040–2077	Assigned by CCAMS
2100	NATO Exercises
2101–2147	Transit (ORCAM) Amsterdam
2200	NATO Exercises
2201–2277	Assigned by CCAMS
2300	NATO Exercises
2301–2377	Transit (ORCAM) France
2400–2477	NATO Exercises
2500	NATO Exercises
2501–2577	Transit (ORCAM) Germany
2600	NATO Exercises
2601–2617	Glasgow Approach
2601–2637	RAF Cranwell
2601–2645	MoD Boscombe Down
2601–2657	Irish Domestic Westbound departures and Eastbound arrivals
2620	Aircraft in the vicinity of Glasgow monitoring Glasgow Approach
2621–2630	Aberdeen (Sumburgh Approach)
2631–2637	Aberdeen (Northern North Sea Off-shore)
2640–2657	Aberdeen (Northern North Sea Off-shore
2643–2644	RAF Cranwell
2645	RAF Cranwell Conspicuity
2646–2647	MoD Boscombe Down
2650	MoD Boscombe Down Conspicuity
2650–2653	Leeds Bradford Approach
2651–2657	MoD Boscombe Down

2654	Leeds Bradford Conspicuity
2655–2676	Leeds Bradford Approach
2660	Thruxton Conspicuity
2660–2677	Aberdeen (Northern North Sea Off-shore)
2661–2675	Middle Wallop
2676–2677	Middle Wallop Conspicuity
2677	Aircraft operating outside Leeds Bradford Control Zone and monitoring Leeds Bradford radio frequency
2700	NATO Exercises
2701–2737	Assigned by CCAMS
2740–2777	Transit (ORCAM) Zurich
3000	NATO Aircraft receiving a service from AEW aircraft
3001–3077	Transit (ORCAM) Zurich
3100	NATO Aircraft receiving a service from AEW aircraft
3101–3127	Transit (ORCAM) Germany
3130–3177	Transit (ORCAM) Amsterdam
3200	NATO Aircraft receiving a service from AEW aircraft
3201–3277	Assigned by CCAMS
3300	NATO Aircraft receiving a service from AEW aircraft
3301–3303	Swanwick (Military) Special Tasks
3304–3306	London D&D Cell
33207	D&D Conspicuity Training Fix
3310–3367	Swanwick (Military)
3370–3377	Allocated to NATS
3400	NATO Aircraft receiving a service from AEW aircraft
3401–3477	Assigned by CCAMS
3500	NATO Aircraft receiving a service from AEW aircraft
3501–3507	Transit (ORCAM) Luxembourg
3510–3537	Assigned by CCAMS
3540–3577	Transit (ORCAM) Berlin
3600	NATO Aircraft receiving a service from AEW aircraft
3601–3623	RAF Benson
3601–3632	Scottish ATSOCA Purposes
3601–3634	RAF Waddington
3601–3657	Cardiff Approach
3601–3647	Jersey Approach
3624	RAF Benson Conspicuity
3625–3627	RAF Benson
3636	Aircraft in the vicinity of Cardiff monitoring Cardiff Approach
3637	Wycombe Air Park Conspicuity
3640–3645	RAF Odiham
3640–3666	RAF Marham
3640–3677	Aberdeen (Northern North Sea Off-shore)
3641–3647	BAe Systems Warton
3646	RAF Odiham Conspicuity
3646–3657	Cardiff Approach
3647–3653	RAF Odiham
3650	BAe Warton Conspicuity
3651–3657	BAe Systems Warton
3660	Aircraft in the vicinity of Warton monitoring Warton Radar
3660–3665	Solent Approach (Southampton)
3661–3677	BAe Systems Warton
3666	Solent Radar Conspicuity
3666	RAF Marham – Visual Recovery
3667	RAF Marham – FIS Conspicuity
3667–3677	Solent Approach (Southampton)
3700	NATO Aircraft receiving a service from AEW aircraft
3701–3706	Norwich Approach
3701–3717	Military aircraft under service from RN AEW aircraft in South-west Approaches
3701–3736	RAF Brize Norton
3701–3747	Guernsey Approach
3701–3767	RAF Lossiemouth
3707	Norwich Basic Service
3710	Norwich Approach
3720	RAF Cottesmore Conspicuity
3720–3727	RAF Valley
3720–3727	RAF Wittering Approach
3720–3766	Newcastle Approach
3727	Aircraft flying outside Brize CTR and monitoring Brize LARS
3730–3736	RAF Valley

3737	RAF Valley – Visual Recovery
3737	RAF Brize Norton Approach Conspicuity
3740–3745	RAF Brize Norton
3740–3747	RAF Valley
3750	RAF Wittering Conspicuity
3750–3751	RAF Valley
3750–3761	TC Gatwick
3750–3757	RAF Wittering Zone Transits
3752	RAF Valley – RIFA
3753	RAF Valley – Low level helicopters
3754	RAF Valley – Special tasks
3755	RAF Valley Radar Practice Forced Landing
3756	RAF Valley Straight In Practice Forced Landing
3757	RAF Valley Rotary at RAF Mona
3760	RAF Wittering
3760–3765	RAF Valley
3761	RAF Wittering/Cranwell
3762	Shoreham IFR
3762	RAF Wittering
3764–3766	Gatwick Tower
3767	Newcastle Approach Conspicuity
3767	Redhill Approach Conspicuity
3770–3777	Western Radar
4000	NATO Aircraft receiving a service from AEW aircraft
4001–4077	Transit (ORCAM) France
4100	NATO Aircraft receiving a service from AEW aircraft
4101–4177	Transit (ORCAM) Germany
4200	NATO Aircraft receiving a service from AEW aircraft
4201–4210	Western Radar
4211–4214	Assigned by CAA
4215–4247	Assigned by CCAMS
4250–4257	Belfast City Approach
4250–4267	Aberdeen Approach
4250–4277	Humberside Approach
4255	Aircraft flying in the vicinity of Belfast City and monitoring Belfast City Approach
4300	NATO Aircraft receiving a service from AEW aircraft
4301–4305	Assigned to CAA
4306	Lee-on-Solent Conspicuity
4307–4317	London Control Non-Standard Flights
4320–4327	Ireland Domestic
4320–4327	RNAS Yeovilton
4330–4337	UK Domestic (Prestwick Centre Special Sector Codes)
4340–4353	UK Domestic (Scottish Special Sector Codes)
4354–4356	Westland Helicopters Yeovil
4357	Ireland Domestic
4357	RNAS Yeovilton Conspicuity
4360–4361	Oil Survey Helicopters Faroes/Iceland Gap
4360–4367	Westland Helicopters Yeovil
4360–4367	RAF Northolt
4361–4367	Liverpool Airport
4362–4367	Coventry Approach
4370–4377	Anglia Radar
4370–4377	Ireland Domestic
4370–4377	RNAS Yeovilton
4400	NATO Aircraft receiving a service from AEW aircraft
4401–4427	Transit ORCAM Brussels
4430–4477	Assigned by CCAMS
4500	NATO Aircraft receiving a service from AEW aircraft
4501	Wattisham Conspicuity
4501	Land's End GNSS Approach
4501–4516	Oxford Approach
4501–4517	Prestwick Approach
4502–4547	Wattisham Approach
4506	RAF Topcliffe
4517	Aircraft flying in the vicinity of Oxford and monitoring Oxford Approach
4520	Oxford Approach Basic Service
4520	Prestwick Conspicuity

4521–4527	West Wales Radar
4530	MoD Aberporth Conspicuity
4530–4546	Plymouth (Military) Radar
4531–4537	MoD Aberporth
4540–4542	MoD Aberporth
4540–4541	RAF Topcliffe Conspicuity
4543	West Wales Airport UAS Conspicuity
4547	Plymouth (Military) Radar Conspicuity
4550–4567	Plymouth (Military) Radar
4550–4567	Isle of Man
4550–4570	East Midlands Radar
4571	East Midlands LARS Basic Service Conspicuity
4572	Aircraft operating outside East Midlands Controlled Airspace/Zone and monitoring East Midlands Radar
4572	Farnborough LARS West frequency monitoring
4573	Costock Helicopters inside East Midlands CTR Conspicuity
4574	Southdown Gliding Club Conspicuity
4575	Southend Airport Conspicuity
4575	Haverfordwest RNP Approach Conspicuity
4576	RAF Colerne Conspicuity
4600	NATO Aircraft receiving a service from AEW aircraft
4601	MoD Ops in Salisbury Plain Training Area
4602–4607	Anglia Radar
4607	Aircraft in the vicinity of Hawarden monitoring Hawarden Radar
4610–4667	Assigned by CCAMS
4670–4676	TC Stansted/TC Luton
4677	Carlisle Airport Conspicuity
4677	Luton Airport Conspicuity
4700	NATO Aircraft receiving a service from AEW aircraft
4701–4777	Assigned by CCAMS
5000	NATO Aircraft receiving a service from AEW aircraft
5001–5012	London Control Non-Standard Flights
5013–5017	Assigned by CCAMS
5020–5036	Farnborough LARS North
5037	Farnborough LARS North Conspicuity
5040–5047	Assigned by CAA
5050	Liverpool Conspicuity
5050	Aircraft in the vicinity of Liverpool Airport monitoring Liverpool Radar
5070–5071	Bristol VFR Conspicuity
5070–5071	RAF Syerston Conspicuity
5072–5076	Bristol Approach
5077	Aircraft in the vicinity of Bristol Airport monitoring Bristol Radar
5077	Sherburn-in-Elmet and Leeds East RNP Approach Conspicuity
5100	NATO Aircraft receiving a service from AEW aircraft
5101–5177	CRC Boulmer
5200	NATO Aircraft receiving a service from AEW aircraft
5201–5270	Assigned by CCAMS
5261–5270	Transit (ORCAM) Dublin to Europe
5271–5277	Transit (ORCAM) Channel Islands
5300	NATO Aircraft receiving a service from AEW aircraft
5301–5377	Transit (ORCAM) Barcelona
5400	NATO Aircraft receiving a service from AEW aircraft
5401–5477	Assigned by CCAMS
5500	NATO Aircraft receiving a service from AEW aircraft
5501–5577	Transit (ORCAM) Barcelona
5600	NATO Aircraft receiving a service from AEW aircraft
5601–5647	Transit (ORCAM) Paris
5650–5657	Transit (ORCAM) Luxembourg
5660–5677	Allocated to NATS as CCAMS redundancy

5665–5677	Assigned by CCAMS
5677	Medical Emergency in France
5700	NATO Aircraft receiving a service from AEW aircraft
5701–5777	Transit (ORCAM) Geneva
6000	NATO Exercises
6001–6037	Special Events (activated by NOTAM)
6040–6077	Swanwick (Military) Radar
6100	NATO Exercises
6101–6157	Swanwick (Military) Radar
6160	Doncaster Sheffield Conspicuity
6160–6175	Inverness Approach
6160–6175	Cambridge Approach
6160–6177	Plymouth (Military) Radar
6161–6167	Doncaster Sheffield Approach
6170	Aircraft in the vicinity of Doncaster monitoring Doncaster Radar
6171–6177	Doncaster Sheffield Approach
6176	Cambridge VFR Conspicuity
6177	Cambridge IFR Conspicuity
6177	Inverness Conspicuity
6200	NATO Exercises
6201–6257	Assigned by CCAMS
6250–6277	Transit (ORCAM) Amsterdam
6300	NATO Exercises
6301–6377	Assigned by CCAMS
6400	NATO Exercises
6401–6457	Swanwick (Military) Radar
6460–6467	Assigned by CCAMS
6470–6477	Allocated to NATS as CCAMS redundancy
6500	NATO Exercises
6501–6577	CRC Scampton
6600	NATO Exercises
6601–6677	Transit (ORCAM) Germany
6700	NATO Exercises
6701–6777	Transit (ORCAM) France
7000	VFR Conspicuity code
7001	Military Fixed-wing Low Level Conspicuity/Climb Out
7002	Danger Areas General
7003	Red Arrows Transit/Display
7004	Conspicuity Aerobatics and Display
7005	High Energy Manoeuvres
7006	Autonomous Operations within a Temporary Reserved Area
7007	Open Skies Observation Aircraft
7010	Aircraft Operating in an Aerodrome Traffic Pattern
7011	Aircraft in vicinity of Southampton Airport monitoring Solent Radar
7012	Aircraft in vicinity of London Gatwick monitoring Gatwick Radar
7013	Aircraft in vicinity of Stansted and monitoring Essex Radar
7014–7017	Allocated to NATS as CCAMS redundancy
7020–7027	Assigned by CCAMS
7030	RNAS Culdrose Conspicuity
7030–7044	Aldergrove Approach
7030–7046	TC Thames/TC Heathrow
7030–7066	Teesside Airport
7030–7077	Aberdeen (Northern North Sea Off-shore)
7031–7077	RNAS Culdrose
7045	Aircraft operating outside Aldergrove CTR/TMA and monitoring Aldergrove Approach
7047–7047	Aldergrove Approach
7047	TC Thames (Biggin Hill Airport Conspicuity)
7047	RNAS Culdrose Conspicuity
7050–7056	TC Thames/TC Heathrow
7057	TC Thames (London/City Airport Conspicuity)
7066	Lydd Approach VFR
7067	Teesside Airport Conspicuity
Lydd Approach IFR	
7070–7076	TC Thames/TC Heathrow
7077	TC Thames (London Heliport Conspicuity)
7100	SSR Saturation
7101–7167	Transit (ORCAM) Brussels

7170–7177	Transit (ORCAM) Luxembourg
7200	RN Ships Conspicuity
7201–7267	Allocated to NATS as CCAMS redundancy
7270–7277	Assigned by CCAMS
7300	MPA/DEFRA/Fishery Protection/METMAN
7300	Civil Contingency Conspicuity
7301–7327	Assigned by CCAMS
7330–7347	Transit (ORCAM) Netherlands
7350	Norwich Approach Frequency Monitoring
7350–7353	RNAS Culdrose
7350–7361	MoD Ops in EG D701 (Hebrides)
7350–7363	Manchester Approach
7350–7376	Bournemouth Approach/LARS
7351–7377	Norwich Approach
7354–7357	RNAS Culdrose Conspicuity
7360–7367	RNAS Culdrose
7362	MoD Ops in EG D702 (Fort George)
7364	Manchester Special VFR Low Level Route
7365	Manchester Barton Conspicuity
7366	Flying in the vicinity of Manchester Airport and monitoring Manchester Radar
7367	As above but for students flying solo
7367–7373	Manchester Approach
7374	Dundee Airport IFR Procedural Approach
7375	Manchester TMA and Woodvale Local Area (Woodvale UAS Conspicuity)
7376	Dundee Airport VFR Conspicuity
7377	Bournemouth Radar Conspicuity
7400	Unmanned Air System/RPA Lost Link
7401	Scottish FIS
7402	RAF Leuchars Conspicuity
7402–7414	TC Stansted/TC Luton
7402–7417	RAF Shawbury
7402–7436	RNAS Yeovilton
7402–7437	Anglia Radar
7403–7427	RAF Leuchars
7417	Cranfield IFR Conspicuity
7420	RAF Shawbury Conspicuity
7421–7425	RAF Shawbury
7426	RAF Shawbury Conspicuity
7427	RAF Shawbury
7430–7437	RAF Shawbury
7500	Special Purpose Code – Hijacking
7501–7507	Allocated to NATS (Prestwick Upper)
7510–7535	Transit (ORCAM) Switzerland
7536–7537	Assigned by CCAMS
7540–7547	Transit (ORCAM) Germany
7550–7567	Transit (ORCAM) Paris
7570–7577	Assigned by CCAMS
7600	Special Purpose Code – Radio Failure
7610–7617	Allocated to NATS (Prestwick Upper)
7620–7677	Assigned by CCAMS
7700	Special Purpose Code – Emergency

Index

An original Finnish Airlines example seen at the Daks Over Duxford event in 2019.

Fighter line-up at a Duxford airshow.

Airline Tail Colours

Gerry Manning

This latest edition of *Airline Tail Colours* illustrates the markings of over 600 of the world's leading passenger, cargo and specialist airlines.

Gerry Manning's updated guide includes full colour photographs of the tail markings, each airline's three-letter code, international registration prefix and the ITU country code and also includes a helpful decode tables to ensure this book is easy and quick to use.

Airline Tail Colours is a handy, pocket-sized guide to the tail colours used by airlines from every corner of the globe, making this the perfect addition to any aviation enthusiast's collection.

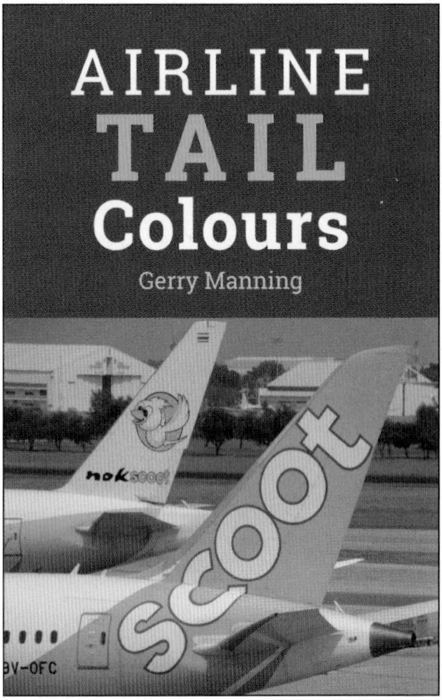

ISBN: 9781910809327
Binding: Paperback
Dimensions: 184mm x 120mm
Pages: 112
Photos/Illus: Over 600
Price: £9.95

Britain's Aircraft Industry

Triumphs and Tragedies since 1909

Ken Ellis

Britain was quick to realise the potential of aeroplanes and in 1909 the Short brothers opened the world's first aircraft factory. From then on the British aircraft industry has maintained a world-leading stance.

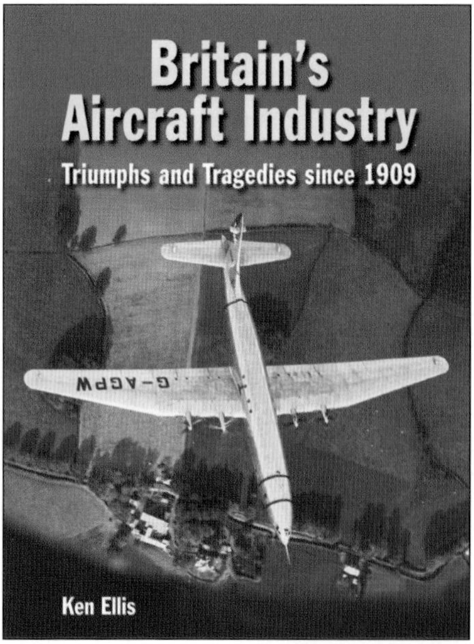

From drawing boards and production lines across the country have come iconic types from the Sopwith Camel to Supermarine Spitfire and Eurofighter Typhoon; Avro Lancaster, the V-bombers and the Panavia Tornado; Handley Page HP.42 to de Havilland Comet and Anglo-French Concorde; Bristol's pioneering Sycamore helicopter to the Lynx and Merlin from Yeovil and many more...

For the first time, here is a readable examination of the British aircraft industry, its heritage and the changes it has had to face, both technical and political. The life and times of the present-day BAE Systems, Airbus UK and Leonardo (Westland); such household names as Avro, Blackburn, Bristol, de Havilland, English Electric, Fairey, Gloster, Handley Page, Hawker Sopwith, Supermarine and Vickers plus less well known manufacturers are covered in detail.

Designers, factories, failures and successes, mergers and closures are all explained, supported by statistical tables and copious illustrations. This is a celebration of a world class industry that remains at the cutting edge of excellence.

ISBN: 9781910809426
Binding: Hardback
Dimensions: 280mm x 216mm
Pages: 368
Photos/Illus: Over 500
Price: £27.95

Civil Aircraft Markings 2021

Allan S. Wright

Now in its 72nd edition, *Civil Aircraft Markings* is the longest-established and best-selling civil aviation book in the world.

At the core of *CAM* is the most complete listing available of all aircraft currently on the UK Register of Civil Aircraft – around 20,000 individual aircraft are detailed in this section alone, from historic biplanes to modern airliners, as well everything in between – including microlights, helicopters, light aircraft, balloons and gliders. For each aircraft listed the registration marks, exact aircraft make and model, and the owner or operator is given, together with space for user notes.

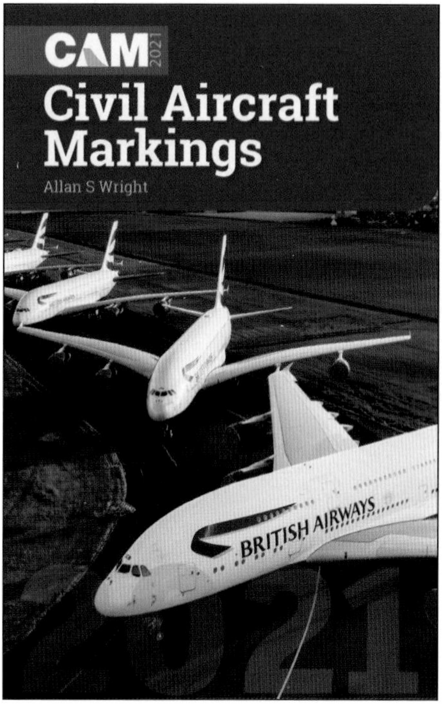

In addition, *CAM* lists other civil aircraft commonly visiting the UK from overseas, which may be seen at British airports, and the latest civil aircraft registers of Ireland, the Channel Islands and the Isle of Man. Furthermore, *CAM* also lists the common Airline Flight Codes, radio frequencies for major UK civilian airfields and the complete British Aircraft Preservation Council (BAPC) register.

Fully revised and updated by one of the UK's most widely respected aviation authors, *CAM 2021* has become an aviation 'Wisden', an indispensable annual publication with a place on the bookshelves of any civil aviation professional, enthusiast and historian.

ISBN: 9781910809891
Binding: Paperback
Dimensions: 184mm x 120mm
Pages: 464
Photos/Illus: Over 30 full colour
Price: £11.95

Military Aircraft Markings 2021

Howard J. Curtis

Now in its 42nd year of publication, *Military Aircraft Markings* is probably the world's best-selling military aviation book.

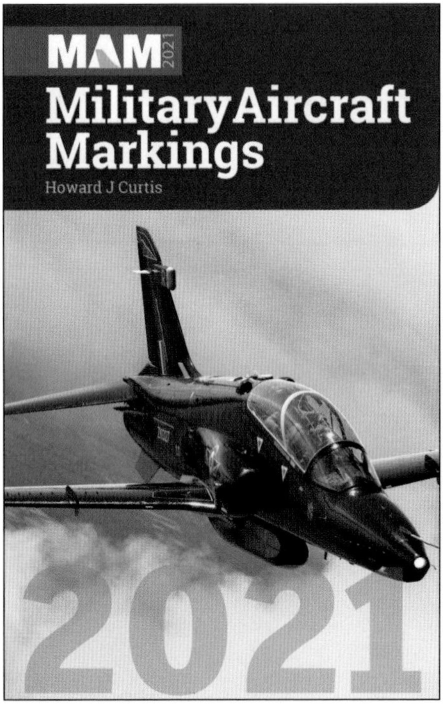

The core of *MAM* is the most complete listing of all aircraft of the UK Armed Forces – the Royal Air Force, Royal Navy, Army and associated units. For each entry the military serial, aircraft type, unit/operator and usual base is given.

Other sections of *MAM* list overseas military aircraft which may be seen in the UK, American military aircraft based in Europe, unit markings and a unit serial number/letter de-code. Also listed in *MAM* are Ireland's military aircraft and historic aircraft in military markings. Additional data such as basic details of the UK's main military air bases, detailed RAF Squadron markings and a maintenance unit cross-reference make up this essential guide to contemporary military aviation in the UK, Ireland and mainland Europe.

MAM 2021 is fully revised and updated by one of the UK's leading authorities on military aviation. It includes a comprehensive listing of visiting aircraft from 'overseas air forces' listings which may be seen during the air display season, together with full colour photo sections. This is an indispensable annual publication for any aircraft enthusiast, historian or student of military aviation.

ISBN: 9781910809884
Binding: Paperback
Dimensions: 184mm x 120mm
Pages: 304
Photos/Illus: Over 30 full colour
Price: £11.95